THE
SUBALTERN
ULYSSES

THE
SUBALTERN
ULYSSES

ENDA DUFFY

University of Minnesota Press
Minneapolis
London

Every effort has been made to obtain permission to reproduce copyright material in this book. The publishers ask copyright holders to contact them if permission has inadvertently not been sought or if proper acknowledgment has not been made.

Published by the University of Minnesota Press
2037 University Avenue Southeast, Minneapolis, MN 55455-3092
Printed in the United States of America on acid-free paper

Library of Congress Cataloging-in-Publication Data
Duffy, Enda.
    The subaltern Ulysses / Enda Duffy.
       p.   cm.
    Includes bibliographical references and index.
    ISBN 0-8166-2328-7. — ISBN 0-8166-2329-5 (pbk.)
    1. Joyce, James, 1882–1941. Ulysses. 2. Politics and literature—
Ireland—History—20th century. 3. Joyce, James, 1882–1941—
Political and social views. 4. Ireland—Politics and government—20th
century. 5. Colonies in literature. 6. Ireland—
In literature. I. Title.
PR6019.O9U6383   1994
823'.912—dc20   93-47083

Contents

Acknowledgments

I would like to thank the following people, who advised, helped, and encouraged me in the writing of this book: Robert Kiely, Fredric Jameson, Sacvan Bercovitch, Bruce Robbins, Tom Richards, A. Walton Litz, Helen Vendler, Seamus Heaney, Marjorie Garber, George Levine, Paul Fussell, and Khachig Tololyan. To the late Allon White, who introduced me to the study of modern culture, I owe a very great debt. My students as well as my colleagues at Reed College, Wesleyan University, and the University of California at Santa Barbara have been an inspiring and challenging audience for many of the ideas I discuss here. The Whiting Foundation and the Wesleyan Center for the Humanities both provided fellowship funds that gave me time to complete this project. At the University of Minnesota Press, Biodun Iginla, Elizabeth Stomberg, Ann Klefstad, and the two readers of the manuscript, Marjorie Howes and Mark Wollanger, have been extraordinarily helpful. Finally, I want to thank Maurizia Boscagli, my best teacher, without whom this book might not exist at all.

Notes on the Text

References to the following works, in the editions listed, are cited parenthetically in the text:

CP *The Collected Poems of W. B. Yeats* (New York: Macmillan, 1956).

FW *Finnegans Wake* (New York: Viking Press, 1939; 1967).

JJ II *James Joyce,* by Richard Ellman, rev. ed. (New York: Oxford University Press, 1982).

Letters I *James Joyce, Letters,* ed. Stuart Gilbert (London: Faber & Faber; New York: Viking, 1957).

Letters II *Letters of James Joyce: Volume II,* ed. Richard Ellman (London: Faber & Faber; New York: Viking, 1966).

P *A Portrait of the Artist as a Young Man: Text, Criticism, and Notes,* ed. Chester G. Anderson (New York: Viking Press, 1968).

U *Ulysses: The Corrected Text,* ed. Hans Walter Gabler, with Wolfhard Steppe and Claus Melchior (New York: Random House, 1986).

Introduction

Postcolonialism and Modernism
The Case of *Ulysses*

Might an IRA bomb and Joyce's *Ulysses* have anything in common? How might an IRA terrorist read *Ulysses?* Or how might a victim of terrorism read the novel, given the opportunity? How can Irish people generally read the novel? Could it be placed at the heart of an Irish national literature? As it has always been seen in some sense as an exception among the masterpieces of patriarchal modernism, could this be because it stage-manages a different kind of intervention within the realities of nation, race, class, even gender? Could its difference make it the representative text, even the original text, of a different strand of modernist writing? The recent history of critical responses to the venerable monolith "modernism" has been characterized by a successive uncovering of modernisms previously unseen; here modernist women's writing and African-American modernism are exemplary. Exploring the relation of *Ulysses* to the colony in which it is set, and the nation that was emerging from that colony at the moment the novel was being written, might we uncover a postcolonial modernism? Could this postcolonial textuality have its origin in early twentieth-century Irish writing, given that the Irish Free State, European yet marginal, was the first postcolonial nation to gain independence from the British Empire in the modern period?

I want to reclaim *Ulysses* in these terms for Irish readers as *the* text of Ireland's independence, and by doing so, return it to readers everywhere as a novel preoccupied, in ways not suspected heretofore by its metropolitan critics, with both the means by which oppressed communities fight their way out of abjection and the potential pitfalls of anticolonial struggles. *Ulysses,* for reasons to do with the politics of its critical reception, has almost without exception been read as a text that ultimately despised the city, the people, and the would-be nation in which, paradoxically, it shows an obsessive interest.[1] I, rather, will read it as the starred text of an Irish national literature. It plays the same decisive role in redefining the issues at stake in imagining an Irish national identity as, to choose at random, Shakespeare's *Henry IV* or Austen's *Pride and Prejudice* does for the English, Cervantes's *Don Quixote* does for the Spanish, or Melville's *Moby Dick* does for the American sense of nationhood. Each of these texts derives its resonance in part from the way in which each accentuates elements at stake in a nexus of material and ideological forces becoming manifest in England, Spain, and the United States at the historical moment when each was written. *Henry IV* educates its readers in the cohesive potential of nascent British nationalism, *Pride and Prejudice* reworks aristocratic matrimonial codes for its newly monied bourgeois readers, *Don Quixote* dwells on the foolishness of traces of feudal decorum to a new renaissance merchant class, and *Moby Dick* recasts the masculine explorer narrative in a grandiloquent American grain. In the case of *Ulysses* the convergence of a historic national transformation and its literary reworking is marked extraordinarily clearly. Joyce's novel was written, as its very last words (beyond the famous syllabic chain of "Yes ... yes ... yes") inform us, between 1914 and 1921,[2] which was exactly the period in which Ireland gained its independence from Britain in a bloody rebellion and anticolonial guerrilla war. These crucial years in modern Irish history witnessed the Irish Volunteer mobilization and gunrunning of 1914, the Easter rebellion in 1916, when whole streets of north-central Dublin were destroyed by shells and over four hundred people were killed, the setting up of the secessionist Sinn Fein Irish parliament in Dublin in 1918, and the guerrilla War of Independence of 1919–21. This war ended with the Anglo-Irish treaty of 1921 that led to the establishment of an independent Irish state. It is striking to think of Joyce writing in 1916 about Bloom wandering down Dublin streets that had already been half destroyed in the Rising. (O'Connell Street, Henry Street, Moore Street, Middle Abbey Street, and Eden Quay all suffered severe damage; in all, there were three thousand casualties in the Easter Rising alone).[3] *Ulysses,* written during the same seven years, encodes successive reactions to the events occurring in Ireland. For example, "Circe," the phantasmagoric tour de force and the episode that is the climax of the novel, was written in nine anguished drafts between June and December 1920 while the Irish guerrilla War of Independence was at its height. The book, which was published in Paris one month before the treaty that guaranteed Irish independence was signed in London, is nothing less, I suggest, than *the* book of Irish postcolonial independence. That it has not been acknowledged as such before this bespeaks the power of New Critical interpretation, which has had an unspoken ideological interest in sustaining an anational cadre, unsullied by any specific politics, of high modernist texts.

Of course *Ulysses* does not render itself up unequivocally as national allegory. Rather, it epitomizes the circumspection and cunning that Stephen Dedalus professed at the close of *A Portrait,* and that would become the hidden weapon even of such postcolonial fictions as Chinua Achebe's early novels, which are replete with what appears to Western readers to be a surfeit of "anthropological" knowledge. For a start, *Ulysses* sets its narrative clock back to 1904, so that it would have to inscribe its tropes of postcolonial difference and community upon an anatomy of the entrenched late-colonial regime that was fostering a full-fledged subalternity in Ireland at the start of the new century. Yet the interruption of the account of colonial everyday life by shock tactics in the prose points up in the text first, the hegemonic might that was being confronted; second, the fragility of the counterhegemonic "native" rebellion; and third, the haphazard possibilities of national independence itself. The text's strategies for delineating the forces at work in Ireland while it was being written may be summed up as follows: the novel relentlessly pinpoints the mechanisms of the colonial regimes of surveillance and the panoptic gaze, as well as the secrecy they generate; it exposes nationalism and other chauvinist ideologemes of "imagined community" chiefly as inheritances of the colonist regime of power-knowledge they condemn; and it mocks imperial stereotypes of the native while it delineates their insidious interpellative power. Against these forces it arrays a relentless interrogativity, born, I suggest, of the text's own perplexity about how to tell of an anticolonial struggle. This interrogativity is epitomized by the multiple generic discontinuities between episodes, which pose the issue of how both postcolonial subjectivity and postcolonial communities might be imagined beyond the peculiarly dependent, "hailed" social and economic status of the colonial territory. In the figure of Leopold Bloom, for example, *Ulysses* takes over the freewheeling quality of that nineteenth-century Eurocentric figure the flaneur, to refashion him as a potential postcolonial subject. In its images of doubly abject women (oppressed first because they are women, and second because they are colonial "natives"), it evidences the continuing sexism of the largely masculinist narrative of postcolonial "freedom." *Ulysses'* post-coloniality means that it is exceptional as a vehicle of social carnival among an array of angst-ridden high modernist texts, but it does not render it, ultimately, an idealist utopian document.

Ulysses distributes the literary effects of modernist defamiliarization on the one hand and an almost archaic strand of realist mimeticism on the other to present the reader ultimately with a postcolonial text. Long seen as a modernist masterpiece, the novel is more interesting in that it is pivotal: it marks, at the heart of the modernist canon, the moment at which the formal bravura of the Eurocentric high modernisms is redeployed so that a postcolonial literary praxis can be ushered onto the stage of a new and varied geo-literature. Joyce's great novel marks, in this sense, a new episteme in what the Irish poet Seamus Heaney has described as "the government of the tongue." Such a claim raises at once a series of questions. The more parochial of these concerns Joyce criticism: it is the issue of why *Ulysses* has not been considered in these terms up to now. It may be answered by considering Joyce's own self-presentation as a member of the high modernist metropolitan mandarinate, and further, how this fitted admirably with the version of modernism as it was theorized by the entrepreneurs of the Joyce industry in the decades after World War II. The second question, more important for understanding the numerous national and transnational literatures from Africa, Asia, South America, and elsewhere now being subsumed under the term "postcolonial," and for evaluating the viability of "modernism" as a literary-historical category, concerns the origins of postcolonial writing and its relation to strategies of textual production generally termed "modernist." This issue can be considered by exploring such matters as the particular role of marginal national literatures within a supposed high modernist monolith, the parallels between guerrilla violence and other modes of anticolonial insurrection and modernist textuality, the way in which common materials of metropolitan culture that are treated in modernist texts, such as consumerism and commodity fetishism, might appear to a colonial writer, and last, the ways in which modernist textual excess, and its mirror image in carnivalesque "displaced abjection," might appear when transmuted from western literatures into their postcolonial counterparts. I will consider these issues in turn, beginning with that of how postcolonial and modernist textualities might be related, before going on to explain in more detail how the

problems and possibilities I outline become integrated into the polyse-
mous textuality of *Ulysses* itself.

Ulysses, Adjacency, Modernism

To understand how a text like *Ulysses,* which for years has been
gleaned for every last attribute of its modernist narrative theatrics,
might have all the time been covertly operating as a postcolonial novel,
or conversely how such a novel, with all its connotations of national allegiance, political awareness, and subaltern sensibility, might have
passed itself off as a metropolitan modernist masterpiece, one first
needs to realize how many formal elements both kinds of writing have
in common. Ultimately, the critic must uncover how and why metropolitan modernist defamiliarizations provided forms that were avidly borrowed for anticolonial and postcolonial literary production. A history
of the many strands of postcolonial writing—one that would outline
the relation between high modernist strategies of defamiliarization and,
for example, South American magic realism, the hallucinatory narratives of the Bothswanan writer Bessie Head, the narratives within narratives of the Somalian Narrudin Farah, or the brilliant fictions of
Salman Rushdie—has yet to be written. The best recent materialist
readings of modernist aesthetics have, however, considered how modern art deployed, even as it helped to elide, material conditions in Europe's colonies. And much recent theorizing of postcolonial literature,
especially the sophisticated poststructuralist work of such critics as
Homi Bhabha and others on hybridity and liminality in postcolonial
narratives,[4] has implicitly addressed the "modernist" tendencies in
some postcolonial writing's estranging and obscure forms. The critic
must engage these two critical projects in dialogue in order to theorize
the modernist *Ulysses* as a postcolonial novel.

Among materialist readings of modernism the work of Fredric Jameson most directly investigates whether the polymorphous perversity of
the canonical modernists of Paris and London colludes with or destabilizes epistemologies of early twentieth-century imperialism.[5] The materialist critique of these modernisms has for years—at least from Georg
Lukács's *The Historical Novel* to the work of critics such as Pierre
Macherey—harbored grim suspicions that modernist obscurity is a
solipsistic aesthetics of compensation; latterly, materialist criticism has

scrambled to reinscribe as politically progressive what successive post-structuralisms have mapped as defamiliarization. Such criticism would read modernist deformations as homologies of the reifying effect of capitalism, the effect by which, as Marx put it, "everything solid melts into air." Precisely because reification forces a separation and a fragmentation of the public and the private, dividing labor from consumption, critics after Kristeva have adamantly refused the idea that transgressive excess, especially in the symbolic arena of literary form, is inherently politically progressive. Particularly when dealing with the canon, in which, as Walter Benjamin put it memorably, "the spoils are borne aloft in the triumphal parade,"[6] a rigorous historicizing is key. In this study, I have taken Fredric Jameson's controversial Marxist periodizing of the fictions of modernity, itself developed from the three stages proposed by Ernest Mandel in his book *Late Capitalism*,[7] as a suggestive point of departure. Post-Marxists may with some reason condemn the literary genealogy Jameson outlines as a regression to a vulgar base-superstructure model, but, admiring its geopolitical focus, its potential for imagining shifting hegemonies on a worldwide scale, and its suggestion of collusion between local genre and international political power, I have taken it as a challenge, and as a pointer to a key aspect of early twentieth-century political and economic development.

Jameson postulates three stages of historical development matched by three strategies of narrative.[8] First, there is the moment of local or national capitalism, to which realism roughly belongs; second, that of monopoly capitalism, or the stage of imperialism, which seems, as he puts it, "to have generated the various modernisms"; and finally, our own period, the era of multinational capital, which has given rise to postmodernism. Being able to imagine that the lived experience of an early twentieth-century character in, for example, an E. M. Forster novel focused on a corner of "little England," owed its form to economic conditions existing elsewhere—in Egypt or the Punjab or the Congo basin—and was bound up with the whole colonial system, allows one to trace in such representations the faultlines at which the everyday life of the home counties was invaded by a nagging sense of the exploitation and oppression that made possible its comforts.

Such a notion works, however, upon a theory of the unsaid; it considers modernist or premodernist obscure prose as a symptom of the reality of exploitation elsewhere, which the strangeness of the prose works to effectively hide. This would seem to envision a textuality almost diametrically at odds with that of a text like *Ulysses* which, I suggest, was written with the forces of anticolonial revolution in view, and which profoundly embodies the subaltern concerns of a postcolonial text. What needs to be understood is how the immediacy and the urgency of much postcolonial fiction make it an appropriate site for modernist strategies of defamiliarized representation. We need to consider how, in a literature from the point of view of the victim, the materiality of violence and the fear it begets leaves its mark on subaltern prose.

Filling the space of and the cries of the revolution's victims has been one of the tasks of postcolonial literature. The shock of the explosion that occurs when no one expects it, the suddenness with which the debris is flying, the groans of the victims, the wail of sirens, the anger at the carnage or the secret pleasure that a blow has been struck on your side or theirs, all must be *retold,* and when the writing comes out of a violent anticolonial guerrilla war, the narration of this specific kind of violence determines the texture of the telling. Frantz Fanon, the most insightful political theorist of the forces at odds at the moment of anticolonial struggle, rightly places this violence—whether the repressive state terrorism of the colonial military police apparatus or the secret guerrilla terrorism of the anticolonial groups—at the heart of his account of the anticolonial psyche.[9] As Lukács pointed out, a crisis is only the intensification of the forces already present in the society,[10] and colonial regimes will invariably have used repressive policies of contained violence to maintain their power. Planted between these two versions of violence, the official state version covert in one way and the guerrilla subaltern version covert in another, writers rendering into words a struggle that is now brought out into the open and intensified find themselves forced toward silence by grim paraphernalias of censorship that match the violence, in that both are very much the effects of the political power dynamics now being contested.

Violence and censorship render fearful much writing out of the anti- and postcolonial contexts. The subaltern writer will have learned in advance that she cannot speak in the ruler's presence, that the ideal the colonist demands of her is silence, that if she does speak she will in all likelihood be considered merely a colorful curiosity within the discourses that the ruler controls. Further, she will be aware that she can only speak through the medium of the oppressor's language, which will always seem compromised. As a member of the subaltern group, she will feel censored by her community, in some sense forced into writing

of the group's subjection and its victories, into producing only the viti-
ated monologic of propaganda. Hence, the official colonial power exerts an extraordinarily repressive force over her very means of literary
production, while the subaltern community would censor her by dictat-
ing her ideological position. At the moment when the formal potential
of the ideology she shares with the subaltern group jars with and grates
against the formal possibilities allowed by the colonizer-controlled language, the material about her—the terror of everyday life in the anticolonial war—generates horrors that stalk the borders of the unrepre-
sentable. When the tripartite censorship of comrade, colonial power,
and horrific event is overcome by the will to write, what results is a text
in which recalcitrance is embodied as the rationale of expression. The
fractured viewpoints, impetus toward allegory, rhetorics of obscurity,
and comic defamiliarizations that enliven the writing make for strategies close to the literary defamiliarizations of metropolitan modernism,
that are set off in the anticolonial moment by a mechanics developed
out of fear. It is partly such fear that empowers the magic realism (as it
has been named) that is probably the most striking formal characteristic of postcolonial writing across any number of cultures.

At first glance it might seem, therefore, that modernist defamiliarization as theorized by materialist critics, and postcolonial defamiliarizing
strategies as I have just sketched them, spring from precisely contrary
impulses: while the metropolitan modernist text's obscurity is symptomatic of its disavowal of those real conditions experienced in the exploited colony that make possible the "refinement" of the society it describes, in the postcolonial text obscurity and novel textual strategies
evidence rather a desperation to be as close as possible to the real conditions out of which the text is constructed. The perceived contrariness
between the two traditions, however, derives mostly from the Eurocentric perspective from which the theoretical model was constructed. As
perceived from the western metropolitan standpoint, the aesthetic
problem is taken to be what the cultural critic Edward Said has termed
"adjacency," that is, the space of contemplation, glorification, subversion, or whatever between the ground of real experience and the aesthetic representation of it in the detached artwork. As a version of adjacency, Jameson's rationale of modernist textuality is an extreme
rendition of the well-worn modernist tale of alienation ("the terrorist
stance of the older modernism," Jameson himself has called it), except
that whereas once the late romantic artist experienced his anomie as

alienation from the decadent confusion of his urban western milieu, in the newer version the modernist text somatizes its politically uncon-scious awareness of a geopolitical exploitative reality from which it is alienated. From this particular logic of modernist representation, the post-colonial text is seen as a utopian mirage in which the problem of aes-thetic distance has been erased, a version of perfectly organic adjacency, a wholly contingent writing out of real lived conditions, much like the goal of "automatic writing" among the metropolitan modernists.

In postcolonial writing, some western materialist critics would have it, this literary praxis has been achieved, and postcolonial writing can there-fore be valorized, with blithe imperial condescension, as nothing less than the inevitable culmination of metropolitan modernism's "struggle." The reality of postcolonial literary production, however, can afford to be less triumphalist. The materialist critique of European high modernism as the political unconscious of western imperialism and colonialism may be granted, as long as it does not collude in a First World-*versus*-Third World radical othering of the colonial periphery, an othering that is ex-actly what it condemns in the cultural exhibits it critiques. More realistic is the view that colonialism itself, as well as the anticolonial conflicts of the interwar years and the postcolonial national formations that resulted mostly after the Second World War, were as characteristic of modernity and its progress — as characteristically modernist — as the more usually cited developments, such as the rise of mass markets, the onset of Tay-lorization and Fordism, the massive efforts to create and satisfy an ap-petite for consumer goods, even the "death of the subject," which are taken as underlying modernism's enlightenment project in the west. In this view, the distinction between metropolitan modernism and anti- and postcolonial literature seems unfortunate, in large part a lingering result of the sundering of "First" and "Third" worlds instituted by impe-rialism itself. Many of the first colonial writers to write in English, from C. L. R. James to Jean Rhys, are clearly "modernist," and many that have followed them since have forcefully deployed narrative strategies devel-oped in the modernist heyday. To such as these, insisting that his mod-ernism must be read in the light of his late colonialism, I now add James Joyce. My perspective is that the works of postcolonial writers like Joyce were certainly not (as is sometimes claimed for postcolonial texts in western languages) servile imitations of inappropriate First World lit-erary models, but rather reactions to a more profound crisis of moder-nity, a crisis that affected them and the milieux they described in their works much more directly than it affected their modernist peers. This closeness meant that their versions of literary defamiliarization have struck new and, to western critics, uncannily familiar notes in the metropole while providing models for further postcolonial writing to follow.

As an extreme example of an apparently new and horribly real social force that in the early twentieth century affected both modernist and colonial textuality, consider the adjacency of terrorism or guerrilla warfare and literature in the period. Terrorism, which first attracted wide attention in the new century with the Boer War and soon after began to be extensively theorized by military strategists, turns out to be one of the characteristic inventions of modern warfare, whose disposition of strategies and representations has a specifically modernist appearance. Terrorist warfare focused on the personal, on civilian life, which it was keen to interrupt and brutalize in the cause of advertising its proponent's vision of the common good. Only at the turn of the twentieth century did terrorism come to be notated in western high fiction, in works such as Conrad's *The Secret Agent*. At the same time it was growing widespread, particularly as a subaltern military strategy in anticolonial wars of independence like the Irish War of Independence of 1919–21.

Only subsequently did terrorism come closest to contemporary western textuality when its strategy of the "propaganda of the deed" came to be matched by the avant-garde's "revolution of the word." Modernist fiction learned what terrorism taught: that to stage the death of the patriarch, no heroic subject need be represented; rather, anyone need only be obliterated, or, in literary terms, a subject needed only to be erased. This obliteration had to be effected suddenly and randomly if shock—the prime strategic effect of both terrorism and modernist textuality—was to work. Only then could either form short-circuit the logical synapses of Enlightenment rationalism and, in a technique that fiction came to acquire in the nineteenth-century sensation novel, appeal to such emotions as wonder, anxiety, and above all, fear. It then fell to postcolonial writing, as that which was closest to anticolonial guerrilla warfare, to represent such shock tactics in fiction.

In this light, in a strong reading, one may read *Ulysses* as a covert, cautious "guerrilla text" in which the violence erupting in Ireland while the novel was being written is in a complex manner homologized by the modernist textual strategies of estrangement that characterize the work. The effect of such homologies upon *Ulysses* becomes visible when we

surrender our comforting concept of the book's unity in an architectonics that Joyce himself (by unofficially presenting his table of correspon-
dences with the *Odyssey*) coyly encouraged readers to find. Hugh Kenner, in perceptive readings of Joyce's modernist narrative strategies, has
already alerted readers to the work's silences,[11] to how much, despite its
loquacity, it refuses to tell. If we look *through* the framework of corre-
spondences (which often only lead, at any rate, to our reading the book,
in Colin MacCabe's words, as "a complex jigsaw puzzle whose solution
is the banal liberal humanism of the critic")[12] we perceive a text whose
mechanisms of order are superficial in comparison to the savage insistence upon the chaotic that we are asked to confront by the shifting
gears of the text. Hence the uncompromising stylistic rupture represented
by each new episode, the author's constant refusal to explain or conceptualize, the straining of realist conventions in the blatancy of repeated
coincidence. Under this kind of scrutiny the book appears as an unpre-
dictable series of elisions, absences, ruptures, abrupt changes, deformations of expression.

One might attribute this to a stern defamiliarization—the term with
which the Russian formalists characterized the political project of the
modernist text—or to a Bakhtinian transgression of the formal and
what it represents.[13] To a writer as interested in concepts of form as
was Joyce, however (as the symmetry of *A Portrait* and the Odyssean
schema for *Ulysses* prove), neither of these account for the perverse
polysemy of the novel. Rather one might hear, in this perversity, the
ambivalent, almost fearful searching of the novelist for codes within
which to encapsulate the horror—and the potential—of the revolutionary moment. It might in this sense be significant that "Sirens," the
first stylistically bewildering episode Joyce wrote, was completed in
1916, the year the rebellion occurred in Ireland. The novel's extraordinary polysemy culminates in "Circe," the grand phantasmagoria of the
book, the episode written and revised during the months when the War
of Independence in Ireland was at its height.

Both the "Circe" and "Sirens" episodes (and others) are fascinated
with the issue of what should be told and what should be kept secret;
this wariness about the value of the information shared by the community is characteristic of any terrorist field of operations. *Ulysses,* in its
provisional mode, works for a start as structural homology of the oper-
ation of the economy of all political information, literary and otherwise, that is acted upon in an anticolonial war. It explores the interac-

tion between information and political power at the moment of revolutionary crisis. The novel effects a redistribution of the textual in the space between the horror of actual violence and the explanations of overtly political discourse, offering a literary praxis at a moment when people needed to conceptualize the possibilities of national freedom in a new state.

Joyce's Irish Politics, 1914–21

If *Ulysses* can be read as a text written out of the postcolonial moment, one may go on to ask why readings of the novel focusing on its relation to Irish political realities have not been central to the text's criticism, especially given its extraordinary interest in Irish matters and the fact that it was written in 1914–21, during the crucial revolutionary period in modern Irish history. The answer is to be found first in Joyce's adroit self-representation as a metropolitan modernist artist and an "exile" from Ireland, and second in the way in which the New Critical stalwarts of the postwar decades who favored Joyce and founded the "Joyce industry" were deeply receptive to the apolitical nature of the "exile" label. Nevertheless, as I will show, one can glean from Ellmann's biography and other sources an ambivalent interest on Joyce's part in the events of 1914 to 1921 that led to the founding of the Irish Free State; this ambivalence meant that *Ulysses*, written in the same years, could become a highly sensitive record of its author's reactions to Irish independence.

James Joyce's self-fashioning stands out among that of the famous male modernists as particularly contrived and well planned. A full-scale examination of his self-promotion, which would be an extremely telling exercise in understanding the relation, in the interwar years, between the male modernists' self-presentation as international stars within the new media cult of celebrity and the subsequent formation of the modernist canon, might begin by looking at the color photograph of Joyce's face that appeared on the cover of *Time* magazine upon the publication of *Finnegans Wake*. As the photographer Gisèle Freund describes it, Joyce posed for this portrait with all the faux grumpiness of an aging star actually eager for the enormous publicity it implied.[14] The photograph marks the culmination of an astute career of self-promotion that began at least as early as the title of his first novel: *A Portrait of the Artist as a Young Man*. What Joyce did, as he describes it in the novel, was to take the general air of *ressentiment* which in the post-Parnell years had become second nature to most, and especially to ambitious young educated males in late-colonial Ireland, and reconstitute it, with the help of the teachings of Aquinas and others, into the famous "Non serviam," to be encoded as the late romantic trope that pits the sensitive apolitical aesthete against his degraded community. Such strategies of co-option would be commonly practiced by numerous postcolonial artists seeking recognition in the metropolitan center, and by Irish figures in particular; in the brilliant game of acting the master's stereotypes of the aesthete better than he could himself, Joyce's best model was Oscar Wilde. With Joyce one could say that the moving myth of the exile that he created in *A Portrait,* which many critics since Richard Ellmann have continued to validate, is a novel collation of generalized nationalism and Jesuit philosophy. Like Wilde's flowers and dandified clothes, it is a front that, imitating Wilde, he kept up with gusto once he could afford it. I think that he admits as much in *Ulysses,* where Stephen, like the young Wilde, strikes an attitude, and Bloom, physically at any rate, resembles Wilde as he looked after he had been released from Reading gaol; see the photographs of Wilde in Rome, as a flaneur who looks shockingly like Leopold Bloom.

Joyce's face on the cover of *Time* magazine marked his gift of his work, and his personality, to his American critics, the majority of whom (although they admired his work in the first place for its necromantic obscurity that lent itself superbly to new critical exegesis) were eager too to admire Joyce the writer as apolitical exile. Perhaps this explains why it has almost wholly escaped critical notice that Joyce's interest in Irish affairs might be the most immediate reason for the nature of the extended development of his novel. Critics have taken at face value Yeats's 1916 letter[15] requesting a grant for Joyce from the Royal Literary Fund, which asserted that "Joyce ... had no interest in politics. In fact at this very moment he is probably absorbed in some piece of work until the evil hour is passed" (*JJ II* 391). They may also have noticed that there are very few references to the Irish situation in Joyce's letters of these years.

That he did, however, follow current events closely is proven by such letters as the one to Mary Kettle written on September 25, 1916, sympathizing with her on the death of her husband in the First World War, and obliquely regretting the death of her brother in Dublin in the aftermath of the Rising (*Letters I* 96, also *JJ II* 399–400). Joyce notes that he read of that death in the *Times*, showing at least that he followed events in the British Isles. He was to regret the shooting of George Clancy, mayor of Limerick, a former friend at the Royal University and the Davin of *A Portrait*, in February 1921. In the autumn of 1920 he followed the hunger strike of Terence MacSwiney, Lord Mayor of Cork, with sympathy. Himself at the time battling with the British consulate in Zurich, he noted MacSwiney's gesture in a rhyme:

> White lice and black famine
> Are the mayor of Cork's supper ... (*Letters II* 16)

That he felt these events to have a particular effect on his writing is shown by his statements about the necessary relation between the artist and his subject matter. Replying to a request from the *Journal de Genève* for an article on the Easter Rebellion of 1916, Joyce commented:

> The problem of my race is so complicated that one needs to make use of all the means of an elastic art to delineate it.... I am restricted to making a pronouncement on it by means of the scenes and characters of my poor art.[16]

In 1921 he was telling the aspiring Irish writer Arthur Power that all great writers "were national first and it was the intensity of their nationalism that made them international in the end, as is the case of Turgenev" (*JJ II* 505). From such statements we can piece together Joyce's conviction that the Irish political situation was a major component of the essential backdrop, the "matter of strict history" (*U* 645) in confrontation with which his artistic ambitions would develop.

Joyce was also aware, by 1916, that the violent revolutionary change in Ireland would make his relations with Irish politics difficult, and hence affect the development of his relation to his artistic subject. Each of his three responses to the 1916 Rising and to the War of Independence that have been recorded hint at Joyce the writer's suspicion that the eminent reversal of Irish political subservience would jeopardize the credibility of the myth of the artist that sustained him. This myth, which he had summarized in the "*Non serviam*" of *A Portrait* and implicitly celebrated in his depiction of a paralyzed Dublin in his short stories, vaunted his alienation from that subservient Irish society. Now the validity of that myth was cast in doubt by events in Ireland. Asked if he did not look forward to the emergence of an independent Ireland, Joyce replied, "So that I might declare myself its first enemy?"[17] Ellmann reports that he followed the events of 1916 with pity, and that although he felt the Rising was useless, he also felt out of things. For a time he told his friends, "Erin go bragh!" (surely with irony), and foretold that some day he and Giorgio would go back to an independent Ireland (*JJ II* 399). Asked by his friend Budgen for his views on events in 1919, he answered, "Tell me why you think I ought to change the conditions that gave Ireland and me a shape and a destiny?"[18] His irony and his rhetorical questions show him somewhat bitter that the initiative of creating conscience had momentarily been taken from him. The events and their perpetrators impressed him: he told Budgen that "I do not want to hurt or offend those of my countrymen who are devoting their lives to a cause they feel is necessary or just."[19]

The fact was that his personal artistic myth (the artist who might be contaminated, who must cry "*Non serviam,*" who will be betrayed) not only made him a figure haughtily self-excluded from local political pragmatism; once set up as a personal gospel, it reduced the relationship between himself and his land to a static one. To create a myth pitting a conscientious and hence motivated artist against a paralyzed society is to deny the society the power to generate its own history. The artist alone, recounting the entropy of the society, is functional and functioning: everybody else is consigned en masse to the "casual comedy" of a society in decline. This stance was underlined by Joyce's self-proclaimed "exile." For most Irish writers closer to home, the immediate reaction to the 1916 showdown was an assimilation of the new radical nationalism, a reaction close to that of the populace in general. Yeats's "All changed, changed utterly" was but the most memorable evidence of this particular metempsychosis. Writers who were to Joyce, as he told his brother Stanislaus, "blacklegs of Irish literature"—the possibly propagandist writers of "the litherary side of the movement" were eager to avow the new mood. The patronizing quality of Joyce's pronouncements on the influence of Irish political developments upon him in the years in which he wrote *Ulysses* are, on the other hand, the rhetorical shield of an artist who found the terms of his art threatened by shifting referents in the dialectic between the artist and his nation.

The continuing evidence of a tremendous burst of political life that issued from Dublin challenged Joyce to shed the romantic myth of the artist he had hitherto professed, and to enter into a new relation with his subject matter if he was to continue to "forge the uncreated conscience" of his "race." This was complicated by the nature of the new politics at home: often it was expressed by violence, which Joyce, if we are to accept as his own sentiment that of both Stephen and Bloom in *Ulysses,* abhorred.

Joyce adroitly concealed his newfound uncertainty about his stance in the present by turning the clock of his novel (that clock which had been lying on its side in *A Portrait*) back fourteen years, to June 16, 1904. That date was chosen partly out of personal considerations and partly because *Ulysses* was originally conceived as a final story for *Dubliners,* in which "Ivy Day in the Committee Room," for example, is set in 1903. When did Joyce first choose that date? We are told of it in the book when Miss Dunne types it out in "Wandering Rocks," an episode, Joyce told Harriet Weaver, on which he had done some work in 1916. By choosing a date that was more than a decade before he began to write, he appeared to elude in his art the claims of the troublesome aspects of contemporaneity. He was able to credibly write in ignorance of events occurring in the years 1914–22, when the book was being written. This is simply to make it, to use Tom Kiernan's phrase, "a retrospective arrangement" (*U* 75, 198), but covertly so. Joyce's deployment of features of the streets like Mr. Artifoni's Dalkey tram, which set off from College Green regularly in 1914 but not in 1904, is in this sense emblematic of the more pervasive deployments in the text of developments in his political consciousness that resulted from his reaction to the events of 1914–21. In selecting 1904, he took advantage of our linear sense of history, by taking the years of the history of Ireland through which he had lived and cutting them in half. Writing, as his brother said of him, "to make things clear to himself,"[20] he folded his own memory over upon itself like the pages of a book, and was therefore able to illustrate his change in attitude in his own terms. The artist had transposed his concerns about his relation to the present age onto the age from which he had originally chosen to be alienated.

By setting the book in a single day, Joyce makes it pretend to be the description of a prolonged moment, which threatens to forget the troublesome concept of linear mutable history altogether. Such a stasis can be appropriately situated in 1904: this year stands at a nadir of political development in modern Irish history, between the parliamentary agitation that saw its finest hour under Parnell in the 1880s and the War of Independence, which ended with the signing of the Anglo-Irish treaty in November 1921. On this template, representing a past history invoked in a plethora of suggestions, images, and explicit reminders,

Joyce gradually inscribed his own implicit history of his reaction to the political changes of the years in which the book was being written.

These changes were taking place in the same years as Joyce was writing *Ulysses*. Joyce first refers to the book in a letter in 1914; by June 1915, when he left Trieste for Zurich, he was beginning the third episode.[21] During 1916 he drafted "Scylla and Charybdis." In October of that year he told Harriet Weaver that he had done some work on "Wandering Rocks," and the "Nostos," adding, "I hope to finish by 1918." By March 1918 he had consigned "Calypso" to Ezra Pound: in May, while the crisis loomed in Ireland, he was working on "Hades." At the end of 1918, as the general election that brought Sinn Fein to victory was being fought up and down the country, Joyce, ensconced in his flat in Paris, was rewriting "Scylla and Charybdis." In February 1919, as the War of Independence threatened, and the first, illegal Irish Dail (parliament) sat in Dublin, he was occupied with "Wandering Rocks." He had just completed "Cyclops" when the *Irish Independent*, the newspaper his characters read in Barney Kiernan's public house, had its offices raided by the IRA in the sort of incident that was by then commonplace in Dublin and throughout Ireland. In early 1920, as the first Black-and-Tans disembarked in Dublin, Joyce was completing "Nausicaa." As he wrote "Oxen of the Sun" through the spring of that year, assassinations, ambushes, and reprisals were the order of the day in Ireland. During the summer and autumn of 1920, while Joyce was writing and revising "Circe," the War of Independence reached its height, with shootings, burnings, and assassinations everywhere. Joyce's friend George Clancy, mayor of Limerick, was shot before his wife in March 1921, when Joyce was writing "Ithaca." At the time when the truce was signed between representatives of the British army in Ireland and the IRA in July 1921, he was adding the "Messianic scene ... Bloom's dream of glory" to "Circe." On October 11, 1921, the Anglo-Irish peace conference opened in London; on October 29, Joyce finished "Ithaca" and his book. About a month later, on December 6, the Anglo-Irish treaty was signed in London. On the following evening in Paris, Valery Larbaud was to claim, during his lecture in Adrienne Monnier's bookshop, that, with *Ulysses*, "Ireland makes a sensational re-entry into European literature."[22] A fortnight after the formal transfer of power from English to native Irish government had taken place at Dublin Castle, *Ulysses* was published in Paris on February 2, 1922. Ezra Pound com-

mented that "Joyce has done an Inferno. He has presented Ireland under British domination." Yet the infernal element in the book may have
more to do with Joyce's relation to what was occurring in Ireland as he
wrote than with that backwards look at British rule in Ireland in 1904,
that the text purports to represent.

Ulysses, *Text of Irish Independence*

Shem, in *Finnegans Wake,* claims to have "cutely foretold ... death
with every disaster, the dynamitization of colleagues, the reduction of
all records to ashes, the levelling of all customs by blazes" (*FW*
189–90). (This last refers to the burning of the Custom House, Dublin,
at the height of the Irish War of Independence; it may also refer to the
burning of the Four Courts in the Civil War that followed the treaty, in
1922). "Kuskykorked ... up tight in his inkbattle house" (*FW,* 176)
while the war raged in Ireland, Joyce was physically distanced from the
events occurring where his book was set, yet the text encodes a version
of the forces at work in what occurred. Let us examine how some of
these forces operate upon the architectonics of the text itself.

If we are to posit *Ulysses* as an original postcolonial text, clearly the
matter of beginning will be crucial. Slip by the intricate symbolist apparatus of Buck Mulligan's mock mass and so on, which critics have almost always taken too seriously, and it is clear that *Ulysses* begins very
unpromisingly—as the tale of three clever young cads getting up.
When Stephen and Mulligan serve the Britisher Haines breakfast, what
we have is two representatives of the new native bourgeois class, a
prominent formation in the latter days of every colony, facing a liberal
colonist proud of his capacity for cross-cultural empathy. ("We feel in
England that we have treated you rather unfairly. It seems that history
is to blame," Haines opines [*U* 17]). When the two Irish, predictably,
speak in vehemently nationalist terms, we soon realize that such talk is
no more than the mirror image of Haines's own deeply racist chauvinism. The nationalist rhetoric is intersected by a deep-seated class resentment, especially on Stephen's part. Yet this is mere ideological prelude.
At the moment when Stephen's students go out to play and he hears the
headmaster Deasy remonstrate with them, at the moment when he
"walks into eternity along Sandymount strand" in "Proteus," an episode
that is diorama rather than soliloquy, and above all when Leopold and
Molly Bloom—characters in an altogether different part of the city—

are introduced, the principle of simultaneous events happening to different people in different parts of the same place—that strategy which Benedict Anderson, in his classic study of nationalism, *Imagined Communities,* sees as the key strategy of the novel to represent the national group—is absolutely decreed here as key to *Ulysses.* (It reaches its height in the multiple and simultaneous urban "love at last sight"[23] scenarios of the "Wandering Rocks" episode.) All of this is narrated as realism: as yet there are no realities to be represented for which the signifying apparatus of imperialist nationalism is not adequate.

This alters, however, almost as soon as Bloom, late colonial flaneur, is put into circulation around Dublin, colonial capital. To understand the fundamental differences between *flânerie* in colonial Dublin, Cairo, or Calcutta as opposed to such wandering in London, Paris, or Vienna, one may compare Bloom's dromomania, his compulsive walking, to the more purposeful tours of Clarissa Dalloway in Virginia Woolf's *Mrs. Dalloway.* In Woolf's novel, *flânerie* exists in conjunction with the plate-glass window—of the florists, the haberdashers, and Home and Colonial stores. It is a convention whereby the Home Counties characters are brought face-to-face repeatedly with the culture of commodities, begging to be consumed, which will structure their sensibilities and ways of being. In the colonial cities, commodities are likely to be in short supply, and only the colonist elite will have the money to afford them; it is by dwelling on this that we can politicize all of the poverty, all the second-hand coats, books, and boots in *Ulysses,* rather than moralizing over Irish stereotypes as do even the best Joyce critics. Next consider Rosa Luxemburg's theory of the imperialist economic order;[24] the centerpiece of her paradigm is the idea that the colonies were necessary to the metropolitan centers as potential markets. Such a theory helps to account for the extraordinary stress on advertisements, and on the obscenity of advertisements to those who cannot afford their wares, in *Ulysses*—an insistent hailing of the natives to persuade them to buy.

Wandering Bloom sees all the advertising hoardings, he meets his peers, and he casts a cold eye on the police. The police presence in *Ulysses* is intense: the novel reports on more policemen, constables, redcoats, plainclothesmen, police touts, possible informers, police barracks, prisons, and even applicants for the job of hangman (in "Cyclops") than do most detective novels. (As such, it works as a novel that turns detective fiction, the late-realist, heart-of-empire genre par excellence, on its head.) Bloom's *flânerie,* I suggest, is a mechanism of escape from the persuasion of the advertisements and the panoptic surveillance of the colony as police state.

Exploring versions of possible postcolonial subjectivity, the novel confronts us with the stereotypes of Irish natives generated by the regime of panopticism. This stereotyping follows the pattern of differentiation described by Mannoni, JanMohamed, and others as Manichean allegory.[25] Centrally in "Cyclops," but also in the generic discontinuity from the early realism toward modernist estranging strategies that mark the text as a whole, realist narrative *tells* the Irish as good bourgeois of the Empire, "like us" (but in fact collaborators), while the more hyperbolic text tells them as savage, degenerate, violent, loquacious, and ultimately, as with the Citizen of "Cyclops," as terrorists. Brokering these extremes, the fact of Bloom's Jewishness is crucial, for it allows us to generate his subjectivity from a general principle of oppression ("And I belong too," he says, "to a race that is hated and persecuted," [U 273]) and not merely from a racist chauvinism (Irish anti-Semitism) always already a mirror of the imperial discourse it purports to oppose.

All these issues — stereotyping, freedom of movement, and imagined communities — crash together in "Circe," which fearfully confronts the actual terrorist violence of the anticolonial struggle, violence that was ever-present in Ireland while Joyce was writing the episode in Paris. Among the fragments, images, and texts that I situate around *Ulysses,* one of the more telling is a poem by Oliver St. John Gogarty, the model for Buck Mulligan in the novel. St. John Gogarty's poem, published in a Dublin daily in 1904, purported to welcome a batallion of British troops that had arrived that day in the city. This Kiplingesque paean, however, was a blind; if the reader took the first letter of each line and read downwards, he or she found a message about prostitutes. A duplicitous text, then: it was either realist or cleverly modernist, and the choice of reading depended on the allegiance of the reader. The "Circe" episode, I propose, enacts exactly the same representational transference as does this poem: it represents the matter of the colonial army, and in the case of "Circe," of violence against it, in a scenario centered on prostitution, abject women, in St. John Gogarty's phrase, "Busy whores." "Circe"'s placing of the figure of the abjected woman at the center of the representational economy of terrorism in the text is repeated time and time again in postcolonial novels since (the Kenyan novelist Ngugi wa Thiong'o's *Petals of Blood* is a good example),[26] and it evidences, I suggest, the inability of a text written at the moment of decolonization to imagine an epistemologically different subject altogether beyond the pale of the colonialist and masculinist discourses the subaltern author has inherited. The figure of the abject woman is rendered in effect as scapegoat, and is made to represent the difference (of the colonial master as well as of gender) that the subaltern fears. Thus as Bloom becomes "the new womanly man" in "Circe," Bella Cohen, "massive whoremistress," becomes not just Bello, and male, but a full-blown caricature of the imperial industrialist: listening to Bello's declamations, one realizes that the language she speaks is a parody of that of Cecil Rhodes himself.

This inability to represent woman as postcolonial other is proven in "Oxen of the Sun," where the text tries every imperial English literary style to tell of Mrs. Purefoy giving birth—and yet cannot manage to represent more than the goings-on of a group of drunken males despite all the versions it uses of the King's English. It is later replayed in "Penelope," where Molly is refused a place in any community of women, although she is granted the final showdown in the text's continuous strategy of radical interrogativity. Questioning every masculinist posture becomes her subjective power. As such she epitomizes perfectly the novel's refusal to hypothesize any utopian ideal of postcolonial community while it enjoys as carnival the subaltern's deft redistribution of forces in the language economy of late-colonial power.

Ulysses, therefore, is not a manifesto for postcolonial freedom, but rather a representation of the discourses and regimes of colonial power being attacked by counterhegemonic strategies that were either modeled on the oppressor's discourses or were only beginning to be enunciated in other forms. Such representations of imperial discourse and the multiple voices that have countered it have been the basic elements of numerous postcolonial narratives since, especially in novels from Africa in the years before and after independence. We may now discern in *Ulysses,* the novel read by metropolitan critics since its publication as the capstone-text of the western (and hence imperial) modernist tradition, rather a blueprint for the staging of the confrontations between the discourses and the material forces at odds in any anticolonial struggle. In proposing the historiographic matrix of decolonization as an appropriate one within which to envisage the political trajectory of *Ulysses,* I claim that the book ultimately escapes the standard anomie of much modernist textuality because it succeeds in mapping some notions of independence, Irish independence, upon modes of producing information that had served the now defeated imperial powers. *Ulysses,* read by the people who are after all its subjects, can enter history as did the Mosaic tablets described by J. F. Taylor in the "Aeolus" episode: as "the tables of the law, graven in the language of the outlaw." Its author's self-reckoning in *Finnegans Wake* is therefore well justified: "He war."

Mimic Beginnings: Nationalism, Ressentiment, and the Imagined Community in the Opening of *Ulysses*

> *Creating a new culture does not only mean one's own individual discoveries. It also, and most particularly, means the diffusion in a critical form of truths already discovered, their "socialization" ... making them the basis of vital action, an element of ... intellectual and moral order.*
>   Antonio Gramsci ("The Study of Philosophy," *Prison Notebooks*)

> *Paradise of pretenders then and now.*
>   Stephen Dedalus (describing Dublin in *Ulysses*)

Enclosure, Imitation

Posted on walls throughout Ireland in late 1920, at the moment when James Joyce was writing the central episodes of *Ulysses* in Paris, this government notice described for potential informers how they might pass important information to British officials (Figure 1).[1] The notice's lively imaginative quality is striking in at least two ways. First, it ingeniously overcomes obstacles by inventing elaborate *formal* procedures. The perceived threat — that the mail will be intercepted — is to be circumvented by placing a message in an envelope within an outer envelope, all to be sent to one address and thence forwarded to another. This particular formal arrangement involves secreting one text, very literally, within others; each succeeding enveloping text, somewhat different from that beneath it, acts to deceive the reader about the cumulative significance of the texts enclosed. The originators of this scheme planned that the well-wrapped letter they describe would ultimately have its real message read, and read only by the specific audience for

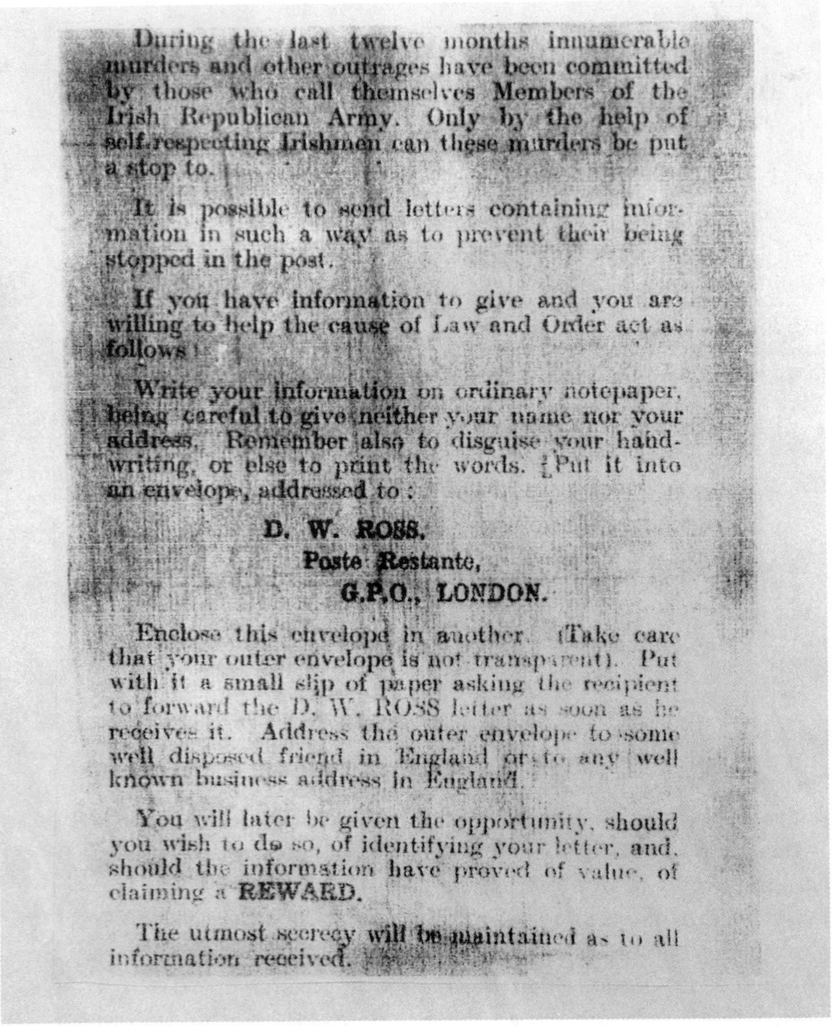

During the last twelve months innumerable murders and other outrages have been committed by those who call themselves Members of the Irish Republican Army. Only by the help of self-respecting Irishmen can these murders be put a stop to.

It is possible to send letters containing information in such a way as to prevent their being stopped in the post.

If you have information to give and you are willing to help the cause of Law and Order act as follows:

Write your information on ordinary notepaper, being careful to give neither your name nor your address. Remember also to disguise your handwriting, or else to print the words. Put it into an envelope, addressed to:

D. W. ROSS,
Poste Restante,
G.P.O., LONDON.

Enclose this envelope in another. (Take care that your outer envelope is not transparent). Put with it a small slip of paper asking the recipient to forward the D. W. ROSS letter as soon as he receives it. Address the outer envelope to some well disposed friend in England or to any well known business address in England.

You will later be given the opportunity, should you wish to do so, of identifying your letter, and, should the information have proved of value, of claiming a **REWARD.**

The utmost secrecy will be maintained as to all information received.

Fig. 1. British government notice displayed around Ireland at the time of the War of Independence, 1919–21.

which it was intended, precisely because of its powers to deceive, to proffer a false message, to that audience that it operated to avoid.

Thus to the notice's second striking feature. Its incitement to deception would have been successful to the extent that it was familiar, to the extent that it invites its readers to take part in a scenario of subterfuge and the secret passing of information that they find commendable, even comfortable. Read this way, the notice might be a page torn from a thriller; its scrupulous directives could easily have been cribbed from an espionage novel. It unfolds as a meticulous detective plot ("write on . . . ordinary notepaper. . . . disguise your handwriting"), and we are charmed by its solicitous details ("Take care that the outer envelope is not transparent"), its local color ("some well-disposed friend in England"), and the mysteriousness of its unknowable character D. W. Ross, possessor only of an ungendered anonymous name. (At this level we want curiously to know: Who is D. W. Ross? What kind of Irish informer would have a "well-disposed friend in England"? How useful was this notice and what kind of responses did it elicit?)

Here is an advertisement soliciting informers whose pitch is an extraordinary kitsch espionage plot. This kitsch element need not come as a surprise when one remembers that this is a document of colonial rule; the procedures and gestures of colonial administrations, after all, were likely to be imitations (often grotesquely or comically exaggerated ones) of procedures developed for use in the home country. This administration-by-imitation gave rise, among British colonists at any rate, to a pervasive sense that their work was a kind of play-acting, and nowhere was this more evident than in the gathering of covert information, a key practice of all colonial regimes. Colonial spying is brilliantly celebrated as play in Kipling's novel *Kim,* for example; there the hero, orphan son of an Irish soldier, who is trained as a child informer, is taught that his work follows the highest code of honor, "the game." It was with this gamelike quality that the notice hoped to intrigue the reader into attending to it. It is this quality that marks it as a characteristic document from the colonizers amid the crises of the final days of the colony, a truncated, indirectly narrated adventure tale that still wishes to realize, in the real world of colonist surveillance, the rhetoric of adventure with which the colonists had always narrated their exploitation as mere exploits. The sense that the notice is playing a game, the basic rule of which is that meticulous attention to matters of *form* will ensure that key information reaches the specific audience for which it was intended among the local population, marks it as a characteristic account from the colonist viewpoint of how information might be passed from one party to another in a dangerous revolutionary moment and in a colonial milieu.

In this chapter I will examine how Joyce, in beginning *Ulysses,* also considered how to pass on information about the matter of the country that was the setting of his novel, at a historical moment (1914–15) for Ireland that was tense with political expectations, on the verge, as events would demonstrate, of revolutionary violence.[2] In the opening of Joyce's text there is deployed both the strategy of enclosing texts within texts on the one hand, and a plethora of imitative, already told tales on the other, which were outstanding features of such covert information-gathering efforts as the British government notice of 1920 appealing for Irish informers. *Ulysses*, it has often been noted, begins with a Joycean crash course on Irish landscapes, politics, and social and cultural life: I will suggest, however, that its viewpoint and narrative at the opening of the novel is highly derivative of the imperial colonist modes it ostensibly condemns.[3] Derivative narratives woo the reader into the text with their familiar ideological resonances; they are supplanted near the end of the third episode of the novel by a demonstration of what the basic conditions for a community built without such derivative interpellating narratives might be.

The principal derivative narratives toyed with and discarded in the opening of *Ulysses* are the familiar ones of nationalism and ressentiment; the primary principle of a nonsectarian community developed in the course of the first three episodes is that of the possibility of imagining different kinds of human subjects existing and acting simultaneously in a complex yet full imagined space. Critics have generally noted how,[4] in the three episodes of the "Telemachiad" that open the novel, the text interweaves some vivid, if ironically cast, tableaus of the colonial oppression of Ireland with a pervasive sense of the alienation of Stephen Dedalus. This alienation, the haughty "*Non serviam*" of the young artist, is a further exploration of the *Bildungsroman* postures of Joyce's *Portrait of the Artist as a Young Man*, which in turn are patterned on literary dreams of engendering bourgeois male subjectivity from Goethe to Samuel Butler. This *Bildungsroman* ethos in the "Telemachiad," however, turns out to be the text's first example of narrative imitation, a blatant transcription of the narrative dynamic of Joyce's previous novel. Because *Ulysses* will treat matters more pressing than the self-satisfaction of the post-Enlightenment young male, Stephen as character soon grew tiresome even to Joyce himself ("Stephen no longer interests me," Joyce told his friend Frank Budgen);[5] the vaunted independence of the artist, no longer sustained by any neoromantic ideology of genius, begins from the opening page of *Ulysses* to congeal into a humbler mock-heroic ressentiment. Stephen comes to harbor a nagging animosity about what he realizes is his inferior social class.

Furthermore, the stereotypical narratives of the oppression of Ireland as a colony—the kitsch symbolism of the old milkwoman, Mulligan's "shoneen" deferential patriotism ("The Sassenach wants his morning rashers" [U 8], the schoolmaster Deasy's Unionist Irishness ("We are all Irish, all king's sons"[U 26]), Haines's condescension and expertise in Gaelic culture (he says that "History is to blame" [U 17] and speaks Irish)—are each imitative of hackneyed tropes of "Saxon greed," the glorification of a medieval Irish chieftaincy, a new respect for folk life, and so on, from the various nineteenth-century Irish nationalist revivals. Fitted inside one another as so many textual integuments, these narratives are soon shown to be in turn contained within the British Victorian and Edwardian discourse of jingoist imperial nationalism. Nevertheless, it is precisely the false promise implied by the parallelling of narrative strands of personal alienation from community on the one hand and nationalist integration within it on the other that, in much the same way as the misaddressed letter described in the colonial notice, allows for the elaboration of an altogether different discourse secreted beneath them. The "Telemachiad" woos us into the novel by flaunting the superficial pleasure of its kitsch, stereotyped versions of communal subjectivity (nationalism) and individual subjectivity (romantic alienation), all the while forcing us to watch while the envelope narratives, each one different from the next, are peeled away. Do not forget that Joyce, as he wrote the episodes of *Ulysses,* was posting them to "some well-disposed friend in England"; in his case, the friend in England was Ezra Pound. Note too that, given their most likely readership, *all* these narratives are "posted to some well-disposed friend in England"—that is, they would be comprehensible to an audience of the colonists themselves. Yet these cosily familiar narratives of personal alienation and nationalist community are soon abandoned. This sloughing-off of the narratives that attract us into the text then leaves its readers with a strikingly different version of the rapprochement between individual subject and imagined community than that with which they had begun. By the close of the third episode, the bitter pleasures of personal ressentiment and resentful nationalism have been supplanted by the suggestion of a simultaneously occurring national life that is at the least a blueprint for the condition of a heterogenous national community whose members coexist peacefully together.

Before tracing this progression in the text, consider how thoroughly the "Telemachiad" is constructed as a tissue of texts within texts, and how slavishly it stages its beginning as a series of imitations in which these enclosed texts imitate each other. In a literary work, the first sign of the enclosure of narrative within narrative is a proliferation of quotation. The opening episodes of *Ulysses,* carrying quotation far beyond the webs of intertextual reference to be expected of works that self-consciously and strategically place themselves within the western high literary canon, adopts quotation-within-quotation as the principle underlying its form. As an example, here is Hugh Kenner's bravura analysis of Buck Mulligan's mocking incantation of the phrase "*Introibo ad altare Dei*" (*U* 3). These are the first words spoken by a character in *Ulysses* — here intoned in Buck Mulligan's sonorous voice:

> Mulligan ... is tastelessly pretending to be a black Mass celebrant, who is going through the motions of an Irish priest, who is reciting from the *Ordo,* which quotes from St. Jerome's Latin version of Hebrew words ascribed to a Psalmist in exile: "Va-a-vo-ah el mizbah elohim": "I will go up to the altar of God." ... So we might set the first words spoken in *Ulysses* inside six sets of quotation marks: " ' " ' " 'Introibo ad altare Dei,' " ' " ' " — a multiple integument of contexts to contain this Hebrew cry for help amid persecution.[6]

The "multiple integument" excellently characterizes the discursive form of the three episodes as a whole. In these episodes, Mulligan and Stephen quote and misquote Shakespeare, Wilde, Yeats, and Meredith at each other; Deasy quotes Shakespeare; the schoolboys recite Milton; Stephen in "Proteus" requotes the lines from Yeats's poem (*CP* 15) "Who Goes with Fergus?" (*U* 41) that Mulligan had already boomed out (*U* 8) in "Telemachus." The characters quote each other: Stephen on the strand repeats Deasy's "All king's sons" (*U* 26, *U* 38) in the fabric of his own thoughts. Throughout "Proteus," indeed, while Stephen mulls "the ineluctable modality of the visible" (*U* 31) on Sandymount strand, he quotes most of the memorable phrases and motifs of the two earlier episodes. Kenner's brilliant archaeology of all these layers of quotation shows us how many discourses Mulligan is mocking; it also implies that the more discourses he mocks the more he quotes, and the harder it is for him to escape, to speak in a new voice beyond any of those quoted. Mockery is revealed as almost a form of mirroring, possessed of only the faintest possibility of the most pallid form of subversion. Ressentiment and resentful nationalism are granted few more forceful weapons than mockery here, as I will show, to counter the discourses they must quote to express themselves.

The "Telemachiad" does not simply canvass the possibility of subverting discourses, then, for that would mean confronting them in their own terms. Rather, it works to lay out the conditions for imagining a community not based on adherence to such master plots; it does this work by exploring the possibilities inherent in its own form. It exposes these possibilities by allowing its opening discursive mimicry, epitomized by layers of quotation, to dissolve into layers of repetition, and then into outright misquotation. Inevitably, the enclosure of narrative within narrative can also easily assume the form of misquotation; the less specific the quotations become — when going beyond the actual repetition of phrases or lines they move to reiterating ways of speaking, genres of representation, whole discourses — the more possibilities exist for such misquotation to occur and for spaces of difference to be opened up. As the "Telemachiad" progresses, the two principal discourses overshadowing the text — that of alienation, which circles around Stephen, and that of Irish nationalism and its representational possibilities through which the larger community is considered — present us with a range of statements, each of which is a misquotation of the other. These misquotations (especially by Stephen in his ruminations in "Proteus") mean that points of reference from outside the original discursive terms of the text are introduced; these in turn suggest a framework with broader possibilities than the derivative discourses originally purveyed. Once the novel makes it clear that it has progressed from quotation as a strategy for endorsing the comfortably familiar, then it has moved from a logistics of "multiple integuments" as the form of its realist representation to exposing such quotation as glib imitation. As such, any reassurances such quotation might possibly have provided that this novel will retail or retell old stories and the ideologies they celebrate are soon undermined.

To pursue a political reading of the novel, we must grasp this relative simplicity of the opening as an issue of the uses of familiarity in a work that soon turns to the defamiliarizing potential of the obscure. The fastidious realism of the discourses in the opening episodes of *Ulysses* means first that they will likely be spoken in dialects already in wide circulation. The delighted shock of *Little Review* editors Margaret Anderson and Jane Heap at the opening words of "Proteus" aside (Anderson cried, "This is the most beautiful thing we'll ever have"), the first episodes of *Ulysses* have always been regarded as less difficult than "Sirens" and those following. The good-mannered familiarity of the opening sequences, moreover, is not only displayed in the carefully layered form, but more fundamentally in the issues the author chose to represent.

Most comfortably familiar in the "Telemachiad" is the way in which the *Bildungsroman* theme subsumes other issues to its own purpose. For a reader eager to settle in with the familiar, it must have seemed as if the project of the first pages of the novel was to prop up the enervated narrative of the *Kunstlerroman*, thoroughly familiar not only from its immediate treatment in *A Portrait* but also in its numerous antecedents in fin-de-siècle British fiction from Gissing and Meredith to Samuel Butler's *The Way of All Flesh,* with an infusion of parallel material dealing with the matter of Ireland. Ireland the oppressed and servile nation now serves as an analogy to the oppressed and misunderstood would-be artist. This would be to use the issue of oppression in Irish politics as a full-dress pathetic fallacy supporting the psychological trauma of Stephen as an ambitious character. Such a story, in which the matter of Irish politics can only be mentioned as the background that enables the development of a psyche, would have been readily familiar to contemporary readers of *Ulysses* and indeed to readers since; Yeats's self-fashioning, and the fashioning of the persona of the politically committed poet by most of his critics, has mostly taken this very path. From the perspective of a politicized Irish reader, however, to juxtapose the politics of an anticolonial upstart territory with such a (in a literary context) familiar, comfortable theme as aesthetic self-fulfillment meant that the politics too would be rendered safe for novelistic consumption.

Nevertheless, if a narrative of resentful nationalism was comfortably familiar, the fact that it was a full-scale modernist work about Ireland did render it novel. By accentuating the matter of Irish history and politics in its opening pages *Ulysses* is an innovative text: for the first time in a work of fiction that clearly aims to be included in an international high literary canon, Irish political issues are canvassed extensively from the native perspective. (Apart from the mixed allegiances of the Mayo landlord and author George Moore, and his mostly Anglo-Irish predecessors who wrote Victorian novels of Ireland, Joyce had few enough novelistic models for such politicking. One might think of his work as a riposte to the skittish treatment of Ireland as backward province in Thackery's *Vanity Fair,* or the maudlin and pessimistic social commentary of Trollope's Irish novels, *The Kellys and the O'Kellys* and *The MacDermotts of Ballycloran*).[7] It is in these opening episodes, therefore, that *Ulysses* marks the "sensational reentry" of Ireland "into European literature," in the limited sense that the French critic and Joyce advocate Valery Larbaud meant when he spoke this phrase during his lecture to launch *Ulysses,* given the very day after the Anglo-Irish treaty guaranteeing the independence of the Irish Free State had been signed in London in December 1921.[8]

Paradoxically, however, the text's outright avowal, at the start, of its interest in Irish nationalist politics from the subaltern perspective is also the first imposing proof that here is a novel that would continue to be interested in the political fate of the nation in which it is set. This avowal, to be clearly understood (as Larbaud and readers since have unequivocally understood it)[9] needed to be spoken within familiar forms; hence the borrowed style with which *Ulysses* declares its interest in Irish politics here is purposely derivative of the discourse of nineteenth-century European and indeed British nationalism. The Irish version of this nationalism, liberally transcribed throughout the nineteenth century by the Young Irelanders and others, from versions in use no further afield than Britain, was elaborated in the two successive Celtic revivals of the Victorian period,[10] and was reaching a crescendo when Joyce was writing these episodes in 1914–15, when organizations such as the Irish Volunteers and the Gaelic League were at the apex of their popularity. To match the discourse of the *Bildungsroman* in *Ulysses'* early episodes, Joyce found that the most hackneyed nationalism—which expressed less the possibilities of a future nation than a shrill resentment of Britain—was quite adequate. In this chapter I will show that the nationalism the novel purveys in its opening episodes is a way of imagining community that has been borrowed by the colonized people from their colonial masters.

Irish nationalism as delineated in the opening of *Ulysses* is a mimic discourse; this mimicry operates within a formal architectonics of text within text, discourse within discourse. Yet even imitation or mimicry, as opposed to mere (unmediated) use, implies a self-conscious redeployment. Through the trope of misquotation within misquotation, this self-consciousness can generate subtle and shocking spaces of difference even as it appears coyly familiar. What remains as Stephen, on Sandymount strand, decides that Dublin is a "Paradise of pretenders then and now" (*U* 38) is a stilted realism, which, as I will show, is considerably out of plumb with the conventional, secondhand ideologies that appear to be its basis.

Subaltern Nationalism as Imitation, Mimicry

Before mapping how these tactics work in the text, I will situate my argument within recent debates on the role of nationalism in representing new communities in postcolonial novels. In this way I can begin to map how subaltern discursive forms reorganize the overt narratives of nationalism relayed in the opening of *Ulysses*.

Anti-imperial revolutions and postcolonial liberation in this century have almost invariably been couched in the rhetoric of local nationalisms; it has been assumed that the nation-state will replace the colonial territory. Thus it is inevitable, as Chidi Amuta puts it, that for literature "national history and national social experience furnish a thematic quarry and an ideological imperative ... especially in post-colonial contexts."[11] Yet Amuta's discussion of the pull of alternative allegiances on African writing, from tribal traditions to the pan-African consciousness that is an impetus in works by such writers as Wole Soyinka and Ayi Kwei Armah,[12] reminds us that the nation and its formation in the postcolonial context constitute a fully *ideological* rather than in any sense an *inevitable* trajectory, and moreover, one imported from the national culture of the imperial master-state.

In this regard we should keep in mind the critiques often articulated by western observers of the inadequacy of postcolonial nationalisms at the very moment when they appear most necessary: from the right these take the form of satirical dismissal of new nation-states with their "membership of the U.N., national anthem and national airline,"[13] while from the left they are expressed as a muted disappointment that these new nationalisms do not appear (once the new state comes into being) to be the force for solidarity that had made nationalism so useful in the previous century to molders of ideology in the newly formed nation-states of Europe. (Contemporary debate on Irish cultural nationalism is also often couched in either of these terms: conservatives' horror at the bloodlust and enduring violence of Irish nationalism alternating with progressives' regret that that nationalism has been stunted and never fully realized because of such intervening ideologies as religious chauvinism).[14] Benedict Anderson, in the most engaging recent exercise of the left critique, his study *Imagined Communities*,[15] explains the failure of postcolonial governments to achieve the ideals their particular nationalism had nurtured as follows:

> Successful revolutionaries always inherit the wiring of the old state: sometimes functionaries and informers, but always files, dossiers, archives, laws, financial records, censuses, maps, treaties, correspondence, memoranda and so on. Like the complex electrical system in any large mansion when the owner has fled, the state awaits the new owner's hand at the switch to be very much its old brilliant self again.[16]

This "complex electrical apparatus" will also include the cultural machinery by which the state consolidates its hegemony, especially the ideology of nationalism itself. It is through nationalism that the new citizen is actively interpellated, just as the old colonial native subject was recruited (mainly by members of an emerging bourgeois class in the colony) to the "struggle for independence." As an ideology, a force by which the subject is convinced of the naturalness of her position, nationalism, despite its role as vehicle of the new state, turns out invariably to have been always already a discourse of the former imperial culture, the very culture it would overcome. In this sense, the long-harbored suspicions of materialist theory regarding nationalist aspirations, particularly the critiques of Rosa Luxemburg and, more ambivalently, Lenin,[17] seem justified; nationalism in this century has shown, in Anderson's elegant phrase,[18] that it can all too often "cut history off at the pass."

It is all the more startling, therefore, to find what may be regarded as the foremost recent manifesto for the study of postcolonial literature lightly passing over these suspicions to insist on "national allegory" as the literary aegis under which a great diversity of texts from different cultures might be seen to have in common an overarching aesthetic-political project. Fredric Jameson's "Third World Literature in the Era of Multi-National Capitalism,"[19] an essay as decisive in the western renewal of interest in postcolonial writing as his companion piece on postmodernism has been for new work on contemporary First-World cultural forms, has disguised to some extent the elegant simplicity of his critical proposal by throwing into the critical debate a term that might easily be confused with "national*ist* allegory." Disregarding longstanding debates on nationalism and its uses in emancipatory political or cultural action altogether, Jameson suggests instead that every postcolonial text, "especially if it develops out of ... western machineries of representation such as the novel,"[20] no matter how mired in the western "aesthetics of expression" it may seem, will in fact invariably stand as an allegory of the national situation:

> Third-world texts, even those which are seemingly private and invested with a properly libidinal dynamic, necessarily project a political dimension in the form of national allegory: *the story of the private individual destiny is always an allegory of the embattled situation of the third-world culture and society.*[21]

With Jameson, as has been noted, attempting "to cash in on the strongest possible interpretation of the Marxist theory of history by demonstrating its prescriptive power for a range of geographically and historically distinct cultural products,"[22] it needs to be asserted that the political matrix he assigns to Third-World texts should apply with equal force, in any thoroughgoing materialist reading, to First- and Second-World documents of culture as well. But this turns out not to be quite the case—Jameson finds in the "backwardness" of Third-World cultures their utopian promise. He builds his analysis on an implicit reading of Marx's modes of production as outlined in the *Grundrisse;* asserting that the precapitalist modes, despite their destruction by the violence of imperialism, survive as "significant vestiges of communal identifications,"[23] he implies that the allegorical act of transference from the apparently private to the communal is more directly inevitable in texts of these cultures. While his choice of the nation as the communal unit grasped by the political trajectory of the text is perhaps more arbitrary (Jameson begins by probing how preoccupied Third-World intellectuals seem today about their national situations),[24] his unsubstantiated faith in the "backwardness" of colonial native cultures allows him to discover even in their contemporary representative texts a certain flowering of social utopian writing, best summed up as the articulation of what Sembene Ousmane in *Xala* (which Jameson rightly admires) calls, talking of a remote settlement of huts and how their inhabitants lived, "The principles of community independence."[25]

The impetus toward understanding the community that Jameson describes, however, might better be called a version of "nationism" rather than "nationalism," for it allows the critic to short-circuit the forceful and embattled historical reality of the European ideology "nationalism" altogether. While he posits a relatively uncomplicated schema whereby communal solidarity is articulated in a postcolonial "national (or nation-ist) allegory," he forgets that nationalism as an imported ideology will almost always have long already existed, and will have forged multiple interpellative links in the colonial territory. Even for the most utopian of writers, nationalism will always, she will discover, have been there before her, eager to proffer for the text an alternative narrative of the relation of individual subject and "imagined community."

The drawback of the directness of Jameson's argument is that it allows him to disregard the considerable ideological interference of pre-existing nationalism (among other "isms") that will in fact mediate, in any given revolutionary colonial context, between the writer and her utopian community-in-solidarity. This in turn is symptomatic of the problems that result from the critic's uncomplicated model of colonial exploitation itself. To imagine colonial political reality as a wholeheartedly brutal oppression of a native population by a colonist class[26] does not take into account the way in which—in the Third World as well as in the First—the penetration of capital stages its victory as a drama of persuasion as well as exploitation.[27] This affects an ideology such as nationalism because, as a liberal bourgeois faith, it is invariably co-opted in the colonies by a new native bourgeois class which, however small, has come into being (despite the violence of colonial oppression) during the period of colonial rule. Nationalism then works in the colony to imaginatively reinvent the "primitive" or "despotic" modes of production that are likely to have long been torn apart and marginalized by the colonial administration, but merely to offer them as so much spectacle through which the masses can be interpellated to the cause of the newly invented nation.

By refusing to invoke class or class consciousness as fundamental categories for understanding postcolonial cultures in the same way that he would deploy them to describe imperial or western national structures, Jameson can suggest an unmediated solidarity between a writer like Sembene and the tribespeople who live under "conical thatched roofs, grey-black with weathering, standing out against the horizon in the middle of an empty plain."[28] By allowing this reinvention of the primitive as a model of the communal to pass without comment, Jameson comes close to reiterating the ideological elision, which serves its own specific class ends in the name of the "national good," of bourgeois nationalism itself. Postcolonial writers, especially those with the utopian intent Jameson admires but who are closer to the lived experience of decolonization and (as Aijaz Ahmad insisted in his eloquent rebuttal to Jameson's argument)[29] alive to the actual contradictions of that experience, are more likely to be disclaiming in their texts those ideologies, such as nationalism, that proffer all-too-easy and manifestly sentimental narratives of liberation. Their texts will rather be aware that these are narratives likely to have been inculcated, albeit with the paradoxical subtlety that is the ruse of capitalist penetration, by the colonial administration in the first place.

Still, the value of Jameson's directness is that he focuses us unequivocally upon an ideal for postcolonial writing, and even if this ideal comes closer to Yeats's call, in "Under Ben Bulben," to "Sing the peasantry" than to the call for distance, the "cold eye" of the Irish poet's epitaph (CP 343–44), here is still the most impassioned recent manifesto for the study of postcolonial texts from a western source. In keeping his critical gaze on specific novels and their authors, and by reconstituting the authors as intellectuals in order to underline their engagement with the national cultures from which each comes, Jameson's argument turns out for our purposes to be more useful in analyzing Stephen as the would-be national intellectual in *Ulysses* than it does in understanding the national community that may be imagined in the text. The most moving quotation Jameson gives us from a third-world text—that from the Chinese writer Lu Xun's "Preface" to his first collection of short stories—turns out to cast a striking light on the significance of the first setting of *Ulysses,* the Sandymount Martello tower:

> Imagine an iron house without windows, absolutely indestructible, with many people fast asleep inside who will shortly die of suffocation. But you know that since they will die in their sleep, they will not feel the pain of death. Now, if you cry aloud to wake a few of the lighter sleepers, making these unfortunate few suffer the agony of irrevocable death, do you think you are doing them a good turn?[30]

Numerous accounts have been given of the symbolic import of the Martello tower in "Telemachus," the squat relic of a coastal fortification system from the period of the Napoleonic wars, "absolutely indestructible" now as in 1904, that stands incongruously among the villas of a middle-class suburban enclave. But we might realize first its role as a prison (Joyce's Dublin version of, and mocking riposte to, the Tower of London), a definitively enclosed space, at once a defensive fort—a bunker—and a prison cell. Stephen remembers the one "cold domed room of the tower" where "Through the barbicans the shafts of light are moving ever, slowly ever ... duskward over the dial floor" (*U* 37), locked by a massive key. When Stephen imagines himself in this room, and then imagines "the panthersahib and his pointer" (i.e., the Englishman Haines and Mulligan as colonial master and dog) locked sleeping within it, with his own vocation being to "Call: no answer," he uncannily reechoes (with a difference) the scenario conjured up by Lu Xun. He also lets us glimpse how the strategy of "enclosure" that, as we saw earlier, is the formal principle governing the text, also epitomizes the sealed-in predicament of the characters represented here.

The difference between Stephen's version and that of Lu Xun is that whereas the Chinese writer has told a fable showing his eagerness, whatever the cost, to engage intellectually with his culture, Stephen's "Call: no answer" is couched as a record of how he has been rejected: the Englishman and his Irish toady, he implies, will in fact lock him out of the tower—that is, deny him the possibility of participating in his own national culture. Lu Xun speaks from a social interest in conditions within; Stephen, the alienated antihero, from an interest in his own status as outsider. Here, however, Jameson's insistence on "the very unusual ratio of subjective investment and a deliberately depersonalized objective narration"[31] in a postcolonial text that seems hellbent on recathecting the national political situation as an individual's psychological crisis, reorients us to see in Stephen's move a gesture of political hopelessness.

And such hopelessness was very much the tone of Irish politics in 1914–15, as Joyce was writing these episodes. This was the period in which the Home Rule Bill, which planned a limited form of self-government for Ireland, had been shelved for the duration of the Great War; it also marked a low point in the development of Irish cultural nationalism, when the movements that had nurtured the various forms of Gaelic culture seemed to have fallen into the hands of middle-class opportunists—the kind of people Joyce castigated with damning realism in his *Dubliners* story "The Sisters." This was the historical juncture in Irish political life when ideology appeared to have outrun action: the latest Gaelic revival had nurtured a desire for national independence, but that independence had not been achieved even in the limited form of "Home Rule" demanded since the days of Parnell by the Irish party, so that ideology risked turning into nothing more than a sentimental affectation of the small new middle class of the colony.

It turns out that, as starred member of this class, Stephen Dedalus's conventional alienation as an artist, which he experienced as personal affliction, can be read back, as Lu Xun did in his own case, as symptom of the national hopelessness that blights the collective consciousness. Jameson describes how the postcolonial artist's sense of futility at the impossibility of a fully realized national allegory is reflected in the mechanics of narrative closure. Spatial closure, however, is not merely a *trompe-l'oeil* closing a perspective at the end of an episode or a book; rather, consider "enclosure" as a phenomenon that is constantly reenacted at every possible level of the text. One can turn Stephen's paranoid sense of being ostracized, his feeling of being outside the pale, inside out: we can read his determined repsychologizing (in the stylized interior monologue of "Proteus") of the politics that he invokes as a strong act of enclosure of such politics within the narrow boundaries of his individual subjectivity. This gesture then becomes another example of the enclosure enforced by the political regime of which he speaks upon all its subjects. One can take the Martello tower as prison to be the all-important image in the "Telemachiad." We can read these three episodes themselves as presenting a succession of literary discourses that attempt to enclose or imprison the psyches of all of the characters within a kind of pale. (The Pale was, in the late middle ages, the small fortified area around Dublin inside which the British colonists protected themselves; from these beginnings, the word "pale" entered the English language). By examining how the mimic discourses purvey derivative ideologies that control notions of subjectivity, one can read Stephen the bourgeois artist as in the last instance a signifier of what Gramsci termed "subalternity": "the feelings of mental inferiority and habits of subservience and obedience which necessarily and structurally develop in situations of domination,"[32] and which Jameson, in the spirit of Fanon, insists is a projection of the economic and political reality that operates in the real world of the beleaguered subject. Following Jameson's argument, we can understand how Stephen's repsychologizing of the political realities he invokes may be read within the broader framework of a politically as well as psychically grounded subalternity.

The mimic discourse Stephen invokes that parallels the alienation he himself experiences as a misunderstood artist is Irish nationalism; to judge its strategic uses in the "Telemachiad" we must ask how, despite its derivation from imperial models, it operates in the colony. This is to consider the ideological static of national*ism,* as a discourse imported into the colony, which Jameson's model of the colonial encounter allows him to ignore. Clearly, this nationalism in its various manifestations cannot be merely discounted as ineffectual mimicry of British-empire jingoism; after all, it is the pivotal myth purveyed at the opening of the novel, the point of discursive departure, and the discourse Stephen invokes in the first place in order to repsychologize it. To come to terms with Irish nationalism in *Ulysses* we must go beyond the problem of the text's closure as Jameson considers it, beyond (and outside) the text itself, to consider "enclosure" within the text as the means by which it turns the mimicry Joyce discerns in the discourse of Irish nationalism into the model of a formal literary strategy. This is the broader formal strategy of mimicry, by which the text encloses its own discursive strands in the overarching framework of the discourses of the culture.

If the explicit mimicry by the characters who populate the "Telemachiad" takes the form of nationalist posturing, if such posturing is repsychologized as a problem of Stephen's psyche, and if this repsychologizing is in fact a projection of a subaltern, structurally determined consciousness, then the real project of the first episodes of *Ulysses* is to recontain this mimicry within the broader project of envisioning subalternity itself. The political force of the first two episodes of *Ulysses* in particular comes from the way the characters' poses are undermined by making visible the discourses-within-discourses as the narrative unfolds in time. Further, this unfolding is continued into the later episodes of the text. Following the "Telemachiad," the shock of the introduction of wholly new characters in the "Calypso" episode, the nervous dispersal and fragmentation of assured stances that takes place when Stephen is among the effete intellectuals in the library in "Scylla and Charybdis" and the garrulous intellectual fraternity of the newspaper office in "Aeolus," and also the transfer of the setting of the novel from the tranquil rural suburb with sea and greenery seen in the "Telemachiad" to the urban networks from Eccles Street to Holles Street Hospital of the rest of the novel, combine, in the fragmented body of the text, into a montage that underscores a growing awareness of the horror of captivity that is already implicit in the enveloping, barricaded textuality of the opening episodes.

We can next see how these episodes' representation of the nationalist ethos evolves into a formal exposé of that nationalism as an exercise in mimicry. This mimicry is a simulation engendered by uncompromising political necessity rather than (as simulation is theorized by current theorists of postmodernity) a version of a culture of excess that has lost its power of referentiality. I will read the episodes' successive gestures of national, class, intellectual, and artistic antagonism as so many deployments of the text's strategy of enclosure — a strategy wholly reinforced by the "Telemachiad"'s spatial imagery (the tower and school as prisons) and its realist proliferation of repetition and quotation, in which each successive requotation enwraps its previous citations. Finally, we must consider the fragmentary echoes of the "Telemachiad" ringing through subsequent episodes in the body of the text, reading in them an acknowledgment of enclosure and imprisonment that wished to pass as ostracism. I suggest that such enclosure is a compensatory fantasy salvaged from the same romantic versions of subjectivity that also gave rise to the notion of nationalist "self-determination." Reading back, one can discern acknowledgments of such simulation in the interstices of the text of the "Telemachiad" itself.

Reverse Racism, Hate, and "Therapeutic Anglophobia"

Ulysses opens with what at first glance seems extremely unpromising material: an account of three pompous, comfortably middle-class young Edwardian white males getting out of bed. The sort of dialogue appropriate to this E. M. Forsterish scenario is that which Mulligan, back from Oxford, dashes off so glibly: "'Thanks, old chap,' he cried briskly" (*U* 3), " 'We must go to Athens. Will you come if I can get the aunt to fork out twenty quid?' " (*U* 4), or " 'Tell that to the oxy chap downstairs and touch him for a guinea' " (*U* 6). The symbolic weight of these young men's self-conscious posturing aside (Mulligan does his trite skit on transubstantiation in the Catholic mass, Stephen fires off his clever line on Irish art as cracked looking-glass before breakfast, even Haines has dreamed elegantly about panthers), this material might have befitted the opening of a story of the sporting life — the kind of caddish world Joyce worked over without any enthusiasm in the *Dubliners* story "After the Race." The preposterous claims that have been made about the symbolic import of the Martello tower — that, for example, it should remind us of one of the Irish round towers and hence of the era when Irish saints and scholars retreated into these structures before the invading Norse—mostly betray a wry critical embarrassment that the tower was, in the first place, nothing more than a fashionably eccentric residence for a group of mildly bohemian young men. The novel, in other words, is insisting on the vacuity of their raffish bohemianism. The opening "Telemachus" episode gives us in its outline the witty parrying of three graduates, a low-to-middlebrow version of the kinds of conversations in, for example, Wilde's *Importance of Being Earnest.* There is no reason, of course, why affected middle-class Irish youth, like every other western upper middle class, should not claim its moment in the canon (although Virginia Woolf disagreed, and famously called Joyce "underbred"); what we must grasp, however, is that Joyce, in beginning his text under this aegis, marks it as embedded in the first place in the artifactuality not of high but of popular culture. The encumbrances of the symbolic apparatuses here may dazzle readers into thinking differently, but the framework presented in the opening episode is first and foremost an ordinary extract from middle-class popular fantasy culture, in its appearance quite as faithful to the popular line, in fact, as anything presented in the scrupulous mimeticism of *Dubliners* or the scenes from popular life in *A Portrait.*

Clearly, the level of Irish everyday life shown in *Ulysses'* opening pages was that closest to British middle-class culture, from which it was mostly derived. (In this context, reading "Telemachus" as a representative British middlebrow turn-of-the-century text, we might compare it to the high imperialist adventure tales of Henchy and Ballantyne, who each used the motif of three young men on an adventure as a basis of successful plots. The first rite of Mulligan, Stephen, and Haines is to go swimming: Baden-Powell would have been proud of them—although in the end only Mulligan takes to the water.) The middle-class texture of the opening tableau, however, is in the first place a background for the rhetoric of nationalism—a resoundingly Irish nationalism—in the text. Just as the prime act of imitation in the "Telemachiad" is the redeployment of the *Bildungsroman* motif of *A Portrait,* so too nationalism as it is displayed in the opening episodes of the new novel takes its cue from the nobly delivered (and preposterous) final declaration of the earlier novel, from Stephen's announcement that "I go to ... forge in the smithy of my soul the uncreated conscience of my race" (*P* 253). Joyce, we know, took extraordinary care with the beginnings and endings of his books; the word "race" was no doubt chosen carefully. Thus the revulsion that the very word, used in a major European fiction, arouses in the second half of this century makes it an excellent place to begin to question the uses of nationalism in this, his next text.

The race to which Joyce refers is not specified, although it has always been assumed that it was the "Irish race" of which he spoke. The idea of an Irish race, which had begun to play a role in nationalist discourse by the turn of the century, had a specific discursive resonance. The issue of race reached a crescendo in both high academic and popular discourses in the west in the early twentieth century, underpinned by Darwin's theory of evolution, strongly supported by the influential eugenics movement. The concept was developed in the context of the ostensible anthropological and ethnographic comparisons of peoples that was part of the ideological underpinning of popular reaction to the major European nations' empire building, which entered its most aggressive phase after the Berlin Conference of 1884. By the early years of the new century, the "scientific philosophy" of eugenics was forcefully in step with the hegemonic project of imperial governance; in 1903, for example, the Physical Deterioration Committee of the Royal Anthropological Institute recommended the setting up of an Imperial Bureau of Anthropology, with an anthropometry section that would collate data on the physical measurements of those races coming under the jurisdiction of the British Empire.[33] Given that the blatant ideological raison d'être of the whole movement in England was the fostering of a belief in British racial superiority, it is hardly surprising that the Irish fared poorly under this scrutiny. The most infamous results were the simianized features given to Irish characters in *Punch* cartoons of the Parnell years, during the Irish land agitation, and after, while notorious comparisons of the Irish to chimpanzees were made in print by (among others) the historian J. A. Froude and the "muscular Christian" Charles Kingsley.[34] It was against this kind of stereotyping that a counterdiscourse celebrating "the Irish race" was developed, in the form of an often Irish middle-class intellectualism that promoted Irish culture as evidence of a rich "racial" heritage. Articles appeared in journals such as the end-of-century nationalist *New Ireland Review* under such titles as "The Race Type in Celtic Literature."[35] Given the relative lack of difference between the Irish and the "home" race (i.e., the English themselves) against whom all colonial peoples were measured, however, it was inevitable that the Irish would be seen to occupy an ambivalent middle ground between the "master" and "dark" races. To this end, a rapprochement was forged in various popular accounts between the various peoples of the British Isles. In the Franco-British exhibition of 1907, for example, the Senegalese and Irish villages, with their respective casts of colorful yet compliant inhabitants, stood side by side; one commentator, however, having deemed the African women ugly, went on to pronounce, "The same flag covers what we believe to be the handsomest people in the world today — English and Irish — who seem to have acquired by some mysterious process of transmission or of independent development, the physical beauty of the old Greeks."[36] Given this easing of the rhetoric of race as a tool of anti-Irishness (a softening advocated earlier by Matthew Arnold himself in his 1867 *On the Study of Celtic Literature*), invocations of the "race" by the Irish themselves in the new century tended to be either aggressive and uncompromising calls for rebellion, as in the writings of Patrick Pearse, who was to lead the Easter rebellion of 1916, or tokens of an extremely generalized national feeling, with archaic overtones, as in the use of the phrase by Stephen Dedalus in the final phrases of *A Portrait*. Yeats, in a similarly histrionic usage, in his Nobel prize acceptance speech to the Royal Academy of Sweden in 1924, was to speak of the years leading up to the rebellion in 1916 as a period when "the race began, I think, to be troubled by that event's long gestation."[37]

Invoking race at moments of high-pitched ardor in early twentieth-century Irish literary discourse was the means of striking the national note with the minimum of committal; as such it was similar to the invocation of Parnell's name (a strategy also practiced extensively by both Yeats and Joyce) in these years: the granting of allegiance to a safely dead hero in order to seem thoroughly politicized yet nevertheless absolved from real political action.[38] The grandiloquence with which the word "race" was deployed in canonical writing should not, however, blind us to the fact that, given the uses to which it had been put, it could never be innocent: it would always suggest a nexus of chauvinist impulses that the term "racism" better defines. The discourse of race in late nineteenth-century Europe had not merely been chauvinistic, but actively directed *against* the peoples that racial theories criticized. Race as a signifier in British fin-de-siècle popular culture reached its apotheosis in the jingoism nurtured by the new mass-circulation yellow journalism that thrived on reporting the Boer War. The Boers (like the Irish) were a "white race" and therefore candidates for outright hatred rather than condescension: J. A. Hobson, in his magisterial 1902 study *Imperialism* (itself tainted with a strain of anti-Semitism),[39] had already perceived jingoism as an "inverted patriotism whereby the love of one's own nation is transformed into the hatred of another nation, and the fierce craving to destroy the individual members of that other nation."[40] In "Scylla and Charybdis" Stephen would criticize Shakespeare's history plays as jingoist, "sail[ing] fullbellied on a tide of Mafeking enthusiasm" (*U* 168); his critique of the most venerated texts in the British canon can be turned back onto *Ulysses* itself, at least in its opening three episodes. The "Telemachiad" of *Ulysses* was a literary construct initially fabricated around the motif of a group of mildly bohemian young men, drawn from popular culture; hence it is not surprising that its nationalist discourses, derived from the invocation of race that works as jingoism, should be propelled chiefly by racist antagonisms itself.

Samuel Chenevix Trench, the model for Haines in *Ulysses,* was a member of an Anglo-Irish family—that is, of an Irish family of English descent;[41] that Joyce made him an Englishman here suggests that he wished the text to be unequivocal about England as the primary source of jingoist, racist sentiment in these episodes, as Haines is made the chief mouthpiece for such sentiments. When Stephen, while he and Haines walk down to the seashore, lets down his guard somewhat to fall in with his visitor's confidences, and declares with feeling that he is "the servant of two masters ... the imperial British state and the Holy Roman Catholic and apostolic church" (*U* 17), the Englishman retreats immediately to the high ground of his own national identity, and instantly reveals his racist attitudes. He gives two responses, the second of which is this:

> —Of course I'm a Britisher ... and I feel as one. I don't want to see my country fall into the hands of German jews either. That's our national problem, I'm afraid, just now. (*U* 18)

Here the matter of Bloom and the "Jewish question" is covertly slipped into the text for the first time, in the form of a declaration of jingoist British anti-Semitism. (It is Deasy, the Irish Protestant Orangeman schoolmaster, who has the dishonor of amplifying it a few pages later, with his infamous joke about why there is so little anti-Semitism in Ireland: "Because she never let them in" [*U* 30]). This anti-Semitism is however, the most direct statement of a racial suspicion also alive (as Haines's word "either" in his statement just quoted implies that he expects) in the sensibilities of Mulligan and Stephen, the two Irish here. Such suspicion is focused effortlessly back onto the British, conveniently exemplified by Haines. Mulligan repeats all of the stereotypes of British brutishness from Irish popular culture: he speaks of Haines, behind his back, as "The Sassenach" (Irish for "Englishman," *U* 8) and "the Saxon" (*U* 4)—these were the names most often given the English in Irish rebel ballads. Benedict Anderson judges that reverse racism played a remarkably slight role in colonial movements, noting as an example that he never heard in the course of his research in Indonesia an "abusive argot word" for either Dutch or white. He compares this to "the Anglo-Saxon treasury: niggers, wops, kikes ... fuzzy wuzzies."[42] In this context, Mulligan's "Sassenach" represents a parlor version of "abusive argot"; it is suggestive of the way in which most of the anti-British sentiment in the "Telemachiad" is couched in the middle-class clichés of Irish popular literary culture. Mulligan later tells Haines that the tower was built when "the French were on the sea" (*U* 15), a reference to a popular ballad, the "Shan Van Vocht,"[43] about the 1789 landing of the French forces at Killala, County Mayo, to aid an Irish rebellion; the centenary of this rebellion had been commemorated in 1898, six years before the year in which *Ulysses* is set, with an outburst of what the Irish historian Roy Foster has termed "therapeutic Anglophobia."[44] "Therapeutic Anglophobia" is exactly what Mulligan, and Stephen also, for all his standoffishness, practice here, and Foster is correct to judge such effusions to be mere rhetoric rather than "an endorsement of separatism."[45] The snide remarks of the two young men sound merely rhetorical precisely because such remarks are callow copies of the racist stereotyping of British middle-class discourse that Haines himself had first voiced.

Racism, the "Telemachiad" implies, will always formulate discourses within discourses, reverse racism, to counter racism, which it is doomed never effectively to oppose because it merely imitates it. The imitation makes for a simulation that sounds, when it is spoken, merely as "rhetoric"; the question then is whether this rhetoric carries a strong negative charge, carries—to be blunt—a charge of hate. Is there real hate of the British purveyed in the opening pages of *Ulysses?* (Here, for example, may be one reasonable explanation for the way in which Joyce was long given such a cold shoulder by those who have shaped the modern British canon, beginning with F. R. Leavis, while he enjoyed such popularity elsewhere.) It comes as a surprise now to read an early British reviewer of *A Portrait* suggesting that the book expresses Irish hatred of England. Yet the notion of hatred, like that of race, cropped up regularly in Irish nationalist polemics. Douglas Hyde, in his influential address of 1892, "The Necessity for De-Anglicizing Ireland," delivered before the National Literary Society in Dublin, insisted, "We must face it as a fact that ... although they copy England in every way, the great bulk of Irishmen and Irishwomen over the whole world are known to be filled with a dull, ever-abiding animosity toward her."[46] Patrick Pearse, in his equally important and coldly passionate oration at the grave of O'Donavan Rossa in 1915 at the end of the Revival period, vowed, "We pledge to Ireland our love and we pledge to English rule our hate."[47]

These protestations of hate are the counterpart, in Irish upper-middle-class rhetoric, of the jingoist music hall songs sung by the masses in London or Manchester; but they are immediately countered, on the part of both polemicists quoted, by a call to disregard all that is disliked about the "foreigner" and to study more intently what is loved in one's own culture. And this is also the strategy that neutralizes any possibility of outright confrontation in the opening episodes of *Ulysses*. Stephen sees Haines as the latest in a succession of British settlers in Ireland since the middle ages; when he characterizes Haines's gaze as a glance askance upon the "wild Irish" (*U* 19) he is quoting a phrase used by such Elizabethan colonists as the poet Edmund Spenser to characterize their Irish subjects. Wary of this glance, he sets himself in a tradition of Irish suspicion of British methods of rule when he recalls three matters that, according to an Irish saying, no Irish person should trust: "Horn of a bull, hoof of a horse, smile of a Saxon" (*U* 19). But he discusses his fear of Haines—and he states forthrightly that it is a "growing fear" (*U* 4)—only with Mulligan, and even then decides peaceably that "There's nothing wrong with him except at night" (*U* 7). Instead, race as a force of antagonism is balanced in the first episode by an insistent focus, beginning with the sardonic discussion of Irish art and Mulligan's wish to "Hellenize" Ireland, on the possibilities of Irish cultural production. This discourse, a muted expression of national pride, is enveloped in the rhetoric of race; it should not seem ironic, therefore, that it too is practiced most zealously by the Englishman Haines, the original mouthpiece of imperialist racism in the book.

Innocuous Hibernophiles and the Ethnographic Encounter

In Haines the "innocuous Hibernophile"[48] *Ulysses* launches in its first pages a scathing indictment of the apparently benevolent ethnographic interest in Irish folk life that was central to the fin-de-siècle Celtic revival. Making Haines an Englishman, Joyce insists that this particular love of Ireland was a discourse with roots in a British rather than a native intellectual project. Rather than despise the Irish—Haines dismisses the possibility with his notorious refusal of the colonist's responsibility, "It seems history is to blame" (*U* 17)—Haines will condescend to them with an academic interest. In this sense he is one of the British conservatives who were accused in the 1890s of "killing [Irish] Home Rule with kindness"—that is, of institutionalizing a benevolent interest to ensure that Ireland would remain united with Britain. The most conspicuous proponent of this approach at the time was Lady Aberdeen, wife of the British viceroy who in 1906 replaced the Dudleys, the imitation-monarchs who drive in state along the quays in "Sirens" (*U* 211). Lady Aberdeen's version of adopted Irish nationalism involved an interest in Celtic Revival high art: Standish O'Grady's play *Finn and His Companions* was given an open-air performance at a garden party at the Viceregal Lodge in the Phoenix Park—possibly an uncanny foretelling, in the same setting, of the glories of *Finnegans Wake*. More usually, however, it meant a display of shamrocky kitsch: at one St. Patrick's ball, Thevin, the viceregal chef, produced an elaborate confection comprising a statue of St. Patrick flanked by lions under an icing-sugar canopy.[49] When the Aberdeens finally left Ireland in 1915, Lady Aberdeen amused the spectators along the route by holding a camera over her head and photographing them as she went by.

In the assiduously self-confident Britisher Haines, *Ulysses* presents us with a figure who exemplifies at once both the never quite successful efforts of British well-wishers like the vicerene to ingratiate themselves with Irish culture, and the local highbrow ethnographers and folklorists of the Celtic revival, of whom Douglas Hyde and Lady Gregory were the outstanding representatives. When Lady Aberdeen held a camera above her head, she was making a record of the Irish people within the parameters of her own conception of how these alien masses could be known; by making Haines an Englishman with a similar interest and naivete, *Ulysses* implies that this kind of imperial intent might be the real basis of the *Irish* folklore movement. Haines plans to visit the National Library, Dublin, on June 16, 1904, and he will later buy a copy of Hyde's *Love Songs of Connacht*—the transcribed poetry of west-of-Ireland peasants in a bilingual edition. Haines's interest, then, is serious, sensitive, and academic, yet his lack of any empathy for the Irish ("An Irishman must think like that, I daresay" [*U* 7] he says at one point) is stunning. It is nothing less than a racially motivated misunderstanding, and it is reciprocated by an equally opaque racial misunderstanding on the part of the Irish natives here.

Ulysses shows how these atavisms actually operate to come between the amateur ethnographer and the folkloric subject by staging a confrontation between the two parties in what is the outstanding set-piece of the novel's first episode. This is the arrival of the milkwoman, and her discussion with the three young men. The folk-ethnographies of the revivalists had often elided the actual conditions of the meeting between subject and informant: Hyde, for example, characteristically introduces new material with phrases such as, "I got this story from Martin Brennan, or Brannan, in the county of Roscommon ..."[50] Through such stratagems, an illusion of complicity, even identification, between folklorist and native informant was sustained. Joyce, however, insists on displaying the reality of the meeting, through nothing less than a clash of genres: he confronts the caddish realism used to portray the three young men at breakfast with the "twilight" glaze of portentous symbolism that diction like Hyde's "in the county of Roscommon" invariably endowed upon the folklorist tales of native life. He shows the old woman at first as she would have been portrayed in, for example, one of Lady Gregory's folklore collections or a Yeats poem inspired by them—as "mythic," in that term's most devalued sense. The milkwoman, overdetermined by such symbolism, is "silk of the kine and poor old woman" (*U* 12); she is nothing less than Mother Ireland, the "Sean Van Vocht" (*sean bhean bhocht,* poor old woman) of the song Mulligan will later quote. Within the mythic strain she might remind us, for example, of the speaker of Pearse's "Mise Eire":

Mise Éire
Siné me ná an cailleach Beara.
Mór mo náir
Mo chlann féin do dhíol a mháthair
Mór mo glór . . .

(I am Ireland
I am older than the old woman of Beara.
Great is my shame
My own family have sold their mother
Great is my glory . . .[51]

From such heights, the old woman is humiliated and made to feel a fool by Mulligan and Haines, in keeping with the caddish realism underlying the scene.

Consider how this scene would have been treated in, for example, George Moore's *Esther Waters,* to see how the clash of British realism and Irish Twilight-text orchestrated here in *Ulysses* achieves its savage effect. In Moore, we could expect the old woman's predicament to be narrated through a clear-eyed realist sympathy. We would know, for example, whether she was a servant on a nearby farm or whether she was in the process of buying out her own holding: the Wyndham Land Act of 1903 had greatly extended the transfer of land from aristocratic proprietors to peasants in Ireland, and could have made this milkwoman a peasant landowner.[52] In *Ulysses,* however, the countrywoman, perhaps the most estranged figure to enter the urban fabric of *Ulysses,* appears (through Stephen's highly derivative ruminations) with full Yeatsian shadow-effects: "A wandering crone, lowly form of an immortal serving the conqueror.... A messenger from the secret morning" (*U* 12). (We hardly hear this cadence in the text again until another, somewhat different version of high symbolism is being plagiarized, in the "Circe" description of the changeling Rudy [*U* 497]). Hence all of her subsequent statements, especially her calculation of the overdue milk bill (on which, again, George Moore would have cast a bitterly realist eye) are comic: she is condemned to being the stage Irishwoman of *Ulysses.* (The inevitable degradation of this stereotyping has already been underlined by Stephen and Mulligan, who have spoken of the folk heroine as Mother Grogan, character in a song,[53] about whom Mulligan tells a vulgar joke.) In this way, *Ulysses* signals that, as an Irish work, it will reject all nativist forms of language, symbol, and subjecthood. Through the tactic of confronting representational modes, it offers a caustic exposé of the differences of class rather than allegiance, which adopting such nativism would elide.

The exposé is masterminded by a snap turning of the joke onto the Britisher Haines himself. Stephen has been daydreaming, trancelike as usual, when suddenly it appears that Haines, thinking that here he should not miss an opportunity for folklore gathering, has attempted to address the old woman in Irish. In one of the episode's most eloquent elisions, Haines's actual words are omitted (*U* 12). Stephen interrupts his trance with the following:

> —Do you understand what he says? Stephen asked her.
> —Is it French you are talking, sir? the old woman said to Haines.
>   Haines spoke to her again, a longer speech, confidently.
> —Irish, Buck Mulligan said. Is there Gaelic on you?
> —I thought it was Irish, she said, by the sound of it. Are you from the west, sir?
> —I am an Englishman, Haines answered. (*U* 12)

It is inevitable that readers would read this exchange as a bitterly ironic comment on the way in which the Irish have had their language taken from them by the colonizing power, to the point where they cannot even recognize it. Virtually all critics have found the fact that in an Irish novel the only character who speaks Irish is an Englishman highly ironic.[54] At first glance this reading is inescapable. Yet reading more closely, we see that the old woman is more canny than she is ignorant. She changes her mind—from "Is it French ...?" to "I thought it was Irish ..." One can read this as servile compliance, a desire at all costs to agree with what the "gentlemen" say—which is, no doubt, how Haines and Mulligan read her words. But it might also have been that she realized that these words were Irish (if only "by the sound of it") but, looking Haines over, guessed that he was not Irish, and knew very well that he was not a western peasant or tweed-clad Irish revivalist, the two groups likely to be speaking the language at the turn of the century. Taking these speculations a little further, it would have been entirely possible that Haines's Irish was spoken with such an appalling accent that the old woman simply couldn't recognize it, or even, to be more kind to Haines, that he spoke the language in, say, the Connemara dialect, while the old woman knew it in the Munster one—for Irish is a language with a number of dialects, each almost incomprehensible to speakers of another. Of course, she claims, "I'm ashamed I don't speak the language myself" (*U* 13), and is probably telling the truth (there were very few Irish speakers left who were natives of Leinster in the nineteenth century, and as such Haines is extremely naive to imagine that the first countrywoman he encounters might know it), but she just might be telling a lie in her eagerness to comply with what the gentlemen expect of her. Or she might be lying to deceive the folklorist, a practice common in rural Ireland at least, where both collectors and informants were so widespread that a whole genre of folktale about tricking the folklorist actually grew up.[55]

I mention all of these possibilities not to discover the truth (it seems impossible to prove one way or the other), but to suggest that we transfer our pity from the old woman, as a figure bereft of her cultural heritage, to Haines, the ethnographer whose sample turns out not to be as exotic as he would have hoped. The text jeers at his liberal pluralism, his eagerness to understand the other culture that his government has for some hundreds of years, as he puts it, "treated rather unfairly" (*U* 17). It decries his apparent concern because, as "Telemachus" has shown, it is worked up from the confident assumption of superiority based on race that was the bulwark of imperial ideology. When Stephen thinks of Haines as "the sea's ruler" (*U* 16), we are being given a critic of culture who would understand a nation that is oppressed by his own — being given, in other words, a mirror-image at the outset of the text of ourselves as critics of culture who would understand others' texts. "Telemachus" illustrates the all-too-easy assumptions that such confidence can generate.

Having come to see how the text invites us to identify with Haines, therefore, we can now understand why the book's opening is suffused with a nationalist sentiment that at times suggests hate. This is not an example of "national allegory" in the sense in which Jameson intends that term; on the contrary, it represents the kind of nationalism as interpellative ideology that Jameson's work on the politics of postcolonial writing is eager to ignore. Rather, this ideology, with its basis in chauvinist racism, whose clichés ring as hackneyed versions of jingoist refrains, is a borrowed discourse, imitated from the chauvinist nationalism of the imperial power. By presenting us, in Haines, with a typical example of the imperial consciousness that fabricates these discourses, *Ulysses* acknowledges at the beginning the degree to which all discussions of "the Irish question" (itself a British phrase) are imitative of British models (of race, national pride, and folklore) designed to condescend to colonial peoples such as the Irish in the first place. On the frontispiece of Kipling's *Short Stories,* published in London in 1903, there is a drawing by William Strang of a giant Kipling holding in his hands a bundle of doll-like Indians, each held by a string like so many puppets;[56] Haines, in the "Telemachus" episode of *Ulysses,* turns out to play very much a similar role, for the various discourses of Irish nationalism here are all based on models that he supplies. *Ulysses* introduces this nationalism at the outset only to expose it as derivative, to signify that it provides a discourse that, as it is a symptom of colonial oppression, can only mimic it, and as such is inadequate to fashion an alternative independent version of an Irish state. To formulate such a version, to break out of the cycle of mimicry and the enclosure of racial discourse within discourse, alternative narrative modes would be needed that seemed ostensibly to have little to do with the matter of Ireland itself, but which rather present narrative forms in which other potential stories might be placed.

Laying the basis for such narrative forms is the task of succeeding episodes of the "Telemachiad." As he teaches and talks to Deasy in "Nestor," and wanders on Sandymount strand in "Proteus," Stephen gradually sheds his morose ressentiment of Haines and Mulligan, as well as his compulsion to mimic his and their already secondhand lines. Instead, he begins to search for significance in the figures about him. In "Proteus" Joyce turns the stream of consciousness, which might seem a perfect vehicle for expressing the last gasps of a shaky western bourgeois identity, into a form useful for observing a whole cast of characters at once, through the eyes of one of themselves. As Stephen notices the two women and the cocklepickers, and as he thinks of his relatives, the novel launches a sophisticated version of the strategy that made many nineteenth-century novels effective national fictions: the ability to show many members of a diverse community simultaneously going about their business, unaware of each other, in a single place. Once the novel moves suddenly from Sandymount to Eccles Street and the whole other world of the Bloom household is introduced in "Calypso," this strategy of imagining different subjects existing simultaneously is shown as key to notating a potential national community. The version of such a community envisioned in *Ulysses* is inclusive and open-ended, well removed from the prescriptive and derivative nationalism heard at the outset of the text. It is the novel forms of these narratives of freedom and inclusiveness that we will explore next.

2

Traffic Accidents: The Modernist Flaneur and Postcolonial Culture

Universal history was born in cities.
                          Guy Debord (*Society of the Spectacle,* 1983)

A whole history remains to be written of spaces — which would at the same time be a history of powers (both of these terms in the plural) — from the great strategies of geopolitics to the little tactics of the habitat.
                          Michel Foucault (*Power/Knowledge,* 1980)

"Want to keep your weather eye open."
                          Leopold Bloom (*U* 234)

Why did Yeats begin "Easter 1916" as a flaneur poem? It is striking that the opening stanza of "Easter 1916" (let us disregard class) might have been spoken by Leopold Bloom. It is not only the timidity of the political outlook ("For England may keep faith ...?" [*CP* 179]), the willingness to lapse into the well-worn and prosaic ("When all is done and said" [*CP* 179]) or even the hint of an advertising slogan in the famous refrain ("A terrible beauty is born" (*CP* 178]), all of which would have been amply worthy of Bloom's heart and mind; it is that the speaker who opens "Easter 1916" is, like Leopold Bloom, a flaneur, wandering through Dublin's streets, meeting men of business, petty bureaucrats, reminiscing. In late summer 1916, when Joyce was imagining one furtive figure loping into the National Library (Bloom in the "Scylla and Charybdis" episode of *Ulysses,* the episode he was then writing), Yeats in "Easter 1916" was recording the recollections of a remarkably similar figure, who had wandered the same streets on his way

to a gentleman's club, very probably one about a hundred yards from
the National Library farther along the same street, the Kildare Street
Club:

> I have met them at close of day
> Coming with vivid faces
> From counter and desk among grey
> Eighteenth-century houses.
> I have passed with a nod of the head
> Or polite meaningless words,
> Or have lingered awhile and said
> Polite meaningless words,
> And thought before I had done
> Of a mocking tale or a jibe
> To please a companion
> Around the fire at the club, ... (CP 177–78)

Here are two important literary works written in 1916, both concerned
with Ireland, and with Dublin in particular; Joyce's novel manifestly interested in *flânerie* and, I propose, covertly relating itself to the insurgency, Yeats's poem focusing on insurgency and, notice, using *flânerie*
as its mechanism of point of view. Why do Ireland's two major writers
turn to the figure of the flaneur to write about Ireland as colony five
years before independence?

By the end of "Proteus," as Stephen forsakes mimicry for observation, *Ulysses* shows itself able to imagine a potential community by representing different subjects simultaneously going about their own business in different locales; by presenting this ability through the figure of
Stephen, himself on the move, it implies too that these subjects will not
be static, but moving also. This chapter investigates the significance of
this traffic. *Ulysses* is, until its closing episodes, very much a novel of
pedestrians; its primary spectacle is that of Leopold Bloom on the move.
Walking is the primary motif in Bloom's representation as a character,
more important than his marriage to Molly, his anxiety over father-
hood, his identity as a Jewish Dubliner. At the heart of *Ulysses* is a particular kind of dromomania—a name, notes Paul Virilio, given to de-
serters under the French *ancien regime,* and in psychiatry to compulsive
walkers.[1] Bloom and the other walking Dubliners might seem typical
turn-of-the-century versions of the flaneur figure who stalks fin-de-siècle continental European imaginations. As I show in this chapter, however, the flaneur of an empire capital and the flaneur of a late colonial

city like Dublin proceed apace under different social auspices. Each is
the effect of structurally opposed sets of economic effects. I will examine how the late-nineteenth-century flaneur of imperial capitals such as
London and Paris was taken by a novel about a late-colonial city, to
be transformed into a figure who could walk by the nets of colonial
interpellation.

The flaneur is one of the most poignant dramatis personae of mainstream European modernism, lifted by Baudelaire from Poe's short story
"The Man Of The Crowd," observed and theorized as he wandered
in the Parisian arcades by the cultural materialist Walter Benjamin.[2]
Now, he is being placed firmly in the foreground by Ireland's modernists as they work to describe realities that are likewise urban, but
which exist beyond the radical anomie inspired by the cosmopolitan
modern city which Benjamin takes Baudelaire's dark and sensual figures to represent. Baudelaire's flaneur is the apparently *déclassé* modernist version of the *homme moyen sensuel,* now allowed to succumb
to "the temptation to lose himself in a flood of human beings," as he
learns "the relationship between unrestrained behavior and discipline"[3]
needed to absorb the continual effect of shock generated by the tech-
nologized cityscape. The flaneur of Yeats and Joyce is this character,
but further, he is a figure who acts as a sounding board for the more
immediate shock of visible political transformation. The Baudelairian
wanderer in the arcades and streets, gazing upon the spectacle of
the city, with its plate-glass windows proffering commodities, its numbered residences (Paris had its houses numbered, Benjamin notes, in the
mid-nineteenth century),[4] its particular configuration of labor and consumption, is a case study in one self-education in the demands and
pleasures of capital at its most ostentatious and concentrated, with
which western modernist literature and theory has been familiar. The
flaneur whom Yeats and Joyce each imagine almost simultaneously also
embodies this reorientation of the individual in the brutally pleasurable
early twentieth-century metropolitan cityscape. His reconnaissance of
the streets, however, among the "grey eighteenth-century houses"
(Yeats) built for the old Anglo-Irish aristocracy, and the "surly front"
(Joyce) presented by such politically symbolic public buildings as the
Anglo-Irish Trinity College, confronts (explicitly in Yeats and, I suggest,
implicitly but no less forcefully in Joyce) the spectacle of late-colonial
domination—educates him in its demands, pleasures, modes. Further,

this is a flaneur-as-subject who is educated in confrontation between the colonial administration and the native population—particularly in Joyce's work.

Yeats, his own allegiance as metropolitan British or nationalist Irish poet at best ambivalent, closes off a nagging awareness of this in a willful strategy of triumphal sloganeering ("All's changed ..."), while his flaneur-narrator turns his thoughts toward leaving the street to enter a club, very possibly the Kildare St. Club, another building certainly connoting allegiance to the ruling colonist power. (This club was the stronghold of British and Ascendancy interests in Dublin,[5] and as a "club"— as in a Kipling story or George Orwell's *Burmese Days*—stood as a symbol of the colonial establishment). It remains to Bloom, on the other hand, to stay in the street, so that the spectacle of the city as colonial and revolutionary nexus emerges in *Ulysses* as its political unconscious. In this chapter I will uncover this "unspoken" Dublin. It is fitting that it is covertly spoken, as it relied on secrecy rather than on display; its impact on Bloom as flaneur can here be made explicit.

The Ideology of Traffic

The opening proposition of this chapter is that the acceptance of shock in an ontological account of city life, or of *flânerie* as a signifier of the twentieth-century subject reacting to such shock, is ultimately essentialist and mystifying. It is essentialist to the extent that it envisions all cities, and their citizens' experiences of them, as largely similar. Consider at the outset the blatant Eurocentrism in Marx's universalizing lament for the modern period (popularized by Berman) as the one in which "*All* that is solid melts into air"[6] (italics mine). One must grasp the metropolitan modernism of Edgar Degas's painting *Place de la Concorde*, Alfred Döblin's *Berlin Alexanderplatz*, Virginia Woolf's *Mrs. Dalloway*, T. S. Eliot's *The Wasteland*, and Franz Kafka's *Amerika*, all of which conjure up *flânerie* as their vision of urban subjectivity, and the theories of the nascent social sciences expounded by Walter Benjamin, Max Weber, Georg Simmel, and Oscar Bie that validate them and whose influence has underlain critiques of modernism from both left and right, as equally implicated in a turn-of-the-century sensibility whose first feature was a triumphal Eurocentrism. Given the continuing hegemony of western concepts in current critical theory (which itself mirrors a radical inequity in the distribution of intellectual capital), it is not surprising that the theories of the early twentieth-century social scientists, impressionistic modernist works themselves, have largely been allowed to stand. Yet the twin notions of "shock," described famously by Georg Simmel,[7] and the *Nervenleben* (nervous stimulation) adduced by Benjamin, which together underpin any account of *flânerie*, imply an ontology of urban experience determined by specific class and political assumptions that has gone largely unquestioned for nearly a century.

The modernist metropolitan artist's or theorist's willingness to engage with the texture of the newly enlarged and busier city marked a degree of disengagement from the question of the political (even geopolitical) factors that gave rise to the new scale and tempo of the metropolis in the first place. The streets of the recently refurbished grand capitals of the new western nations and soon-to-be empires had been broadened or newly built as monuments to imperial power, and also as spaces commodious enough to accommodate the vast new traffic of (partly colonial) trade and business. No sooner had these European cities become national and imperial capitals in the mid-nineteenth century than the metropolitan street as the tableau vivant of western representation entered a new stage. With the building of the massive new street systems—the Ringstrasse in Vienna, the Grands Boulevards of Baron Haussmann's Paris, along with the completion of l'Enfant's plan in Washington and the widening of the Mall in London from Buckingham Palace to the new Admiralty Arch by the Queen Victoria Memorial Committee between 1906 and 1913[8]—images of commodious and busy streetscapes proliferated. Avowedly modernist works focused, fascinated, on what Kafka termed *Verkehr*—"traffic";—the word in German also means "commerce, exchange, circulation, social and sexual intercourse, even tourism and epistolary correspondence."[9] Within such a constellation, the crowded movement of the street became an underlying metaphor for the choking quality of the shared experience of modernity. The subjects with whom the texts populated these streets were machines measuring what Benjamin termed *Nervenleben,* the nervous stimulation generated by the shock of the traffic-crowded cityscape.

Yet such modernist flaneur-pieces as Degas's canvas *Place de la Concorde* might usefully be set over against contemporary (and, despite the marshaled trappings of tradition, newly invented) pageants like Bastille Day, which was held for the first time in 1880, or the triumphal processions of Queen Victoria's Golden and Diamond Jubilees, of 1887 and 1897.[10] These processions aimed to imbue the citizen with a sense of awe at the boulevards and vast new piazzas as spectacles of imperial power; self-consciously high metrotexts worked to overcome the citizen's fear of the grand new scale of the metropolitan thoroughfares. Both, however, depicted the street not only as an aggressive, shocking arena but simultaneously as a site of gratification, where the lone individual could lose herself in the crowd. This new kind of pleasure to be gained by "losing oneself in a flood of human beings,"[11] first put into words by Poe and Baudelaire, was recast as a positive force. The ideological project shared by both official processions and high art was to replace what Engels, with typical early Victorian revulsion against the new urbanism, had described in 1844 as the "repulsive horror of the streets," with an emphasis on the energizing frisson generated in the individual in the ever-stimulating, shocking city.

   "Traffic is an artwork endowed with such strong and various charms that it can never be fully explained"[12] wrote Oscar Bie in 1905. To read traffic as a painting or sculpture as Bie does (a project such Italian Futurists as Balla and Marinetti would fully realize) epitomizes the closeness of such social observers as Bie to the artistic project of the period; its willful aestheticizing[13] of the new reality, however, also suggests a fear of the forces that the traffic—the moving mass—might unleash. In this light, the very invention of *flânerie* as a literary phenomenon— grounded in a residual appeal to the snobbery of bourgeois individualism—may be read as a last-ditch attempt to dispel the threat of the mob's velocity in the street, "where for a moment it stops being a cog in the technical machine and becomes a motor (machine of attack) in other words, a *producer of speed*."[14] Bie, in his 1905 *Gesellschaftliche Verkehr* (Social intercourse),[15] for example, is eager to aestheticize the crowd while he insists on its key role in informing the actions of each of its members: "the spectacle of human traffic ... its rhythmic patterns of people in social motion, ... the noise that rises up from the street ... the confusing tempi of life ... all represent the summation of individual rhythms and their timetable in the book of their artfully stylized motion, the product of an infinitely complex codification of mass traffic." The crowd, by the turn of the century, had at once to be encouraged to partake of the freedom of the street and domesticated in its use. What was needed was art-as-timetable, which could tabulate the flow of traffic in a city of movement. (Conversely, the timetable itself was being revised as art: this was the era of the travel poster.) The flaneur as representative subject in turn-of-the-century fictional narratives of the city stood for a compromise between the desire to aestheticize the crowd—to *represent* it—and to codify or *control* it. (Or rather, it aimed to control the crowd by an act of imaginative will, under cover of the aesthetic apprehension of its novel charms.) It is therefore not surprising that in many modernist city-narratives the writer reaches the point of dispensing with the flaneur—peripatetic consumer of the delights of the crowd, as intelligent and blasé as Simmel, in *The Metropolis and Mental Life* (1903) had described him—altogether, and instead attributes the role of envisioning the crowd to the narrative itself. At such moments, at the very point of the disappearance of the flaneur, describing the crowd's delights is forgotten and the text's project to control it is made key.

This, in effect, is what occurs in Yeats's "Easter 1916" after the flaneur-narrator thinks of retelling the street stories in the club, and it is a point at which that poem brackets its specifically Irish (and postcolonial) political concerns to partake of the crowd surveillance that it shares with many European metropolitan high modernist works, from Eliot's *The Wasteland* to E. M. Forster's *A Room with a View*. Numerous modernist texts stage the death or incarceration, the bundling indoors, of their most interesting flaneurs (one might read all Kafka's fictions as an attempt to question, while it rehearses, such incarceration), but this is the turn that is absolutely refused in *Ulysses;* in fact, the unreserved quality of the text's gift of Bloom to the streets is what makes *Ulysses* such an exceptional high modernist text. (Bloom, much more wholeheartedly than the Yeatsian "I," can claim to be a "smiling public man" [*CP* 213]—without any of the sham bashfulness with which Yeats burdens that self-characterization.) To show how this works in practice, compare for a moment the way in which one glimpse of a cityscape is narrated in *Ulysses* with the representation of similar scenes in the work of both Kafka and T. S. Eliot.

First, consider the photograph of O'Connell Bridge, Dublin, in 1902 (Figure 2). It is a structure of the new, modernized urban order: newly widened (it had replaced an older, humpbacked bridge, torn down in 1872), adorned with ornate gaslamps, the most modern tramlines in

Fig. 2. O'Connell Bridge, Dublin, early twentieth century. Lawrence Collection, National Gallery of Ireland.

Europe, and tramcars bearing advertisements for "Holloway's Pills and Ointments." Before seeing how it is figured in *Ulysses,* consider how the bridge, as crossing, recurs in modernist texts as a point at which the writer can tabulate, in the aftermath of the demolished city gate or customs-point, the traffic flow. Eliot, famously, watches as

> Under the brown fog of a winter dawn,
> A crowd flowed over London Bridge, so many,
> I had not thought death had undone so many.[16]

Kafka's first major story, "The Judgment"[17] (1912), ends with the sentence, "At that moment an unending stream of traffic was going over the bridge." Both writers envision the crowd as an anonymous mass, as seen from a distance; into this mass, Eliot interpolates Dante ("I had not thought . . ." borrows from *The Inferno*) to suggest his own sense of the unreal city as underworld, while Kafka, with only his own inspiration, told Max Brod that in writing his sentence he was thinking of a "giant orgasm."[18]

Now consider how we reach the O'Connell Bridge in *Ulysses.* The approach (of the pedestrian Bloom) is almost unnoticed: "His slow feet walked him riverward, reading" (*U* 124, opening of the "Lestrygonians" episode). (Bloom crosses the bridge on the side nearest the viewer in the photograph; going toward Westmorland Street, he moved from the left to the right of the scene shown. He would have fed the gulls over the parapet before us.) Bloom does not notice any crowd, as he peruses a flier for a preacher from the United States, Alex J. Dowie (*U* 124). He goes on to spot barrels of Guinness stout bound (by barge on the River Liffey below him) for England, and apples piled high, which he surmises — it is early June — are from Australia. He remembers Molly's thoughts of Spain. He sees the Ballast Office timeball and reads Dunsink (Irish) as opposed to Greenwich (English) time.[19] He sees Stephen's sister Dilly Dedalus in tatters, an advertisement for Kino's eleven-shilling trousers on a rowboat in the Liffey, and the gulls that he feeds with a Banbury bun. All he sees leads him to ruminate: Dilly on the evil of large families, Kino's advertisement on the idea that "All kinds of places are good for ads" (*U* 126). Which is to say that the stream-of-consciousness technique turns the morose observations of Kafka and Eliot inside out: the reader's eye is no longer on the bridge or the crowd (as Benjamin said of the crowd in Baudelaire, it is so pervasive that it is scarcely ever mentioned explicitly), but on the series of images caught by Bloom's gaze.

Here, Bloom's ruminations and observations function much as did those of Stephen discussed in the previous chapter. Rather than having omniscient narration work to provide a panopticism with a wish to control the masses, the view from a single subject provides an equalizing gaze upon an heterogeneous group of people, activities, and spectacles. Note that the line of vision, then, of Joyce's and Eliot's texts is directly opposite: one in fact looks out upon the vantage point of the other. Eliot surveys the scene of the bridge; his gaze parallels the desire of Sherlock Holmes, who exclaimed to Watson, "My dear fellow, If we could fly out that great window hand in hand, hover over this great city, gently remove the roofs, and peep in at all the queer things that are going on ..."[20] The poet's vantage point allows him to view the masses from above (as from a balloon or an airplane); he makes a sociological observation. Joyce's, on the contrary, is outwards and upwards: the bridge becomes the platform before an open cityscape and a varied spectacle. Bloom is not disregarded as a particle of the homogenized urban masses: he sees advertisements, apple-sellers, people moving through the grandiose cityscape, and he also considers England, Spain, Australia, other places. In this sense, his stream of consciousness does not represent the latter end of objective narration, fading in a pall of subjective language; rather, it shows itself to be a fresh and fertile ground for the creation of a radically new and independently narrating subject. Just as Stephen's soliloquy in "Proteus" encapsulates a multitude of spectacles of others around himself, so too Bloom absorbs the diversity of activity that surrounds him. Combined with *flânerie,* the freedom of movement, it grants Bloom the opportunity to see a vast series of spectacles in his own way.

Ulysses can clearly be read as *the* example of an early twentieth-century flaneur-novel, because of its manifest aim to characterize a city and because Bloom seems the very personification of the most characteristic modern persona, the man of the crowd. I suggest, however, that its very success in this mode makes it exceptional. For the metropolitan high modernist text, the imaginative invention of the flaneur was from the beginning a doomed enterprise. The particular entrapment-by-narrative involved in flaneur representations is aptly symbolized by this figure's first and perhaps most famous representation, in the short story by Edgar Allan Poe. No sooner had Poe's "Man of the Crowd" been given the freedom of the streets than he was followed, restricted in his movements by being always watched. Poe's hero was managed by that narrative apparatus whose thematics and plotting epitomize surveillance and control: the detective story. Much Eurocentric modernism was interested ultimately in controlling, even as it appeared to develop, the novel subjectivity of those to whom the freedom of the streets has been given; thus representations of the flaneur and the detective-story idiom have from the first gone hand in hand.

Ulysses' single-day setting, its primal image of a perambulating turn-of-the-century bourgeois male, has meant that it has been seen as a relatively typical set-piece of early twentieth-century metro-representation, a literary counterpart to the famous photographs taken by Zola in Paris, Monet's *Les Parapluies,* or films like Karl Grune's *Die Strasse* (The street, Germany, 1923). Rather than read Dublin in 1904 (or in 1914–21, when the novel was being written) as simply another European city whose streetscapes had received a newly rationalized impress of insidious modernization, however (the sort of cityscape now opened to the postmodern, nostalgic gaze by the monochrome photographs of Fox-Talbot and William Lawrence in Dublin[21] or Atget in Paris), I wish to read it as one of the first cities of the colonial "other world," the world that largely made the expansion of the European capitals possible, and a city that was soon to be itself a capital of a newly independent postcolonial state.

In turn, Bloom — particularly if one reads the story of his being cuckolded, humiliated, and disregarded as tragedy — may readily be seen as another hemmed-in flaneur under surveillance, so that *Ulysses* becomes the text of his incarceration and defeat. On the contrary, however, I will read Bloom's *flânerie* as aggressive, emancipatory, and the blueprint for a potential version of new postcolonial subjectivity. I will claim that the enlivened, reborn flaneur in Joyce's text is formed out of a model for the representation of the urban subject that more Eurocentric modernists were chiefly concerned to suppress. As such, we might say that the gift of high modernist writing to newly emerging Third World representation was this loping, dark-clothed estranged figure that European writers at the height of empire had created but of whom they had from the beginning been afraid.

To suggest such a cross-transference of representational forms from texts whose unconscious political agendas are very much at odds begs a series of questions. Why, in the first place, should the flaneur in the colonial or postcolonial city be capable of being imagined as a more fully or freely sensuous and self-constituting subject? Would it not seem, rather, that the flaneur in the colonial city would be more rigorously under surveillance in the real conditions of a colony, if not in a text? Why is the figure in the colony—which I suggest is Bloom's milieu—receptive to a richer spectacle? Why should it be the colonial flaneur who realizes the full potential of *flânerie?* To answer these questions, it is necessary to understand more fully the actual relationship between a subject like Mrs. Dalloway,[22] going out to walk through the West End of London, and a flaneur-figure in Delhi, or Dar-es-Salaam, or even Dublin: between the cosmopolitan European flaneur and his colonial counterpart. That the second figure in this relation was up to now invisible does not mean that he did not exist, or rather, that he (or she) could not be invented. This invention—by a simple transference from the empire's discourse—was a fitting gesture of early twentieth-century cultural appropriation; I will now explore how it came about.

Confronting the Imperial Flaneur With his "Native" Counterpart

There are in *Ulysses* some minor moments of pleasure that seem like glimpses of an antiquarian mode. These involve scenarios in which alien discursive strategies of the text collide: those moments when a First World flaneur is confronted with this character's colonial counterpart. Dublin, like any colonial city, was a warehouse for the last, worn-out relics of empire *flânerie:*

> A onelegged sailor crutched himself round MacConnell's corner, skirting
> Rabaiotti's icecream car, and jerked himself up Eccles street. Towards
> Larry O'Rourke, in shirtsleeves in his doorway, he growled unamiably:
>   —For England ...
> He swung himself violently forward past Katey and Boody Dedalus,
> halted and growled:
>   —Home and beauty. (U 185)

The "Wandering Rocks" episode, which includes this passage, is the novel's central entr'acte, and the key staging ground for confrontations between this kind of figure and his local counterpart. There is, for example, Cashel Boyle O'Connor Fitzmaurice Tisdall Farrell, whose wandering eccentricity well represents the only means by which any of

Yeats's "Olympian" colonist class are allowed to enter Joyce's text, as comic flaneur relics of another time. (O'Connor Farrell is pictured passing the Kildare Street Club [*U* 201], the bastion of the Anglo-Irish aristocracy and the club very possibly sought out by the narrator of "Easter 1916".) In what follows O'Connor Farrell encounters the blind stripling, a flaneur but unquestionably a native. In fact, as a piano-tuner, the blind stripling is one of the workers in the book:

> He [O'Connor Farrell] strode on for Clare St., grinding his fierce word. As he strode past Mr. Bloom's dental windows the sway of his dustcoat brushed rudely from its angle a slender tapping cane and swept onwards, having buffeted a thewless body. The blind stripling turned his sickly face after the striding form.
> —God's curse on you, he said sourly, whoever you are! You're blinder nor I am, you bitch's bastard.
> (*U* 205–6)

O'Connor Farrell, the Baudelairean flaneur grown senile, has lost his suppleness in the crowd which Benjamin admired in his ancestor; the blind stripling, on the contrary, despite his handicap (even because of it) has special skills for finding his way through the streets. In such scenes, which litter "Wandering Rocks" (in this episode, when the linear narratives do not bring such opposites together, the cubist juxtaposition of narrative planes does so) the dead end of a metropolitan empire *flânerie* is faced off against the tentative first versions of a late-colonial subject as a ceaseless walker in the city. Stalking O'Connor Farrell are the ghosts of the more confident flaneurs of high European modernism; in *Ulysses*, however, these appear as caricatures like the canting Father Conmee, Mrs. McGuiness whom the clergyman encounters in Mountjoy Square ("A fine carriage she had. Like Mary, queen of Scots, something. And to think that she was a pawnbroker!" [*U* 181]), Mr. Denis J. Maginni, "professor of dancing &c, in silk hat, slate frockcoat with silk facings, white kerchief tie, tight lavender trousers" (*U* 181), and the sandwichmen, each wearing one large-printed letter, who advertise the stationer's H.E.L.Y'S. (*U* 187). These are all props left over from an earlier production.

The blind stripling, on the other hand, aggressively claiming his right to the streets, is one of the masses who now stakes a claim for himself as an individual. This group includes Mrs. Breen, the harried woman whom Bloom meets soon after he crosses O'Connell Bridge, and her husband who carries lawbooks about the city on June 16; most from the crowd of petit-bourgeois males who congregate in the afternoon at the Ormond Hotel; Stephen; Mulligan and his circle; and above all Bloom himself. There is one other highly memorable flaneur in *Ulysses*, mysterious because it appears he is not sure which group he belongs to: he is the man in the macintosh, who wanders throughout the city without the spectator's confidence of the empire flaneur or the determination of his colonial "native" counterpart. As such, the man in the macintosh may be the IRA terrorist as gunman or bomb-carrier in *Ulysses*. Such men were conventionally shown in trench coats or macintoshes in photographs from the 1916–21 period, and like this figure, they wished to be inconspicuous. Certainly, as Joyce worked on the later episodes of *Ulysses,* the figure in Dublin itself most like the man in the macintosh was Michael Collins, key leader in the War of Independence; Collins, as "the most wanted man in Ireland," was famous for nevertheless evading the British security forces while he crisscrossed the city in civilian clothes. If the man is Joyce's proto-gunman (and even the text's covert allusion to covert figures like Collins), then the old metropolitan flaneur is indeed being thoroughly recast in a late-colonial context.

Why should the figure of the western flaneur, stock hero of European modernist texts, have proved so amenable for kidnapping by a text that, I propose, comes out of a late-colonial rather than a high-imperial context? Why should it have been possible to degrade the older flaneur — who had earlier behaved with such subtle and knowing elan on the streets of London, Paris or Vienna — in a novel set in Dublin? If Dublin was a late-colonial city, why should a novel written at the moment when that colonialism came to an end, written from the subaltern viewpoint, have found this flaneur a useful figure to abduct as the basis for a representation of potential subjectivity within another economic order? Under what conditions — the texture of life in the late colonial city — did it show the subaltern flaneur to operate? How did it alter the pattern of the *flânerie* of the metropolitan capitals to make it appropriate for a colonial urban center? To understand how this transference from the concerns of the subject at the center of metropolitan reality to those of the subject at the periphery — both epitomized by a walker at large — took place, one needs to consider why this crosscultural exchange of literary figures should have occurred at the heart of the modern period. *Ulysses*, by making a spectacle of the old *flânerie* for us as it inaugurates the new, challenges us with these questions. We have seen how a conventional view of *flânerie,* as the representative subjectivity of an implicitly progressive European modernism, is often not borne out in practice in such Eurocentric modernist texts as *The Wasteland,* which turn out to suppress the freely wandering figure as they survey the masses. This *literary* control of the flaneur in the empire capitals was paralleled by a *literal* control of those to whom the freedom of the street was granted in the colonial centers. But the strolling figure at the heart of an empire had also to be constituted as a scene of gratification (Mrs. Dalloway, for example, buys her flowers) and the mechanics of this gratification, built around the possibilities of consumption in a city of commodities, were what the subaltern text seized, in order to reformulate them as the mechanics that would make possible a postcolonial subject.

The *flânerie* of metropolitan modernism was an education in consumption; at the same time, the avant-guardist impulse of such literature (or its elitist puritanism), affected to despise such gratifications. With the high modernists staging a critique of Victorian aggrandizement, the flaneur was allowed into their texts as the last "character," in the sense of that term derived from nineteenth-century bourgeois realism. Thus the flaneur exists in metropolitan modernist works as the last hostage of realism whom the modernists (Döblin in *Berlin Alexanderplatz,* Woolf in *Mrs. Dalloway*) could not bear to let go: as such, in their texts, she or he invariably operates as a nexus for the nostalgic desires to which the commodity pitched its pleasure. As a figure he embodied, therefore, in a fateful contradiction, both the stark pessimism of would-be oppositional modernist art that still harbored him, along with an appetite, however attenuated, for the decadent pleasures that this art would righteously forego. This rearguard, perverse pleasure in the commodity is epitomized in the flaneur-as-cipher by the way texts focus on how he surrenders his consciousness to the pleasurable logic of the commodity economy. The text's own conscientious rejection of these superficial pleasures, in turn, is signified in the single, pointless motor-activity to which it condemns him: his compulsive walking. These two defining features of the western modernist flaneur—the surrender of individual consciousness in favor of a reception of pleasure before the proffered commodity; and the unending, repetitive movement on foot—are precisely those abducted by a literature interested not only in modern metropolitan reality but also in the matter of colonial rule and anticolonial insurgency. As with the sad harlequins painted by Picasso, the modernist literary text was always ready to vitiate the flaneur's pleasure in consumption. As a narrative sign this figure occupies the space, as the theorist of architecture Manfredo Tafuri puts it, between Munch's "The Scream" and El Lissitzky's "Story of Two Squares," between "the anguished discovery of the nullification of values ... [and] the use of a language of pure signs, perceptible to a mass that had completely absorbed the universe without quality of the money economy."[23] This western walker stands at the moment at which individual consciousness ceases to be important or even necessary: at the point when the spectacle of commodities (theorized by Guy Debord fifty years after the fact)[24] successfully proffers itself as a substitute for the hapless anomie originally induced by the realization of the end of values as such.

This is apparently the point at which we find Bloom in *Ulysses*; his own abandonment of "values," as has been pointed out by the critic Franco Moretti,[25] precludes him from feeling any profound anguish at Molly's adultery, and whose stream of consciousness, as Kenner and others have shown, may more appropriately be called a stream of unconsciousness, or rather, a stream of ruminative reactions to a plethora of the proffered signs that constitute the city itself. Yet Bloom (precisely because this is the first postcolonial novel, rather than the last metropolitan one) does not suffer from an anomie induced by the loss of (western, metropolitan, empire) values: as a subaltern subject, he had never had confidence in such values to begin with. What is key, rather, is the way in which First-World values, and the First-World *flânerie* that marks their disintegration, are dependent upon the economic realities that the colonies represent. The different urban milieus of the empire capitals and colonial cities exist as mirror images of one another; they each need the other in order to function, and for each, the truth of its existence is to be found in the condition of the other. The metropolitan pedestrian's moment of surrender of consciousness turns out to be that at which, for the colonial subject, the whole network by which his consciousness has been interpellated is exposed; compulsive walking turns out, for the colonial subject, to be a convenient signifier that would at once replicate and overcome those former networks of control.

The figure of this western flaneur, thrown up specifically by the imperial modernist imagination, can function in colonial and postcolonial texts to exemplify the other that is a contemporaneous colonial subject precisely because of the congruence, in the early years of this century and at the historical moment when the empires were about to be broken apart, of the histories of the senses of both the metropolitan citizen and the colonial subject. The flaneurs imagined by Baudelaire or the *flâneuse* of the opening pages of Woolf's *Mrs. Dalloway* are both confronted with the spectacle of a capitalism that is manifestly *metropolitan* — confronted, that is, with an economy that functions vaingloriously at the heart of grand empires as triumphal spectacle. (Woolf's Miss Kilman in *Mrs. Dalloway,* for example, goes to shop at the Army and Navy Stores. Mrs. Dalloway looks forward to meeting Peter Walsh, who has come back from India.) For the inhabitant of the capital of an empire, however, that lingering experience of separation designated by Durkheim "anomie" or by Marx "alienation," which touches Woolf's characters to the quick, may itself in the last instance be characterized as the individual's experience of the forceful disjunction of colonial production and home consumption insisted upon by imperialism, which kept the exploitation of the colonies absent from the conspicuous consumption of their wealth in the metropolitan centers.[26] And the fictional metropolitan flaneur, moreover, ultimately (as with Mrs. Dalloway herself) marks the bearable limit of anomie and of character as autonomous individual consciousness altogether. It is crucial to realize that the reaching of this profound limit in the education of subjects in the imperial center is predicated on a further intensification of control over the "native" subjects in the colonial periphery.

In the opening decades of this century, then, flaneurs from the empire and the colonies look into the kaleidoscope of capital's spectacle from opposite ends: the flaneurs of Woolf and Baudelaire are presented with the imperial city and its wares, a spectacle from which a primary source of its wealth, the colony, is elided; Yeats's and Joyce's walking antiheroes are shown, on the contrary, the colonial city, in which the pleasure of consumption is always overshadowed by a more explicit evidence of exploitation. The oppression sensed by the colonial native (as described by such postcolonial writers as Frantz Fanon and Aimé Césaire)[27] on the other hand, stems from his or her subjection to a regime that enforces the exploitation of raw materials for the benefit of the colonist power, the "liberation" of the work force for similar ends, and the consumption only of the excess production of the imperial centers.[28] The listless anomie of the metropolitan is predicated on exactly that absence (of the colonial reality of the production of wealth) which functions as the sole presence for the other. At the late moment of high imperialism, the metropolitan citizen and colonial native face each other in a version of Hegel's master-slave relationship, in which the identity of the master is the slave, and the identity of the slave is in the master.

The western flaneur's surrender to consumption (which corresponds to the moment of the jettisoning of conscious will by, for example, Mrs. Dalloway) is, for the subaltern, the point at which he is finally won away from any ideology of "self-determination" and can be fully and completely interpellated by the colonial regime. In order for imperialism as a stage of capitalism to function as an economic mechanism, realizing the commodity culture at home is predicated upon creating an interpellated native subject in the colony. When this occurs, the colonial subject also, and simultaneously, loses her identity as an individual consciousness, so that her subjectivity is not now to be found (as the stream of reaction proves) in any "inner" or politically conscious direction, but rather in the mass of stimuli with which this further disempowered individual is bombarded. We can see this vividly at work in "Wandering Rocks," where Bloom, ostensibly, since the fourth episode of the book, the central character, appears now only in a series of sidelong glances from the narrator, and in a story told by a passer-by who spies him searching through a book-cart (U 192–93). Bloom as unheeded flaneur wanders through this episode; what we come to know of him in it we infer from his milieu.

Is this then not the same outcome for the native flaneur as for this figure's empire counterpart, which we noted earlier in the texts of Kafka and Eliot? Not quite. The metropolitan flaneur had to contend merely with the authorial eye withdrawing in disgust until it took in, at a suitable distance, the masses as a whole, whereas the native flaneur had to contend with actual webs of intense surveillance by the forces of colonial rule. Both the metropolitan and colonial figures are the victims, at this historical moment, of a loss of individual autonomy. For the metropolitan, however, this loss is at least couched in a rhetoric of novel freedoms: particularly the freedom to "choose." (Take "travel literature," the most First World of all genres: this was also the moment when the

European masses were given access to the pleasures of mass transport in popular tourism.[29]) For the colonial native, however, the new freedoms granted as the colony becomes more successful (hence more submissive) are always merely the countersign of a more thorough if less evident control. The native's interpellation as a subject at this stage occurs not by exposure to numberless commodities in a carnival of desire (as is the case with the First-World citizen in Paris or London) but first, through a concerted and fundamentally repressive regime of the control of knowledge and surveillance, a gaze of power-knowledge exercised at every level of the subject's existence. This is what the late colonial text represents; whereas Eliot simply draws back, aghast at the masses, Joyce examines this regime in detail. In "Wandering Rocks," for example, the network of covert information extends from the secrets of the confessional harbored by the Jesuit Father Conmee to the official secrets communicated to Corny Kelleher, undertaker, by the North Strand policeman (U 183–85). Ulysses, as I will show, is built around webs of official and unofficial secrets that act as barriers, customs-points, and silent inspections curtailing the freedom of movement of this native colonial flaneur.

At the same time, this terrific and apparently total interpellation, while appearing to mark the colonial government's final success of its project to dominate the native, turns out, paradoxically, to be the latter's version of an opening for freedom. The access to pleasure and the forgetting of anomie on the part of the First-World citizen must be paid for by her colonial counterpart with a complete availability for colonial interpellation. The metropolitan flaneur has paid for his pleasure with a surrender of consciousness. The flaneur in the colonies, on the other hand, turns out to be a figure representing the key stage in an approximately reverse progression. For this latter subject, the moment of total interpellation by a colonial regime of surveillance is the one in which spaces are opened for at least the possibility of an accession to consciousness of his position. (He has, in Lukács's terms, now reached the point at which reification can be comprehended, as he has now "no ideals to realize.") This is the postcolonial discovery of the text: it is signified in the native flaneur by his abduction of the second trait of his metropolitan counterpart: the compulsion to movement.[30]

Neither in its discourses nor its practices had colonialism witnessed much willingness to allow mobility to the colonial native. On the contrary, while the western novel from *Don Quixote* to *A Passage to India* had used travel by the metropolitan heroine or hero as a form of education, metropolitan texts with colonial settings had insisted on the *captivity* of—the power of incarceration over—the native, from Robinson Crusoe, whose thought on seeing Man Friday's footstep was that he would now have a servant, to the chained laborers whom Marlow remembers under the trees in *Heart of Darkness*. (Reacting to such traditions, any depiction of movement in a postcolonial novel must be regarded as a kind of celebration. This partly explains why *Ulysses* is so thoroughly a text that glories in continual moving about). The urge to dominate native populations and to coerce them into productive labor was, nevertheless, not only at odds with metropolitan liberal discourses (nineteenth-century British colonial activity in Africa was justified as a means to end the slave trade, for example), but contradicted, too, the utopian impulse behind colonialism: ultimately, to render the colony a more perfectly organized version of the homeland itself.

Rosa Luxemburg, among others, theorized that the final aim of colonial endeavor was to open the colony as a further pool of consumers. If this was being achieved in any of Britain's colonies in the period of high empire, it was being achieved in Ireland, the oldest and "most advanced" British overseas possession. We need not see Bloom, who buys little that is more expensive than a bar of soap and pays for, but forgets to return to collect, the ointment for Molly,[31] as one of the first colonial consumers in high literature (whether Molly occupies that role will be considered in chapter 5 of this study), but, in his job as canvasser of advertisements for the *Freeman's Journal,* he is employed to help put in place exactly such a system. A wandering canvasser, he is uncomfortable in the sedentary, regular post Molly wishes for him. As a "commercial traveler," he seizes and exploits the freedom of movement allowed the native in the latter stages of colonialism by the apparently benevolent imperial regime. In this colonial flaneurdom, he replicates and subverts that first "voyage out" (to use Virginia Woolf's phrase) of the colonists themselves that made the founding of the colonies possible. The book's title and structure reinforce this. The *Odyssey* has been called both the first novel and the first narrative of imperial voyaging; in Joyce's *Ulysses,* the first major antiimperial novel of this century, Odysseus's wanderings are mimicked by the native, but with the callow and solemn disregard for the original that announces a new departure. The first colonist classic is transmuted into an original anticolonial text.

Now this postcolonial *flânerie* is not a mechanics of desire (for the pleasurable commodity), but rather the velocity of evasive action. It is not the last convulsive version of the quest narrative, but rather an original narrative of escape and departure. Remember that the utopianism of the ruling colonist was based on the dream of establishing a new polis in a landscape from which the native population would be entirely obliterated. Freeing the natives, as a preliminary to establishing the colony as a society of consumers that, realizing the colonist's ideal, perfectly matches the home, contradicts the image of the colony as a territory whose natives can never have the rights of the citizens of the homeland. In the period of advanced colonial rule, the freed native, although no longer under coercion, is likely to be subject to an intense system of surveillance by the colonial administration. It is to this system that Gayatri Spivak alludes when she notes that Foucault's studies of European institutions of intense surveillance were unconscious allegories of the more pervasive and territorially widespread panopticist regimes in every colony.[32] Such a system of concerted surveillance operated in Dublin both in 1904 when the book is set and even more so in 1914–21, when it was written, and through it the apparently harmless Bloom, and the other ineffectual and tenuously bourgeois males who wander the city, weave a path that is part acquiescence and, potentially, a mechanism for evading a system that would ideally have them placed in a fixed abode. Their *flânerie,* mimicking the original voyage of the colonists, is a prime image of the attempt of the native to escape the webs of knowledge of the colonist regime. We will now consider how webs of surveillance were shown to operate upon the flaneur in different ways in empire and colonial literary texts, and explore how, in *Ulysses,* Bloom and the other native flaneurs move toward the end of native *flânerie:* the breaking of the bounds imposed by the imperial regime.

Finders Keepers: Holmes, Bloom, and the Flaneur as Consumer

Webs of surveillance operated in metropolitan texts to tabulate and encourage the proprieties of consumption necessary for the smooth running of a commodity culture; in colonial texts, on the other hand, they operated to suppress the native population, who were promised rather than granted a share in the metropolitan abundance of commodities. An example of the first is a Sherlock Holmes story by Arthur Conan Doyle, "The Adventure of the Blue Carbuncle," first published in the *Strand Magazine* in 1891;[33] my example of a colonial text encoding the webs of state surveillance in the colonial territory is the "Sirens" episode near the center of *Ulysses*. Conan Doyle's "The Blue Carbuncle" is a suggestive example of how the imagination of the metropolitan bourgeoisie dealt with its vision of the webs of official knowledge in fin-de-siècle culture: they structured it around the valuable commodity. The "Sirens" episode of *Ulysses* shows the native perception of how webs of information operated in the new century in a colonial setting. These perceptions are generated in the first instance by the genre and locales of each set-piece; they arise from the interactions of their fla- neurs with "the encompassing and politicized spatiality of social life"[34] portrayed in each work. Doyle's text is a detective story set in Holmes's lodgings and in the night streets of London. "Sirens" is set in the quay- side streets in the center of Dublin and then in the Ormond Hotel; it de- scribes how an hour is passed by a large cast of characters on a June afternoon. Both texts offer a specialized reconnaissance of *flânerie:* they elucidate, in ways specific to the metropolitan locus of the one and the colonial locus of the other, the course of education in consumption on the one hand and of exploitation on the other that was the raison d'être of each version of *flânerie.*

"The Adventure of the Blue Carbuncle" tells how Holmesian non- chalance operates to discover that a theft occurred, and to locate the stolen jewel and the thief. In the first moments of the story, Holmes closely reads "a very seedy hard felt hat"; he then hears that the goose that had been found with the hat after a street fight turned out to have a recently stolen ("its value can only be conjectured") blue carbuncle in its crop. Holmes locates the owner of hat and goose, and traces the bird, through a Covent Garden stall, to a poultry keeper on the Brixton Road. Before going there he accosts one James Ryder (the "head attendant" at the hotel where the carbuncle had first been stolen) who clearly knows that the diamond should be in the craw of the goose. Back at Baker Street, Ryder confesses ("he burst into convulsive sobbing") to the crime; wondering what to do with the carbuncle after he had stolen it, he had forced it down the throat of one of the geese in his sister's flock, only to later walk off with the wrong fowl. When he realized his mistake, the geese had already been sold; this was how the diamond had luckily fallen into the hands of Holmes. Compared to this tightly plotted diversion (from the Christmas greetings that Watson had ostensibly come to deliver to Holmes), the diversions of "Sirens" may seem diffuse. The action, or series of activities, takes place between 3:38 and 4:30 on June 16, 1904;[35] it opens as two barmaids in the Ormond Hotel discuss the viceregal cavalcade that has passed along the quay outside. Simon Dedalus enters. Bloom wanders along the quays, buying twopence worth of notepaper in Daly's stationers, spotting Blazes Boylan as he enters the Ormond bar. Bloom also enters the hotel with Richie Goulding; they eat dinner together in the dining room. Meanwhile Dedalus and a group of his friends gather round the piano: the episode culminates with Ben Dollard's rousing rendition of the rebel song, "The Croppy Boy." Bloom, thinking of Boylan who has driven off to meet Molly in Eccles Street, and writing under a pseudonym to one "Martha Clifford," listens to the song from the dining room; he walks out before it is over, and passing along the quays, farts happily as he goes.

Yet there are telling similarities — clues — that locate both these texts in the genre of detective stories that feature flaneurs. In both, for example, the hotel is key: in "Sirens" the bulk of the action occurs there, while in "The Blue Carbuncle" it is from a suite in the Hotel Cosmopolitan that the diamond is first stolen. Both tales describe much walking about the city, spotting others from a distance, although in "Sirens" this occurs mostly in the early pages, whereas in the Holmes story it takes place in the second half of the tale. Both stories valorize seeing, hearing, using one's senses to the utmost. "Sirens" begins with an overture in words-sounds, and constantly harps on hearing and seeing: "His spellbound eyes went after ..." (U 219), "Bloom heard a jing, a little sound" (U 220), "Pat, waiter, waited, waiting to hear, for he was hard of hear ..." (U 225), and "Look: look, look, look, look, look: you look at us" (U 231). The Conan Doyle story focuses on seeing as observation: when Holmes challenges Watson to consider the battered hat, his friend returns it to him "ruefully ... 'I can see nothing,' said I." Both narratives are constructed as stories within stories: in "The Blue Carbuncle" the initial focus is the friendship between the doctor and the detective, while the tale of the theft intervenes; in "Sirens" the story of how Bloom passes another hour is interrupted by the tale told in the song "The Croppy Boy." These similarities create a framework that can be used to discover how "Sirens" might be a detective story, once one has understood why this new genre, as epitomized by "The Blue Carbuncle," processes knowledge of the metropolitan turn-of-the-century city as it does.

The similarities of the two tales act as foil for the acute differences in the ways in which knowledge of the social space is processed by each. First, "The Blue Carbuncle" is a mystery, a tale in which, at the outset, no one (except the unknown criminal) knows anything; no one is aware, even, that a crime has been committed. In "Sirens," on the other hand, it is taken for granted that everyone knows much about the business of others. (The "difficulty" of the text for most readers is that they find themselves inducted into this society of common knowledge: they are expected to know, for example, that Daly's was a stationer's, and that Rostrevor, where Miss Douce has just spent her holidays, is a seaside resort in County Down, 60 miles north of Dublin — and in a county that, after the Anglo-Irish treaty of 1921, became part of Northern Ireland.) In the Holmes story, we do not even hear that there has been a crime until the fifth page, and then only when Holmes reads about it from the newspaper. This recreates a world of the isolated "private" individual in the city, who would be ignorant of information of common interest altogether were it not for the newspapers. In "Sirens," however, people continually gossip about each other. As he hears Ben Dollard's voice, for example, Bloom ruminates "Other comedown. Big ships' chandler's business he did once ... Now in the Iveagh home. Cubicle number so and so. Number one Bass did that for him" (U 232). Earlier, Ben Dollard himself had gossiped about Molly: "The wife was playing the piano ... for a very trifling consideration and who was it gave me the wheeze she was doing the other business?... Yes. Is she alive? — And kicking" (U 221). The Holmes story traces a progress in the public knowledge possessed by private individuals. Holmes begins complacently ignorant, gleams scattered clues, collates them into a narrative, and resumes anonymity once the puzzle is solved. "Sirens" is a narrative mechanism that allows the mingling of private and public lives; it is propelled by the presumed desire of the characters, narrator, and readers to know as much as possible about everyone else. The economy of knowledge in "The Blue Carbuncle" presumes a split between public and private; in "Sirens," it does not.

The economy of information in "The Blue Carbuncle" is structured around the clue; in "Sirens" it is structured around rumor. What effect has each of these devices in presenting information? In the detective story, the clue is a trace left by the guilty party upon a commodity. The clue, in "The Blue Carbuncle," cannot exist unless imprinted upon a commodity, giving the commodity a new aura by rendering it a signifier in a chain of knowledge. The tallow stains on Mr. Henry Baker's hat, for example, tell Holmes that its owner does not have gas installed. The clue endows the commodity with an aura—of mystery—because it fastidiously refuses to be a transparent signifier: like a modernist text, it conspicuously flaunts its obscurity. Thus the clue is in complicity with the commodity, in the way that this latter exists in a capitalist culture of overproduction, for the commodity too guards its aura as its passport to the pleasurable world of exchange and its refutation of its materialist origins in the realities of production. The clues of the detective story, too, ease the commodity's *entreé* into the circle of exchange, for a clue implies that the significance of one commodity is to be found in another: in the detective story, the chain of signifiers is a chain of commodities. In "The Blue Carbuncle" the hat leads to the goose, the goose to the carbuncle—and the carbuncle (via advertisements in the evening newspapers) to suppliers of fattened geese, and to the Alpha Inn, where "on consideration of a few pence every week we were each to receive a bird at Christmas."[36]

The detective story, then, finds the answer to the riddle it has proposed itself in the circle of exchange, the relations of shopkeepers, buyers, and sellers. It shows itself cognizant of the way advertising mediates between the grubbier milieu of actual exchange and the fetishization of the commodity itself. The Countess of Morcar has advertised a £1,000 reward for her jewel in the *Times,* and Holmes later locates that owner by placing advertisements in the "*Globe, Star, Pall Mall, St. James' Evening News, Standard, Echo,* and any others that occur to you."[37] This detective story plots itself by simply turning the commodity around on its usual path: instead of moving from trader to consumer via advertisement, its progress in the story is from (illicit) consumer to trader, also through a calculated use of advertisements, but also, in the plot, via clues. The effect of this reversal is to uncover the mechanics of supply, but to conceal the realities of actual production.[38] We are, as western consumers, familiar with the coy narrative of desire by which the product, advertised by the merchant, inter-pellates the buyer; strikingly, Conan Doyle's story fabricates a narrative of the reverse movement from commodity to trader.

Guiding this reverse movement, the clue is not a trace of the crime it-self, but of its perpetrator: it points to a single human subject who at-tempted to short-circuit the circle of exchange by stealing the commod-ity imbued with the richest aura of all, the carbuncle ("Just see how it glints and sparkles," cries Holmes). The role of the advertisement in mediating the conventional progress of the commodity from seller to consumer is granted to the *clue* when that movement is played back-wards, from consumer to circuit of exchange. By pointing to an individ-ual criminal (and a good rule of the detective story is to have only one criminal),[39] the clues reassure the investigator (detective or reader) that blame can be assigned to an individual, that the loss of a significant commodity can always be contemplated as the fault of an individual (mis-)consumer. Moreover, while the commodity aesthetics engineered by the advertisement interpellate the consumer by generating desire, the cognitive aesthetics of the clue in the detective story cajole the reader by appearing to appeal to her intellect. It is the ruse of realism in the story, the lure of transparency, the promise that the detective and the reader will be granted unprecedented powers of surveillance, when in fact the commodity will never become transparent to the point of betraying its origins in production, and the force that actually propels the plot is the aura (the mystery) attached to the jewel, the goose, the hat — to all the commodities in the text. We are hoodwinked into believing that we are engaged in a progression of rational deductions toward a criminal, when all the while we are being more deeply immersed in the aura of commodities. This subsumption of both "rationality" and human sub-jects (the criminal, the detective, the reader) to fetishized commodities is, then, an excellent example of reification spreading out from the com-modity and hiding the material bases of the society shown in the story. Since both the validation of the detective's powers of intellect, on the one hand, and the possibility of divining the identity of the criminal on the other are both lodged, through the mechanism of the clue, in the commodity itself, an equivalence is implied between commodity and the human subjects of the story. Both criminal and detective — each flaunting his own uniqueness, which the story never allows to develop even into the realist version of subjectivity described by the term "char-acter" — are rendered commodities themselves. As unique commodities, they are parasites upon the aura of the (stolen, returned) commodity at the heart of the text.

If the detective story is propelled less by Holmesian bravado than by the powerful fetish of the commodity, from where does the commodity garner its aura? Clearly (and here again one sees how the detective story and the commodity cannibalize each other) in the first instance, from the crimes committed in the name of the object itself. This is the carbuncle's chief attraction for Holmes: " 'It is a bonny thing,' said he. 'In the larger of the older jewels, every facet may stand for a bloody deed.' "[40] Second, the commodity in the text derives its aura from simply being close to other commodities. The carbuncle signifies only "crime" and "immense value," so that the hat and Christmas goose together generate the other, more familiar powers of the commodity aura in the text. These powers revolve around the opposed urban attractions of the home and the street. The goose, given to the policeman, suggests family, celebration, home: "a good fat goose which is, no doubt, roasting in front of Peterson's fire."[41] The line of vision of the detective story must, however, extend to the space of the whole city, and as such the hat is more interesting. For it is the hat of a flaneur, to be worn in the streets, a hat knocked off the head of a man in the Tottenham Court Road in "one of those whimsical little incidents which will happen when you have four million human beings all jostling each other within the space of a few square miles."[42] Nevertheless, when Holmes reads the hat he is at pains to stress the domesticity of its owner: the tallow stains suggest an owner who "walks upstairs at night probably with his hat in one hand and a guttering candle in the other."[43]

The place of commodities in the text is assuredly the home; the place of detection, however, is the streets. Even the criminal knows this, as when he tells of the horror of being in the street with the stone in his pocket: "Every man I met seemed to me to be a policeman or a detective, and for all that it was a cold night, the sweat was pouring down my face before I came to the Brixton Road."[44] Yet Holmes insists on eliciting Ryder's confession in the comfort of the Baker Street lodgings: The implication is that the streets are safe (despite such "whimsical little incidents" as a stranger having his hat knocked off by "a little knot of roughs"),[45] but that the place of commodities and the subject who enjoys them is home and fireside. The fin-de-siècle detective story, invoking the scene of the domestic to effect closure, is locked within the expectations of nineteenth-century realism. In bringing home its flaneurs, it works, like Eliot's poem, to curb their freedom of the streets. Mediating the Victorian and modern strands is the flaneur as detective, who is denied a family but still assures us of his allegiance to home, or at least to a fixed address, his credential as respectable defender of the proprieties of consumption.

Next, consider commodities as integers of information in the economy of knowledge, and the home as the scene of this economy, in the "Sirens" episode of *Ulysses*. "Sirens" is hardly a commodity-centered text: the few objects on display here are notably ambivalent as consumer goods. The most striking is the seashell Miss Douce has brought back from her seaside holiday (*U* 231): part transplanted natural object, part souvenir, you hold it to your ear and (apparently) hear the sea's roar. There is also the tuning fork, which the blind stripling has forgotten, and the sheet of paper on which Bloom writes to Martha Clifford, provided free by the hotel. Neither does "Sirens" betray any thorough allegiance to home; only Boylan, the seducer, jingles off to Molly's and Bloom's home in Eccles Street. The Ormond Hotel as locale is an imitation home for all comers. In "The Blue Carbuncle," on the contrary, it had been from a room in the Hotel Cosmopolitan that the Countess had had her jewel stolen: a hotel, Holmes's text implies, is hardly a secure habitat for the subject who defines herself through her possessions. (A subgenre of twentieth-century fiction — from Virginia Woolf's first novel *The Voyage Out*, set partly in a South American hotel, to Elizabeth Bowen's *The Hotel* and Thomas Mann's *Death in Venice*, showing the debilitating, albeit educational, effect of hotel living — endorses such caution.) We might presume that in presenting dilapidated, ambivalent versions of commodity and home as the paraphernalia of its narrative, "Sirens" operates to transgress the material certitudes laid down by works like Conan Doyle's story. To the extent that this transgression demarcates a difference between the status of the home/commodity nexus in London and in Dublin, it is one of the pleasures of the narrative. Remember, however, that transgression, as Foucault points out in his moving essay on Bataille,[46] works in the last instance to reinforce and reconfirm the original experience of limits. It would be hasty to assume, for example, that since the Holmes story, constructed out of the sensibility of the metropolitan center, dealt in the proprieties of consumption, therefore "Sirens," set in the periphery, exposes in any direct way the mechanics of production. On the contrary, objects such as the seashell that Lydia, the barmaid, has brought back from Rostrevor take their places in the carnival of commodities even more brazenly than the Countess of Morcar's precious stone. The seashell is a *gadget*,[47] a commodity that pretends to use value (it can be used for "hearing the plash of the waves, loudly, a silent roar" [*U* 231]) while being utterly useless; more, it is a souvenir, an object whose aura derives from no feeling more powerful than nostalgia. Such seductions of the commodity do not, however, mitigate its power: this too is a reified society where the commodity exerts its power as object of desire.

Such reification in "Sirens," however, comes about in a more complex fashion than in the narrative economy of "The Blue Carbuncle." There the clue pointed through the commodity directly to a subject, the criminal: hence an equivalence was posited between the criminal as flaneur and the product, so that the criminal was by implication commodified also. In "Sirens," however, the seashell's "clue," its "silent roar," (*U* 231) is only an illusion ("The sea they think they hear. . . . The blood it is. Souse in the ear sometimes," (*U* 231) as Bloom, ever the amateur scientist, trying to sound Holmesian, but not succeeding, explains). Its significance, rather, is guaranteed by a story—in fact a confession—from Miss Douce:

> From the forsaken shell miss Mina glided to her tankards waiting. No, she was not so lonely archly miss Douce's head let Mr. Lidwell know. Walks in the moonlight by the sea. No, not alone. With whom? She nobly answered: with a gentleman friend. (*U* 231)

Stories like this within "Sirens" have been characterized as clichéd;[48] more specifically, they epitomize a consciousness wholly interpellated by the version of commodity culture the seashell souvenir aptly represents. Doyle's story, while it commodified its flaneur characters to match the consumer goods upon which the story was built, held itself aloof as a master narrative, an act of surveillance of the culture, itself above suspicion. "Sirens," however, by twisting the spiral of commodification so that its representative objects interpellate rather than equal the text's human subjects, and by appealing to stories within the text to explain the significance of the objects rather than vice versa, makes us realize that these stories, and the texts in which they are set, are the most commodified artifacts of all.

It is easy to see how the detective story, as possibly the most mechanically reproducible of literary genres, could smoothly occupy the role of fin-de-siècle commodity text. On the other hand, "Sirens" as commodity is unlike the seashell souvenir it describes, in that it flaunts its artifactuality—its status as human production—rather than proceeding with the linear narrative in which the text of *Ulysses* had mostly, up to this point, been composed. Joyce himself called the episode a "fuga per canonem,"[49] and the onomatopoeic overture with which the text begins, as well as the mercurial sliding from one narrative perspective and even scene to another—in short, its self-conscious high modernist estrangements—all flaunt this episode's commodity form. Further, the gush of sentimentality and retrograde nostalgia in the stories it contains—the tragedy of Ben Dollard, former shopkeeper but now an inmate of the Iveagh home for indigent alcoholics; the platitudes in Bloom's letter to Martha Clifford ("Accep. my poor little pres enclos ...: p.o. two and six" [*U* 229]); above all, the fatuous loneliness of Bloom as he contemplates the encounter between Boylan and Molly ("Yet too much happy bores" [*U* 228])—display "Sirens" as a commodity-text delighted to show off the most puerile compensations of a reified culture: structures of feeling as cheap thrills. This carnival of nostalgia carries us to the most sentimental story embedded in "Sirens," a tale of an unintended and shocking confession, the ballad "The Croppy Boy," which is sung by Ben Dollard.

Before looking at the song, however, consider two questions. Why, despite the fact that it purveys fewer and less valuable commodities than "The Blue Carbuncle," does "Sirens" flaunt their commodification to the point where its own story and the place of (story)telling in general come into question? Its very sirens, the barmaids, are behind a counter; they sell drinks, and desire. Second, what role does *flânerie* have in negotiating these wagers of representation in "Sirens" as text? To understand the peculiarly heightened depiction of the meager pool of consumer products in "Sirens," and in *Ulysses* in general, recall the utopian aim of colonial endeavor: to render the colony a more perfect copy of the "mother country." In the particular historical circumstances of fin-de-siècle capitalism, this meant the fabrication in the colonies of an even more seductive carnival of commodities than existed in the metropolitan center itself. Given also, however, the actual scarcity of many consumer goods in the lives of the natives in the colonial hinterland, a strange tension was bound to develop between the utopian intent (of what might have been) and the more impoverished reality. The disparity between wished-for consumer carnival and the reality of impoverished lives, as in the Dedalus household where the daughters starve, accounts for the shrill intensity and pervasiveness of advertising in late-colonial Dublin, a phenomenon *Ulysses* amply documents. (Consider, as a single example, Bloom's idea for a "transparent showcart with two smart girls sitting inside" as an advertisement for Hely's stationers [*U* 127].) With British-made consumer goods on display, but with so few having the money to buy them, advertisements strove to attach themselves to any political and social movement, and particularly to assert their Irishness, in order to be effective: Bloom's plan for the shopkeeper Keyes's advertisement, for example, calls for a design of crossed keys, a reference to the Manx (Isle of Man) parliament, and by implication, as he points out, to Irish Home Rule. Consumption is treated ambivalently throughout *Ulysses*; it is either confined to the ephemeral, like the seashell, the penny Banbury bun Bloom throws to the seagulls over the parapet of O'Connell Bridge (*U* 126), the underwear he would like to purchase for Molly, or to the consumption of food or drink, which is surprisingly often found disgusting in the text (*U* 139). No one goes on a shopping spree in Dublin on June 16, 1904. Ultimately, I suggest, consumption is treated as a token of betrayal (hence Bloom's fastidious account-keeping [*U* 584] may be forgiven): the significance of consumption as betrayal reaches its apotheosis in the most comic and ambivalent commodity in the text, appropriately a home product, Plumtree's Potted Meat. The potted meat, which Bloom and the readers of the novel encounter first only as an advertisement (*U* 61), turns out, when Bloom finds the crumbs from the meat-jar among the bedsheets (*U* 601), to be the sign of his marital betrayal at the hands of the bounder Boylan.

More often, Dublin as colony is merely the site where an advertisement substitutes for the commodity and so fails to interpellate the flaneur as consumer. The blindness of the piano-tuner stripling, in this sense, epitomizes the oblivion of the native to the call of the commodity — as in the following example, a poster advertising Mermaid brand cigarettes:

A stripling, blind, with a tapping cane came taptaptapping by Daly's window where a mermaid hair all streaming (but he couldn't see), blew whiffs of a mermaid (blind couldn't), mermaid coolest whiff of all. (*U* 237)

A commodity culture constructed only from advertisements, however, hails its subjects rather than reaching them directly through desire.
Such hailing in lieu of consumption makes for a culture propelled, to
borrow Baudrillard's phrase, by "the ecstasy of communication."[50] When
it is not really the goods themselves that are on offer but rather the evidence that they exist,[51] the conditions are set for a colonial culture that
often turns out to be uncannily similar, in its simulations of the real, to
that described as the predicament of contemporary western societies by
theorists of the postmodern. The critic can speculate that the mixture of
pervasive social control and mass-cultural forms that now characterizes
aspects of the lived experience of western societies has been familiar in
the west's colonies for much longer—in a real sense, this mixture was
originally tested there. This also partly explains the fascination with
colonialism of recent materialist theory. Still, this colonial culture of
communication gives those it addresses, the native would-be consumers,
the opportunity to respond, first at the same level—that of communication—rather than at that of consumption, which they cannot afford.
The native would-be consumer, not waylaid into actual consumption, is
in a better position than her imperial counterpart to answer back to the
address of the advertisement. This is what occurs, and throughout the
text of *Ulysses*, it is associated with *flânerie*. Father Conmee, for example, walking toward Fairview at the opening of the "Wandering Rocks"
episode, seeing the advertisement on the hoardings at Annesley bridge
for a music-hall appearance by the blackface performer Eugene Strat-
ton, ruminates on "the African mission ... and the propagation of the
faith and ... the millions of black and brown and yellow souls.... It
seemed to Fr. Conmee a pity that they should all be lost, a waste, if one
might say" (*U* 183).

Of course Conmee's interest is another aspect of colonialism—pros-
elytizing religious missions; he stands as one colonial native who would
assume the mantle of the colonist master to appeal to other natives,
while he himself is being appealed to in the advertisement. His is a good
example of the limited opportunities for a native consciousness to offer
the advertisement a thoroughly effective counterhegemonic address. The
popular-cultural forms of the native population—the songs, sayings,
stories, mores—that carve out a more independent cultural space, are
significant bearers of any refusal by the native group to be interpellated into the pleasures of colonialism. And it is one of these, the song

"The Croppy Boy"—not a text composed out of some ideally pure "native" culture which at any rate did not exist, but rather out of a native culture experiencing a late colonial period of deep interpellation by the colonist regime—that is presented at the core of the "Sirens" episode.

"Our Native Doric": Native Consciousness of the Colonist Gaze

The song "The Croppy Boy" is a rebel ballad telling a tale from the rebellion of 1798; it was one of many such songs popularized at the centenary of that rebellion, a celebration that would have been relatively fresh in the minds of the audience in the Ormond Hotel in 1904. (It was also one of the songs chosen by Joyce himself when he appeared on the same concert platform as the famous Irish tenor John McCormack in that very year,[52] with Nora Barnacle in the audience.) The ballad tells of a young rebel, or croppy, who on his way to battle stops at the house of a priest to confess his sins. The youth confesses, and then asserts, "I love my country above my king." He is ready to be pardoned when the figure dressed as the priest throws off his cassock and stands revealed as a "yeoman captain"; the youth is captured and led away to be executed. Clearly this text is as deeply inflected by the sentimentality of commodity culture as any product the Victorian metropolitan sensibility was likely to produce. (And we know that even British turn-of-the-century music-hall audiences were deeply affected by pathetic Irish emigrant songs—although Irish war songs in British variety shows were likely to be jingoist assertions of Irish loyalty to the crown.)[53] The song's listeners are, as Bloom observes, "All lost in pity for the croppy" (*U* 235). The nationalist ethos of the song, in other words, has been as profoundly implicated by the colonist promise of carnival commodity as any other aspect of Irish native sensibility, so that it can be served up handily with the other trappings of that culture, promising a plentitude that it does not deliver, in the hotel. Yet it is striking that its stock tale of an Irish rebel's capture and defeat by the British is itself told as a tale of telling—a story of the danger of telling too much to the ruling powers of the colonist regime. This text within the text of "Sirens" recounts the tale of an Irish rebel who tells too much to one who had appeared to be a figure in authority and an ally, who had appeared to be on his side. As such, it turns out to be a cautionary subtext addressed to the narrative of the episode as a whole—that narrative of colonial would-be consumption.

The extraordinary sentimentality of the song makes it uncompromisingly a product of the simulated commodity culture being foisted on the Irish colony. But this process of commodification in the colony only reached the point of being promised: it was stalled at the moment of advertising, and what existed in the colony was a milieu not of consumption but of communication. In this context, "The Croppy Boy," despite its predictable softness, shows a canny awareness that, first, this communication will take place in both directions, not only from the British regime in power and its allies to their colonial subjects, but also from these subjects back to the rulers; and second, that the native response to the advertisement must be cautious, secretive, careful, if it is not to be self-incriminating. It shows an awareness that the colonist advertisement culture, despite its appeal to the delights of consumption, in fact operates as a thoroughly repressive apparatus: from the point of view of the native subject, it is a trap. It points us to the other aim of the colonial endeavor: to keep the local population subjugated. It also shows that the utopic and dystopic aims of colonialism—creation of a world more perfect than the one at home, and controlling the local population into serving this ideal—are, as they affect the natives, at any rate, one and the same objective. Although the song is as maudlin as the commodity culture whose svelte promised pleasures it tries to imitate with the pathetic exaggeration of the subaltern mimic, it shows all the time that the seductive promise of the advertised commodity must be regarded in the colony with suspicion. Generally, in recent historicist literary criticism, the critic discovers that it is the form of a text that undermines the text's explicit content; in "The Croppy Boy," however, it is the content of the song that stands as a reprimand to the pseudo-commodified, would-be reified form of the piece itself and to the sentimental company in which it is sung.

Returning to the "Sirens" episode as a whole, however, one discovers that the perspectival slippages in the episode's form work to emphasize that the message of the song echoes, at least for the readers, through the setting as a whole. "Tap. Tap. Tap." goes the cane of the blind stripling, a flaneur but with a purpose now, returning to the hotel to reclaim his tuning-fork, like a drumbeat issuing an ominous warning, as it echoes, even if faintly, the drumbeat of the call to rebel. The return of *flânerie*, which we hear only as "Tap. Tap. Tap." (*U* 253) interrupting the singing of the ballad, is no accident at this point. The episode as a whole has deluged us in the fragile commodity pleasures promised by the colonial regime, symbolized primarily by the regimen of the hotel itself, from whose curtained windows, as the episode opened, the two barmaids had watched the British viceroy and his party drive by. In imperial Paris, the flaneur looks into the plate-glass window at the consumer luxuries; in colonial Dublin, the women serving drinks peer out the window at the conspicuous symbols of colonial power. Now the song has reminded us of the other side of the colonial endeavor, the inevitability of colonist repression of the native population. And both of these are brought together not only in the song as warning, but in the listener's reaction to it. Everyone in the hotel is successfully "hailed" by the ballad, which, like an effective advertisement, works by repetitions ("They all know it by heart" [*U* 234]): it stirs up what Bloom describes as "The thrill they itch for" (*U* 234), just as an advertisement tries to elicit more desire without delivering more tangible rewards.

When Ben Dollard starts to sing, the hotel grows quiet; everyone listens. The exact locution the text uses to describe this is as follows: "But wait. But hear." At this point the significance of waiting, a word repeated mantralike in the episode up to now, becomes apparent. All the listeners are frozen into postures of waiting, now: Bloom, who has been about to leave ("Must go prince Bloom told Richie Prince" [*U* 237]), is momentarily held, while "Bronze, listening by the beerpull, gazed far away" (*U* 233). The song, with its Latin tags of the confessional, as Bloom comments to himself, "holds them like birdlime" (*U* 233). But waiting has had a second meaning in this text: it has also signified servanthood—"Pat, waiter, waited, waiting to hear" (*U* 225). As the song ends, it does so again: "Miss Douce composed her rose to wait" (*U* 236). Waiting as wishing for consumption, waiting as servitude: interpellation by the advertisement text and the repression that goes with it in the colony are united, when this song is sung amid the gestures of waiting. To be interpellated, in other words, is to be stilled, to interrupt the progress of one's *flânerie*. And the story told in the song itself upholds this: the youth, in transit, off to war, was captured because he made the mistake of stopping in his journey. His final words before the "yeoman captain" reveals himself are "Now father forgive me and let me go." As such, *flânerie* returns to this text as the mechanics of independence.

"Tap. A youth entered a lonely Ormond hall." The blind stripling, type of a new potentially independent postcolonial flaneur who because of his very blindness can refuse the interpellation of the colonist promise of consumer culture, becomes now, as a rebel "youth," a version of the "youth [who] has knelt to tell his sins" of the song. It is left to Bloom, however, to truly resume this *flânerie*. As the song ends he does so. Getting up, he feels the discomfort of the commodities he has bought and must still buy: "Soap feeling rather sticky behind. Must have sweated: music. The lotion, remember. Well, so long. High grade [he is thinking of his hat]" (*U* 235). He walks by the barmaids whose very natures seem circumscribed by the culture of objects: "By rose, by satiny bosom, by the fondling hand," as well as by the waste of that culture: "by slops, by empties, by popped corks ..." (*U* 235). And then:

> Up the quay went Lionelleopold, naughty Henry with letter for Mady, with sweets of sin with frillies for Raoul with met him pike hoses went Poldy on. (*U* 236)

Poldy is still surrounded by the bibelots of the culture from which he walks away, and indeed he always will be. He is flatulent from his own consumption of food, and he is soon seeing further examples of commodities in "Lionel Marks antique saleshop window" (*U* 238). But by now it is the grim aspects of this culture that he notices, in the "frowsy whore" whom he fears will recognize him (final image, in "Sirens," of two human subjects degraded and commodified) and in the second-hand castoffs in Lionel Marks's window: "battered candlesticks melodeon oozing maggoty blowbags. Bargain: six bob" (*U* 238). And it is here that "Bloom viewed a gallant pictured hero.... Robert Emmet's last words" (*U* 238). Granted, it is easy to read Bloom's infamous farting as he reads — "Pprrpffrrppffff" (*U* 239) — as a mockery of Emmet's own words, and by extension of the nationalism of "The Croppy Boy," which tells of the rebellion of 1798, for Emmet's speech marked the rhetorical high point of the ensuing rebellion of 1803. But it is more accurate to take Bloom's response, his private moment of carnival, as the reaction of the flaneur to the commodification of Emmet's statement in a junkshop window. For Emmet's words, like the rebel song, also concern telling ("When my country takes her place among the nations of the earth, then and only then, shall my epitaph be written"): they are a direct injunction to the Irish colonial population not to tell.

And "Sirens" itself, as the first "obscure" episode of *Ulysses* that Joyce wrote, works to obey this injunction. It is in the innovative form of the "Sirens" text that the cross-purposes of native *flânerie* and colonial commodity culture are fully exposed. By interposing snatches of Emmet's speech and "The Croppy Boy" among the leftovers of the fragile consumer culture (or merely advertisement culture) that the colonial regime would impose, *Ulysses* ensures that it will only be audible to those who already know it beforehand, to those who are in on its secret. Much criticism of "Sirens" has paid little attention to the song that rests at the heart of the episode, because to anyone unfamiliar with it, it is almost lost among the narrative interpolations and the recorded ruminations of Bloom. An example:

> ... Met him pike hoses. Philosophy. O rocks!
> *All gone.* All fallen. *At the siege of Ross* his *father, at Gorey* all his *brothers* fell. *To Wexford,* we are the boys of Wexford, *he would. Last of his name and race.*
> I too. Last of my race ...
> *He bore no hate.*
> Hate, love, those are names ... *Tap.* (*U* 234, italics mine)

This reports, apparently through the consciousness of Bloom, but with a momentary break for the stripling's tap, the lines from the song:

> At the siege of Ross did my father fall
> At Gorey my loving brothers all.
> I alone am left of my name and race
> I will go to Wexford and take their place.
> I bear no hate against living thing ...[54]

As such the narrative gaze operates like an extremely sensitive, lively movie camera, moving from room to room in the hotel, focusing now on Bloom, now on the avid face of the barmaid, now on Ben Dollard, and occasionally on the progress of the blind stripling through the streets. It is a camera-narrative as flaneur, which darts among the crowd attending to what it will. This *flânerie* of the very gaze of the text itself, part of the project Joyce grandly characterized as "exploring the resources and artifices of music and deploying them in this chapter,"[55] is what renders this the first episode of the novel that its original readers, beginning with Ezra Pound, found difficult, and to which they immediately objected. When Harriet Weaver, Joyce's British benefactress, wrote to say that "Sirens" "seems to show a weakening or diffusion of some sort,"[56] Joyce replied that "I do not know in what other way to describe the seductions of music beyond which *Ulysses* travels." Escape from seduction, then, is what the flaneur perspective—with a lingering glance here, a last look there, the typical behavior of even Baudelaire's flaneur—achieves in "Sirens." And this, the first true flaneur-text written for *Ulysses,* was composed in the early months of 1919, as the guerrilla War of Independence, which was to end with the founding of the Irish Free State, was beginning in Ireland. As the city and the nation about which Joyce wrote were moving away from the seductions of colonialism, *Ulysses* and its hero enact a textual and a literal *flânerie* that enable them to fly by the particular interpellative nets of the colonial state.

Envoi: Evading The Pleasures of Colonialism

The implicit model of colonial administration often implied in postcolonial literary criticism takes the colony to be a space in which the state apparatus is relentlessly panoptic, a territory where forms of rigid despotism and crowd control were ruthlessly put into effect. It is in this spirit that Gayatri Spivak reads Michel Foucault, in whose archaeologies, as she states, "The clinic, the asylum, the prison, the university, seem screen-allegories that foreclose a reading of the broader narratives of imperialism."[57] The panopticism Foucault describes, in his studies of heterotopias-at-home as state regimes of control, was perhaps also the major form of power exercised by colonist governments, but it would require us to falsely limit our description of life for native and colonist populations if we were to suggest that it was the only one. (In terms similar to recent work on the importance of class, models explaining hegemonic systems in terms of exploitation, and not merely oppression, are needed).[58] Rather, the lived conditions of the colony, at least in the last stage of imperial power, were played out as an *excess* of the forms of life in the imperial center. It offered at once a gaudy commodity culture that was a shrill imitation of that "at home," and at the same time enforced a regime of surveillance, the consequences of which will be explored fully in the next chapter, that felt it was necessary to keep the native population more thoroughly in check. (In this sense, we might see Jean Baudrillard's concepts of simulation and hyperreality as equally appropriate, complimentary models for theorizing late-colonial reality as the panopticism and surveillance of Foucault). Neither the strategy of advertising the joys of consumerism nor that of covertly enforcing a regime of surveillance could be as successful in the colony as in the imperial center. The exaggerated commodity culture could not exist in practice in the colony because of the dearth of commodities and of the money to purchase them, and could only carry on as a barrage of advertisement, its intensity celebrating only the impossibility of its goal. Meanwhile, the state's surveillance could never be complete because of the intransparency of the native population.

Both systems, however, were integrated: just as the informer, for enforcing the system of control, would be offered a reward, as the notice cited in the first chapter of this study was pleased to state, so the subject who accepted the rewards of the commodity culture would indirectly be an informer, or at least a kind of traitor. In the end Walter Benjamin too connected the flaneur to the police informer; note that both the criminal and the detective, in the metropolitan detective story, are two flaneurs who battle wits at opposite ends of the regime of social control over commodity exchange. Both Benjamin and the detective-story writers reduce the flaneur, potential bearer of a liberated subjectivity, to those contingencies of crowd control that also preoccupied much metropolitan high modernist work. In the native colonial text, however, the flaneur carries on as one who will not be a consumer — who is flatulent at the image of a secondhand commodified nationalism for sale in a junkshop window — because consumption on these terms, he knows, would be a degraded kind of collaboration. This nationalism-for-sale at second hand is not simply an ideology on the imperial model, as was that of Haines and his canny mimic, Buck Mulligan; rather, it is now presented not only in the mind-set but also within the very structural determinants of the imperial culture itself. In this sense, escaping interpellation by this commodity is a bid for freedom: hence the intense *flânerie* of Bloom. The song itself, for all its advertisement-like cheap nostalgic thrills, had told him so. When the text, following its hero, at the moment of the beginning of the independence struggle, resorts to an energetic literary *flânerie* itself, it too is escaping the nets of the metropolitan consumer culture that knew how to interpellate customers who were thinking of home, and were stationary, with a fixed point of view.

3

"And I Belong to a Race ...": The Spectacle of the Native and the Politics of Partition in "Cyclops"

> Only a subject which includes all individual subjects will be capable of embracing an object (society as a whole).
> Emile Durkheim (*Les Formes elementaires de la vie religieuse*)

> — *What is your nation, if I may ask? says the Citizen.*
> — *Ireland, says Bloom. I was born here. Ireland ...*
> — *And I belong to a race too, says Bloom, that is hated and persecuted. Also now. This very moment. This very instant.*
> James Joyce ("Cyclops" [*U* 272–73])

The Colonial Subject in Postcolonial Writing

This photograph of "An Irishman with a lump on his neck" (from the *Dublin Journal of Medical Science* 60, 1875)[1] is horrifying not because the man's deformity is displayed, but because the medical record is cast in the genre of the formal Victorian portrait (Figure 3). The image comes from the pioneering phase of medical photography, before the genre was sufficiently conscious of its utility to emphasize it with connotations of the scientific, by draping the patient or suggesting a stark, decontaminating minimalism. The usefulness of the photograph as medical evidence is at odds with such features as the sitter's street clothes, the oval frame, and the setting of the subject in profile. These are all borrowed from the classic genre of Victorian portraiture, the studio portrait of the respectable bourgeois. Suggesting this genre, in turn, highlights a further contrast: it exposes the person in the photograph as ragged, pathetically unkempt. It renders what is visible beyond the bare functionalism of the photograph rife with uncertainty: the pose is that

Fig. 3. "Irishman in top hat with a lump on his neck," taken by James Robinson, D.D.S., Dublin, Ireland; albumen print, 1874. From *Masterpieces of Medical Photography,* Joel Peter Witkin, ed., captions by Stanley B. Burns, M.D. (Pasadena, Calif.: Twelvetrees Press, 1987).

of a gentleman, but the connotations are those of a beggar. This conno-
tative emphasis is upon the sitter's Irishness. Sporting a caubeen, di-
sheveled clothing, and a simianized face, as drawn in countless Victorian
cartoons in *Punch* and American magazines,[2] this photographed man
would have been instantly recognizable as Irish to the British gaze. Posed
as a gentleman, his otherness is comically accentuated in contrast to the
generic ideal. By placing him in profile, however, the photographer also
suggests the exotic or mysterious quality of his sitter. Nineteenth-
century portraiture favored views of the full face; profiles were reserved
for sitters considered marginal or romantic, especially women or poets —
consider Julia M. Cameron's famous photograph of Tennyson.[3] The
stock signifier of the inscrutable available to realist portraiture in both
painting and photography was the deflected face. The profile pose denies the viewer the reassurance of empathy: the subject gazes into an
unknown distance. This anonymous deformed Irishman, showing half
his face, signifies the possibilities and the plight of his otherness, looking away into a space we cannot see.

This photograph exemplifies representations of late-colonial subjects:
it suggests otherness by splitting the utility of the photograph from the
connotations of the pose. In earlier chapters we have seen how a late-
colonial author might begin to envision a community of diverse individuals and groups, and how such versions of subjectivity as the flaneur,
garnered from imperial models, might be turned to account in writing
from the periphery. In imagining a postcolonial subject, however, the
author from the colony had a further major obstacle: it was necessary
first to face down the stereotypes with which the colonial native had
been characterized in the minds and discourses of the colonizers. For
the author of *Ulysses* the question was this: How could a native writer,
at the critical moment of decolonization, take a model of the self as
grim as the one given in the photograph and re-represent that subject as
a worthy member of the polis that is about to come into being? Writers
who portray Irish characters in the last years of British rule in Ireland
either replicated or reacted to models typified by the man's photograph;
hence, for example, the grotesque native servants in Somerville and
Ross's *Some Experiences of an Irish R.M.*[4] With the task of imagining a
new subject, however, which became urgent at the moment of revolution, native writing faced a crisis. At this point, a nervous fracturing,
strategies of splitting that curiously mirror the split subjects of colonist

representations of the subject, begin to appear in both literary and popular works.

To trace how Irish writers reworked the colonist version of the native subject at the moment of postcolonial independence, I will read three representative texts where such a subject is canvassed: the "Casement diaries," Yeats's poem "The Municipal Gallery Revisited," and, finally, the "Cyclops" episode of Joyce's *Ulysses*. The first two represent (the first in detail, the second in passing) one insurgent colonial subject, Roger Casement, an organizer of the 1916 rebellion who was executed for treason. The Casement diaries are strange and garbled documents covertly publicized by the colonial power in order to portray Casement as not merely a terrorist but a wholly degraded native subject. The scandal to which their covert publication by British government sources at the time of Casement's trial for treason in 1916 gave rise, and the subsequent allegations from Casement's supporters that they were forged by the government, bring into relief the issues at stake in constructing the late-colonial subject as either barbarian or hero. Conversely, Yeats's paean to Casement—his poem "The Municipal Gallery Revisited"—betrays the poet as curiously of two minds about how he might portray a heroic subject. His "images of thirty years" (the revolutionary years) are of two kinds: the insurgents shown in profile whom he does not name, and the artists, staring from the canvases, whom he names often. Why does this split exist as the political unconscious of his poem? Finally, why is the "Cyclops" episode of *Ulysses,* which was written between the 1916 Rising and the War of Independence of 1919–21, perhaps the most glaringly split text in the whole high modernist canon? Not only does it pit Bloom and the Citizen against one another, but it directly confronts inflated and degraded styles. By flaunting its disjunction, I will suggest, between strongly demarcated split subjects as "characters," and its radical transgression as style, "Cyclops" breaks the mold of the colonial "native" to make way for a version of a postcolonial subject.

First, however, a warning, and an excursus into the well-worked theoretical field in which this chapter situates itself. My specific context is research, particularly by feminists, that contests the jettisoning of the subject in the broader field of poststructuralist theory.[5] Materialist criticism has always distrusted the subject, although it has seldom hesitated to use it as a working category. Adorno called it "a mere limited moment" of "western peephole metaphysics ... imprisoned for all eternity to punish it for its deification."[6] Since Althusser's adducement of the "interpellated subject"—the mere effect of an ensemble of structures 'hailed' or interpellated by such ideological apparatuses as churches, education systems, and states—has exposed the unrigorous quality of the Marxist notion of subject-as-consciousness (as in the phrase "class-consciousness"), suspicion of the subject as the site upon which ideology stakes its claims has, if anything, deepened. These suspicions are echoed in the deconstructionist assault on the metaphysics of presence: here is a key perspective shared by materialist criticism and deconstruction, camps otherwise often at odds.[7] Still, the category "subject" continues to return as the repressed of politically conscious poststructuralism. The subject as category is insistently foregrounded in work that articulates the status of women's, postcolonial, and U.S. minority writing as empowering discourse. Still, Adorno reminds us that "it is the very wall (of metaphysics) around the subject that casts its shadow on whatever the subject conjures";[8] we need to read with suspicion when *any* representation of a colonial hinterland focuses intently upon individual subjects. We need to ask, in terms of Lyotard's two master narratives,[9] whether the subject-centered discourse is a narrative of the unity of (hegemonic) knowledge under the guise of a narrative of the liberation of humankind.

High modernist texts like *Ulysses* have found their readers in the poststructuralists of both left and right precisely because criticism of modernist master texts is willing to celebrate the eclipse of the traditional subject as "rounded character" (in E. M. Forster's term). Heteroglossic high modernist texts seem starred sites in which the effort "to break the compulsion to achieve identity"[10] is at last actively being achieved. Totalizing interpretations of modernist estrangement, however, found little to celebrate beyond the temporary release afforded by the Rabelaisian carnivalesque noted as a novelistic pleasure by Bakhtin;[11] to subvert entrenched language codes is not necessarily to attack official law. Instead of imputing the death of the subject as character to high modernist polyphony because its lack of transparency "disrupts" perception of that subject, we can discern how there develops a challenge to the hierarchy of discourses in a work by mapping the specific literary mechanisms by which the master narrative is decentered there. In modernist texts, as in Adorno's modernist theory, the subject is certainly under duress; to enjoy the utopian comedy of a novel like *Ulysses*, however, we need to be sensitive to how defamiliarization reconfigures the subjects and stereotypes familiar in the society out of which the novel was composed. *Ulysses* works to supply in advance, in the novel, what has been called for in critical theory: "a whole new logic of collective dynamics, with categories that escape the taint of some mere application of terms drawn from original experience."[12] This comic-political novel can plunder heavily stereotyped subjects from the high-pitched discourses of late colonialism that articulate them, and by pitting them against one another can initiate an original collective dynamic worthy of the post-colonial nation, the Irish Free State, which was founded at the same historical moment that *Ulysses* was being written.

Place the photograph of the sick man side by side with the "Cyclops" episode of *Ulysses*, to consider how the novel's subject-representations are liberating rather than repressive. In "Cyclops" too we meet the would-be Victorian gentleman — Bloom himself. We have the wild Irish peasant — the Citizen. Whereas in the photograph these were merely implicit sources, however, whose reticence rendered them an embarrassment, in "Cyclops" they are explicit results whose staged struggle is, as I will show, liberating. In the photograph they were both superimposed on a single subject, so that the contrast effects his degradation: here they are separated, individually analyzed, and surrounded by a diverse group of commentators, hangers-on, lawyers, and litigants whose variety suggests at least alternative models of subjectivity and dynamic interaction. Moreover, the two stereotyped subaltern modes of subjectivity represented by Bloom and the Citizen have their difference accentuated by the writerly strategy of composing the text in two glaringly and comically opposing styles at once. When the low style, in key with the Citizen's milieu, rubs shoulders with the high style that poses as repeated attempts to attain an ideal of bourgeois respectability, we reach the moment when the difference between the vulgarian native and the civilized native (Caliban versus Ariel, Black Skin, White Masks), which has been discerned again and again in representations of the colonial subject, is finally made visible in the form as well as in the narrative of a canonical literary text. Hence "Cyclops" makes its own revolution in world literature, and in that of Ireland: the moment when the contradictions between two modes of production become visible, and are shown to contest each other, at the center of cultural life.[13]

To infer once more this savage/civilized dichotomy in colonist representations of the native or in the mentality of the native writer is, however, to do nothing more than to display an Althusserian interpellated subject characterized by a simple dualism. In a criticism worthy of Joyce's novel as a text of decolonization, the key question remains: How can this split subject be accepted by the text, not merely subverted—with, for example, the satiric and carnivalesque impulses for which it is so easy to celebrate *Ulysses*—but in fact transformed into the image of a counterhegemonic subject worthy of a new community? Colonist representations of the subaltern have been reconnoitered in terms of Manichean allegory since O. Mannoni analyzed the Ariel/Caliban division[14] in *The Tempest* as a colonist stereotype, in a study written against the background of the Franco-Algerian war. It has been used to describe British stereotyping of Irish subjects by, among others, Seamus Deane in his *Field Day* pamphlet "Civilians and Barbarians."[15] The ambivalence of such othering for colonist discourse and for contemporary subaltern historiography has been examined carefully by both Gayatri Spivak and Homi Bhabha.[16] To grasp how this dualism has not only been manipulated but also, *overcome* in texts of the modern period and since, the critic must understand the mechanisms that produced it in the first place. It is the mechanics of interpellation of these subjects, rather than the mere fact of their existence, that Joyce adroitly reconfigured in the confrontation staged in "Cyclops." The infamous dismissal recorded in "Telemachus"—"It seems that history is to blame"—was uttered, as we have seen, by the colonist Haines, whose name approximates to "hate" in French. In the first chapter we saw how the novel toys with versions of the subject as consciousness and as bearer of ideology, before diffusing them in a vision of community based on multiple, simultaneous differences. In the second chapter we saw how the subtle suasions and the repressive apparatuses of a colonial regime are each avoided by the colonial native as urban dweller, who uses in this escape a version of the *flânerie* of members of the master's culture. At this point, an archaeology of the discourses that fabricated the barbarian/civilian split in the colonist's vision of the colonial native are needed if the mystifications of Haines and his ilk are to be fully overcome.

Archaeologies of the Subject as Terrorist

The subject as barbarian/potential gentleman portrayed in the photograph was produced by superimposing two discursive genres: the scientific record that would show him in his degraded actuality, and the genteel "art" genre of the formal portrait whose standard was the British bourgeois. The medical photograph is an exemplary new product of the systems of surveillance, record-keeping, and statistical computation developed in the second half of the nineteenth century. In the colonies, as in Ireland, the first mechanism of state control was the police. Various state-run enterprises put into effect in the course of Victoria's long reign—the national schools, the Ordinance Survey, the legal system of Resident Magistrates backed up by armed police—had, as Deane puts it, "a highly Spenserian aim in view—the civilization of the wild natives."[17] (Strikingly, the police force, developed at the same time as the camera, was quick to use the new technology of its day. Irish terrorists were photographed for police files in the late nineteenth century.) The police, official dealers in information, were occupied with the collection of evidence. Such evidence was an officially monitored discursive genre, collected by the law-enforcement authorities, modulated in the legal system through the ritual of the public trial. Evidence presented by the police at a trial aimed to incriminate one version of the colonial subject-as-barbarian: the criminal. If the crimes were committed against the colonial authorities, the criminal was characterized by one of the terms used in the nineteenth century for what is today called a terrorist. Since both law trials and terrorists are major concerns of Joyce's representation of colonial subjectivity in "Cyclops," I will show in a moment how the discourse surrounding evidence worked to create the idea of the terrorist.

The other discourse that we must take into account to understand the "Cyclops" strategy of reconfiguration is that represented in the photograph by the suggestion of a gentleman's portrait. If the regime of bureaucratic surveillance delineated the native barbarian, the native as potential civilian was suggested by genres with pretensions to gentility and ultimately to art. These were the burgeoning range of discourses that heroicized the Irish. They followed a direction pointed out as early as 1867 in Arnold's monograph *On the Study of Celtic Literature.*[18] They grew at the same time as the regimes of surveillance in nineteenth-century Ireland; their most forceful expression was the strongly Gaelic and, latterly, militant strand of the second Celtic revival.[19]

The mythologizing strains of the late nineteenth- and early twentieth-century revival, apparently so esoteric and nostalgic, might seem quite unrelated to a mode so apparently humdrum as the early portrait photograph; consider, however, Samuel Beckett's characterization of the movement as an "antiquarian" interest bred of the "altitudinous complacency of the Victorian Gael."[20] Revival historicizing has convention-

ally been characterized as the inspiration for "the fight for national independence" (in Yeats's words, "Did those words of mine send out / Certain men the English shot?"). Its modes of heroic endeavor, nevertheless, emulated imperial glorifications of the subject: the antiquarian
researches of Douglas Hyde, founder of the Gaelic League, in the west
of Ireland have an ideological intent not all that different from the researches of Thomas Hardy in Dorsetshire. Suggesting, in the end, a sti-
fled ressentiment, in its attempt to delineate a folk tradition that will
outdo the elite art of the colonist culture, this art betrays its own ambivalence because it is incapable of creating an independent subject: it can
do so only in the master's terms.

Before considering how these parallel regimes that would make of
the Irish native either a barbarian or a hero are uncovered in "Cyclops," I will consider how they operated in practice to represent one
colonial subject—Roger Casement—as terrorist. I wish to show how
his ambivalent status as bourgeois gentleman and alleged terrorist at
once lent a nuance of hysteria to his portrayal under both rubrics. In
1916, two years before Joyce wrote "Cyclops," Casement, a well-
known public figure with a minor role in the Easter Rising, was hanged
for treason. It is fitting, then, that he is named in "Cyclops": "those
Belgians in the Congo Free State ... that report by ... Casement....
He's an Irishman" (*U* 274). This refers to Casement's career as a colonial inspector and opponent of colonial exploitation in the Congo; because *Ulysses* is set in 1904 it elides the fact that Casement soon after
threw himself into condemning colonialism in Ireland. Thus, Joyce's
tribute to him in the book—with that "decency" Seamus Heaney has
Joyce impute to Irish writing[21]—leaves unsaid Casement's career in
Irish insurgency, his execution, and his diaries. I will here use these
Casement diaries,[22] unspoken texts of "Cyclops," as an example of evidence, to examine how a product of the police regime of surveillance
operated in practice in revolutionary Ireland in 1916. We will then look
at a discourse that would heroicize Casement, the commemorative reference to him in Yeats's *Last Poems*.

Colonial Subject under Surveillance: The Casement Diaries

The Casement diaries are no doubt the most striking papers from the
archive of police evidence of Irish insurgency in the 1914–22 period.
Their management and "publication" at the time of Casement's trial

turn out to be a caricature of how more quotidian police evidence was handled in terrorist trials.

The diaries were a tattered set of notebooks allegedly found by the police after Casement's arrest. Written during his inspectorates in Africa and South America, they were not part of the prosecution's case and were not mentioned in the courtroom during Casement's trial. To forestall a movement to prevent his execution, however, their contents were leaked to newspapers in the months between his sentencing and his execution in the summer of 1916. They were seen to detail—mostly in garbled shorthand—homosexual encounters between Casement and others, mainly in African and South American ports of call. This managed, limited making-public, first of the typed extracts from the diaries and then of photographed pages, bore results. Casement was lambasted in the British press as "a man with no sense of honor and decency ... [living] a foul private life ... He is a moral degenerate."[23] The recasting of the terrorist as a barbarian subject had begun.

These diaries, in their orchestrated, secret "publication," operate to create a subject out of a collection of texts, against a background of the assumed fact of Casement's guilt. The diaries accentuate the inference of Casement's difference: imputing homosexuality to him is to repudiate him under the sign of a pervasive otherness, in this case, to mark him with one version of the barbarian stereotype. When the diaries created a scandal, the focus was diverted from the act of treason for which he was condemned by the official law, to a repudiation of his complete being as a subject. Convicting him as "a moral degenerate," the diaries remove Casement's guilt from the arena of moral or political choice to the most plausible denominator of individual subjectivity, the desiring body. As the rebellious-patriotic martyrdom is transformed, by insinuation, into a discourse of forbidden sexuality, Casement's choice of political action is pictured as the merely predictable expression of an inner secret.

The Casement diaries are obscure not only because of the garbled shorthand in which they are written, but also because of the "official secrecy" with which they were made public in the summer of 1916. This secrecy was regarded with suspicion by Casement's supporters, especially the Irish patriotic faction: they asserted—plausibly—that the diaries were forged. This startling claim (intriguing enough that over twenty books have been written on the controversy since)[24] also opens striking critical possibilities. It forces one to look at the diaries as an invented, fabricated text, a pastiche of the life of their purported author, composed of a collage of descriptions collated by an anonymous scriptor for the strategic ends of a ruling power. The moment that the diaries' forgery was asserted was a moment of awareness in Lukács's sense: a moment in which those "who have no ideals to realize"[25] were enabled to see the truth of their masters. It represents seeing through a reified commodity, when reification defines the effacement of the process of production. The rereading of the diaries as forgeries insists on revelation of the process of their fabrication. Drawing attention to the missing author, to the text as pastiche, to the strategic uses of obscure prose, this might seem to be a reading of the diaries as if they were a modernist text. The police, conversely, had read the diaries as the *exposé* of a villain; their expectations were those of readers of realist novels.

Yet those who suggested that the diaries were forged, as it turned out, merely aimed to discredit the government to the extent that it denied Casement his destiny as hero in the national struggle. The forgery hypothesis was advanced to render Casement a martyr, sacrificed at the hands of an imperial regime that would libel its enemies through fraud. This formula mantains the focus on Casement as an independent but nevertheless subaltern subject. It maintains the gaze upon his body, as was proven when the government of the Irish Republic in 1966 chose to celebrate the fiftieth anniversary of the 1916 Rising by arranging the return of Casement's remains from Pentonville Prison in London. Casement was given a state funeral in the rain through Dublin. This oppositional reading of the diaries, then, turns out to be a preliminary version of the heroicizing discourse that we shall consider in Yeats's poem.

First, however, consider the dilemma we face as readers of the diaries today. To us reading them now, they may or may not have been forged, and this knowledge locks our reading into a disabling ambivalence. The diaries' contents are trite and mundane, but in the process of their making-public on the one hand and their reception (with the forgery allegation) on the other, they graphically expose the split between native and colonist versions of the insurgent subject. The confrontation between the two views almost made explicit the barbarian/civilian split between the two representations, but in fact what occurred instead was that the controversy was ended by smothering that split in the nationalist dramaturgy of sacrifice and a more vehement subalternity. No new image of the subject was evolved. Casement as insurgent or terrorist becomes a figure locked in doubt. He remains the nationalist hero, of whose shade Yeats could write some years later:

> What gave the roar of mockery
> The roar to the sea's roar?
> *The ghost of Roger Casement*
> *Is knocking at the door.*[26]

Yeats's Split Subject: "Municipal"/"Terrible"

Yeats's hero-making of Casement is contained in a sidelong glance: a look, in his poem "The Municipal Gallery Revisited," (CP 316–18), at a painting of Casement standing in the dock at his Old Bailey trial. When the poem contrasts sidelong glances and full-face looks, however, Casement is placed between those whom the poet is willing to name and those whom he is not. His furtive image brokers the regard and disregard for the revolution that tempt the poet.

The face in profile is a common signifier in many heroicizing representations of Irish revolutionary insurgents; Yeats himself was photographed in profile. Virtually all the photographs[27] of Patrick Pearse, the "visionary" 1916 leader, show him in profile—this was, revisionists assert, because of a squint that he wished to conceal. The deflected glance is also a staple of the painting of the Irish revolutionary period. Sean Keating's canvas, "Men of the South,"[28] which shows a posse of guerrillas by a road, places all of its six subjects in profile. Yeats mentions a companion-painting to this work as one of the "images of thirty years" in the opening of his "The Municipal Gallery Revisited." It is remarkable how many of the paintings from the revolution to which he draws our attention are centered upon the deflected face. His phrase "pilgrims by the waterside" refers to John Lavery's "St. Patrick's Purgatory,"[29] which shows virtually all of its subjects with faces averted as if in shame. The profiles in these pictures are matched by Yeats's deflected glances at them in the first one-and-a-half stanzas of his poem. Both portrait pose and poet's glance are meant to suggest an ineffable heroism. Yeats characterizes such a pose here with the adjective he had used to name the unimaginable in insurgent heroism in "Easter 1916": the word "terrible." There he saw "a terrible beauty"; here the figures represent "a dead Ireland ... terrible and gay."

Yeats next mentions Lavery's painting of Roger Casement, his face "half-hidden by the bars." Casement in this painting is shown directly facing us: his face is the focus of the painting. It is the court officials who are shown in profile. Yet the power of this direct gaze is modified by the bars of the courtroom dock that narrowly frame the face. Once Casement has been noticed, however, quite abruptly the poem changes. Yeats realizes, as it were, that he has moved from the room with the pictures of the revolutionary insurgents to one hung with portraits of his friends: the high bourgeois and aristocratic artists and patrons with whom he created the Irish literary revival. Augusta Gregory, Hugh Lane, and John Synge: their portraits are all painted in a modified impressionist turn-of-the-century style, and all the subjects stare directly, confidently, from the canvases. There is not a deflected glance among them. Looking back at the first stanza we see that Yeats had foreshadowed his attention to portraits painted in direct front-face when he spoke of two Irish politicians:

> ... Griffith staring in hysterical pride
> Kevin O'Higgins' countenance that wears
> A gentle questioning look ... (CP 316)

Griffith was one of those who signed the Anglo-Irish treaty of 1921, which provided for Irish independence (Molly Bloom acknowledges in her soliloquy that Bloom had named him as "a coming man," (U 616) and O'Higgins was a forceful leader of the new state; Yeats here marks the zealous confidence displayed by the insurgents when, for the first time, they could look directly at the painter or into the camera.

Casement, who is named here and who does stare (although not hysterically) from the canvas, occupies in this poem the space of difference between the heroic style ("terrible ...") in which Yeats describes the anonymous, profiled insurgents and the more intimate mode in which he speaks of the artistic elite. The poet repeats his friend's names insistently — John Synge and Augusta Gregory are each named three times — but the lines dealing with the insurgents preserve anonymity: "a revolutionary soldier ... An abbot...." The exceptions are Griffith and O'Higgins, the new state's politicians whom Yeats admired — and Casement. Naming Casement here corresponds to Lavery's gesture of showing his full face in the courtroom scene. Still, Casement is present despite a double erasure: the haste of Yeats's glance and the obscuring of his face by the bars of the dock in the painting Yeats had seen. (Joyce repeats this gesture when he erases Casement's career between 1904 and 1916 in the reference to him in "Cyclops.") Yeats does focus on Casement's insurgency — and he names him — because Casement was not a bourgeois revolutionary ("From counter and desk") but a member of Yeats's own caste, the lower gentry: an Irish Protestant distinguished by a knighthood won for colonial service. Yet he does not emerge as a subject with claims to be, to use another of Yeats's adjectives, "noble" (as in the phrase "O'Leary's noble head" [CP 300]). Rather, suffered to appear under repeated deflections, he is, as the poem has it, "guarded."

Yeats is guarded too, in revisiting the Municipal Gallery in which he searches for new versions of postcolonial subjectivity. The attempt of the poet to formulate such new versions slips apart into a series of oppositions. Unwilling to adjudicate between the connotations of the insurgent images ("remorse or rest," "abbot or archbishop"), neither can Yeats locate certitude in the program of the artistic elite: their images are "permanent or impermanent," Lady Gregory possessed "that pride and that humility," and he himself "childless, ... thought 'My children ... ' " The last stanzas face the divisions with desperation: the fox cannot foul the lair of the badger, there was the "dream of the noble and the beggarman." But the fox/badger image is "out of Spenser" (British colonist poet par excellence in Ireland), and the dream is merely remembered, a dead letter in the postcolonial Ireland in which the poem was written. Here is a version of the same splitting we have seen in colonist representation: beginning with the split between the insurgent class and the class of artists and "founders," (another version, if muted, of the split between barbarian and civilian), Yeats does not manage to unite them into some ideal new subject in which the beggar and the nobleman are one. Thus the "self-same" excellence will not return, ideals are couched in the past tense, and the gallery is a plebeian "municipal" institution. "Municipal" is a term that resounds with Yeats's disgruntlement here (Ulysses itself, he might have felt, was altogether a "municipal" novel); it rings with the poet's own shame at not having conjured up a pantheon worthy of a higher adjective.

At the close of the poem, however, Yeats makes a gesture full of pathos and courage. He places his own authorial accomplishments before us as a test case ("You that would judge me") for a worthy postcolonial subjectivity. And, at the last, he locates his worth not only in saying but also in community:

And say my glory was I had such friends. (*CP* 318)

This rings out the poem on a conventional phrase, standard as an epitaph (and notably more conventional than Yeats's own epitaph in Drumcliff churchyard), but it also posits the idea that community might be the foundation of a new desirable subjectivity. Yeats still only finds worth in a grouping with the civilized, finding the halls hallowed because of them; yet his attempt to include both insurgents and artists in his "municipal" pantheon allows him, in the last lines, to look us fully in the face in the manner of those portraits that unflinchingly, if hysterically, focus the direct gaze.

Yeats is willing here to look at the frightening otherness of insurgency and the horror of guerrilla terrorism; such willingness is what makes possible heteroglossic modernist reconsideration (beyond heroicizing "altitudinous Victorianism") of the colonial and postcolonial subject. This does not imply sympathy for the gunmen or even for their aims, merely a refusal to dismiss them as barbarians or to leave their description solely to the evidence-gathering of the police. Yeats's own "Easter 1916," for example, despite (as we saw in the previous chapter) its uneasy introduction of the flaneur figure, has been criticized[30] for cloaking willful violence in a discourse of mythic martyrdom, and the poem stands, even today, as probably the most extraordinary glorification of terrorists in the high literature of this century. Yet for a poet of such divided allegiances as Yeats (he was "happier than Sophocles" that Queen Mary had attended his play *Cuchulain* in Lady Cunard's London drawing-room when news reached him of the 1916 rebellion in Dublin)[31] it is a complicated attempt to come to grips with the phenomenon of insurgent terrorism. Later, bemoaning the terror of the Irish Civil War of 1921–22, he would still speak of one terrorist gunman as an "affable irregular" (*CP* 201). It remained to Joyce, however, who left Ireland as some of his friends (as he notes in *A Portrait of The Artist*) were joining earlier versions of these irregular forces, to consider Irish nationalist terrorism in its meeting with daily life in more thorough detail.

"Cyclops," in confronting the insurgent in order to imagine his eclipse in a new community, exemplifies the adjacency of an early twentieth-century discourse on terrorism and the literary movement that is termed modernism. A full history of the discourses of terrorism and of the various stereotypes of the terrorist, key to representing the colonial other, remains to be written. Meanwhile, one may note that the shock tactics of modernist writing, which undermine a single point of view, upon which terrorism itself, and stereotypes of terrorists, thrive, allow for new representations of guerrilla action. Or, noting that high literary modernism and the discourse on terrorism both come into their own in the early years of this century, I suggest that both guerrilla tactics in warfare and new levels of obscurity in prose are each symptomatic of a new willingness to transgress the apparently partitioned spaces occupied by the modern subject (for example, public versus private, or individual versus collective spheres). Terrorists, from the troublemakers of Yeats's "Meditations in Time of Civil War" to the comic figures in Evelyn Waugh's novel *Scoop,* came to signify the limits of otherness in some modernist texts. (Think also of writing on the Spanish civil war.) The term "guerrilla" had been coined as early as Napoleon's Spanish campaigns;[32] the terrorist as stereotype, however, grew familiar between the two world wars. T. E. Lawrence's "The Science of Guerrilla Warfare," for example, still a key text in theories of terrorism, appeared in *Encyclopedia Britannica* (the eleventh edition), in 1929.[33] (Before the terrorist there had been the anarchist—as in Conrad's *The Secret Agent*—and the assassin—as in Sarajevo in 1914.) Since then the terrorist-guerrilla has become the most familiar token of the Third-World other as barbarian. He is almost invariably shown as a lone individual, masked, dark, frightening. Nowhere more than in this terrorist stereotype does Adorno's suspicion of subject-making as a deflection from more viable political concerns seem more appropriate.

Yet in a high modernist work like Yeats's "Meditations in Time of Civil War" (CP 201), the fear of terrorism (and fear, Adorno and Horkheimer insisted, is the propelling emotion of modernity)[34] is challenged by a will to understand the context that gave rise to the terrorist's aims. The high modernist text joins the colonial subject as terrorist (product in the first instance of police evidence), and its alter-subject the heroic gunman as martyr (created out of models of heroic individualism that mimic those of the colonist), in a discourse that neutralizes the horror of the one and the pathos of the other. Beyond the terrorist, a subject worthy of an independent postcolonial community might then be uncovered as the work imagines it into being.

"Cyclops": Readings and Difference

Critics of the "Cyclops" episode have always remarked upon, but never satisfactorily accounted for, the text's most striking badge of courage: its split into two clashing styles. While the two styles taunt each other on every page, the critical strategy is invariably to depend on the narrative of one rather than that of the other; the realist *récit* of the Nameless One is invariably the half of the tale to which critics defer. Dismissing the interpolations as mere parody, they pose as sympathizers for the embattled subject Bloom.

Joyce's friend Frank Budgen inaugurated this critical line. "He is in the position of the Council schoolboy caught wearing the Harrow tie,"[35] he commented on Bloom in "Cyclops," betraying mostly his own cultural and political milieu as well as his expectations regarding his and the novel's readership. Budgen sees Bloom in this episode as a respectable man fallen among vicious nationalists. Reading "Cyclops" as the tragic tale of an individual ostracized by the group, as the moment when Bloom is placed in the stocks by the male society of Dublin, Budgen set the course that readings of the episode have followed since.[36] Following the dubious lead of the realist narrator in the episode, and laughing (with some nervousness) at the parodies in the interpolations, critics invariably characterize "Cyclops" as the set-piece in which Joyce, with the heartfelt agreement of his readers, sends up chauvinistic and ignorant Irish nationalism. In this critical chorus the Citizen, the major spokesman for that nationalism in the episode, is derided with a gleeful vengeance for his mistreatment of Bloom. The Citizen is the Irish terrorist in *Ulysses,* and certainly "Cyclops" is the episode of the book that confronts Irish nationalist terrorism. Many critics, however, with Bloomlike nervousness, retreat behind Poldy's own cliches — "But isn't discipline the same everywhere …?" (*U270*). They thereby implicitly dismiss the elaborate and hilarious interpolations as merely a surfeit of satire.

These readings are inadequate both because they choose the realist narrative half of "Cyclops" as more important than the other, and because, as I will explain, there is in their own postion a suggestion of the very chauvinist feeling they condemn. Rather, it is the juxtaposition of the interpolations with the realist text that makes the episode unique. As Hugh Kenner points out,[37] the presence of the interpolations has never been satisfactorily explained; he ascribes them, following the critic David Hayman, to a shadowy writer-in-the-mackintosh who flits through the text from "Sirens" on as the "arranger."[38] Poststructuralists, on the other hand, see the interpolations as merely disruptive, as a barrage of displacements designed, as Colin MacCabe puts it, to convince the reader that he or she "can no longer pass through signifier to signified, can no longer bathe in the imaginary unity of a full self but must experience him or herself as divided, distanced, as other."[39]

Yet the two halves of the text, its two styles, must be granted equality because this episode sets the sights of its objectivity at the horizon of "race." ("I will forge ... the uncreated conscience of my race," Stephen Dedalus had said.) For a writer, the first racial characteristic is linguistic. In "Cyclops," the two races represented are the Irish and the Jews, and the first tokens of linguistic difference in "Cyclops" are constructed around stereotypes of Irish and Jewish speech. The narrator, just before the first interpolation, imitates one Geharty, then Moses Herzog:

> Geharty:
> *Tell him, ... I dare him and I doubledare him to send you round here again or if he does ... I'll have him summonsed up before the court, so I will....*
>
> Herzog:
> *He drink me my teas. He eat me my sugars. Because he no pay me my moneys?*
> (U 240)

Colonial discourse takes race as its first signifier of difference, and this is replicated in the very language of this episode. To read with justice, we can hardly find one parodic and not the other. Focusing on the realist narrative, most readings do precisely that: this exposes their second inadequacy. In castigating the chauvinism of the Citizen and his ilk, critical readings tend (with politeness) to sound chauvinist themselves. Stereotypes of Irishness appear. For Michael Seidel, for example, "The Citizen is all Irish brawn, a true Norseman ..."[40] Harry Blamaires sees Alf Bergan as "full of Irish mockery and laughter."[41] To Hugh Kenner, Joyce's "second narrator ... is Irish if not 'all too Irish': a fluent performer, a touch malicious ..."; Introducing "Cyclops," Kenner speaks of "sullen patriotic rage" as an Irish characteristic that is still irksome.[42] This is "real Irish fun without vulgarity," (U 252) as the "Cyclops" interpolation on the preparations for a patriot's execution puts it. Yet a criticism of the racism in "Cyclops" that toys with such stereotyping itself can hardly be trusted as the just word on Joyce's text.

Previous readings, then, have two weaknesses: they tend to regard the interpolations as secondary and embellishing rather than equal to the Nameless One's narrative, and they betray, despite their best intentions to prove that the episode mocks chauvinist nationalism, traces of an anti-Irish attitude themselves. To overcome both prejudices, we must give an equal place to both halves of the text, and accord equal respect to both "races" described here. It is Leopold Bloom, of course, who represents *both* the Irish and the Jewish peoples in "Cyclops"; his status as a subject on both planes signifies racial diversity (as opposed to colonial split subjectivity) here. Recognizing this racial diversity is key to the success of this episode's project of imagining a postcolonial subject. First, however, Leopold Bloom (he himself asserts it) is an Irishman. The text represents his subject-position as an Irish person by placing him in contrast to a character named merely "The Citizen," who is especially imported into the novel in this episode alone to suggest this contrast. Elucidating Bloom's Irishness in this way — in the historical moment of 1904, when Irish nationhood was merely an idea — displays him as a subject by deploying in dialogic contradistinction exactly those split stereotypes (barbarian versus civilian, Caliban versus Ariel) which we have already noted in representations of the colonial subject such as the portrait photograph, where the contradiction between the stereotypes is occluded.

Bloom "I feel so lonely Bloom"(*U* 235) of "Sirens" might have served as the alienated antihero of any western modernist tragicomedy[43] born of the decline of European liberal capitalism; as such, his antiheroic genealogy stretches from Henchard in *The Mayor of Casterbridge* to Decoud in Conrad's *Nostromo*. Yet to represent him as a subject in late colonial Ireland in 1904, and more so in the revolutionary milieu of the country in 1919, when "Cyclops" was written, required that Joyce employ topoi less familiar to mainstream literary currency. Bloom was indeed a subject of the British empire, but specifically an Irish one, a subject of a late-colonial regime; he could only have been fully represented within the split categories that we have seen as characteristic of other late-colonial portraits. The value of "Cyclops" is that, rather than eliding these categories as was necessary if a master text was to preserve its political unconscious intact, the split was highlighted as the opening principle of representation. Bloom and the Citizen are the Ariel and Caliban of *Ulysses*, the two sides of colonist portraits of the colonized other now presented together by a native writer. Further, Joyce exacerbates the distinction between the two by making it not merely a point of narrative but also a basis of style, so that the style in which the episode is written is radically split also. The vulgar narrative of the Nameless One seems closest to the world of the Citizen, while the hyperbolic officialese of the interpolations matches the officious, bourgeois mind of Bloom.

Consider how well Bloom and the Citizen fit the stereotypes of barbarian and civilian in this spectacle. The Citizen is the culmination of every degraded stereotype of Irish savagery. He is a lazy insolent drunkard, yet a great talker. He may even be a peasant, with his holding in Wicklow (U 269), and he looks it, with his spitting, his bits of broken Irish, and his "mangy cur," Garryowen. He is full of the chauvinist nationalism that British reasonableness professes never to understand in the Irish. As "old Fenian" he embodies the version of Irish subjecthood most feared by the colonial power: the terrorist rebel. Seething with resentment and anger, erupting in a gesture of violence, he represents the Irish terrorist in *Ulysses*. Joyce, recreating this 'Citizen,' cannot but have had some sense of irony, of defiance of the forces that built this stereotype in the first place.

Bloom as colonized "civilian" is a more subtle construction. Whereas the Citizen exists solely as a type, Bloom as stereotype here exhibits only one register of a persona delineated throughout the novel. This very subtlety is a symptom, however, of the "angelic" face of colonial subjectivity. The Citizen dwells in his barbarian's bitterness, viciousness, and what Kenner grandly calls Pyrrhonism (the art of the put-down, an "Irish" art, that Kenner himself finds exasperating);[44] Bloom believes in reasonableness, sobriety, respectability—he refuses to drink but accepts a cigar—and platitudinous charity. He believes in science rather than in myth—erections in the hanged are physiological, he insists—would go in for lawn tennis rather than the Gaelic games being banned by the police, and advocates reasonable love rather than "force, hatred, history, all that ..." (U 273). He is a genteel Arnoldian liberal. With his constructive spirit, adamant sincerity, and antipathy to all Pyrrhonism, one feels that he would have done better among the English than at home. He visits the public house to meet Cunningham, Nolan, and the Orangeman Crofton, who work in Dublin Castle, the seat of British rule in Ireland, and who arrive at Barney Kiernan's in the "Castle car."

Focusing on this division, the episode is a pageant where the apparatuses of panoptic surveillance by which the colonial regime creates its
split subject are all on show. "Cyclops" is heavily patroled by the police. In the opening line we hear of "old Troy of the D. M. P." (The
Dublin Metropolitan Police [U 241]), soon, of "a constabulary man in
Santry" bitten by Garryowen (U 243), of Denis Breen's search for a "G-
man" (the detective branch, U 246), of the "posse of ... Police superin-
tended by the chief commissioner in person" (U 252) at the hero's execution, and "the baby policeman, Constable MacFadden, summoned
by special courier from Booterstown" (U 253) who restored order, even
"Constable 14A" who "loves Mary Kelly" (U 273). The police populate the episode sometimes in burlesque guises; the army, also much
present, is "the garrison" (U 240). The Nameless One passes "the garrison church"; Arbor Hill, next mentioned, was one of the chief British
Army barracks in Ireland. Hynes and the narrator pass Linenhall barracks: Dublin appears a strongly garrisoned city. The army as "the men
and officers of the Duke of Cornwall's Light Infantry" (U 282) appear
in the second-to-last interpolation to clear the "*debris.*" Both police
and army, key to the regimes of surveillance and control, are strongly
etched here as foils to the portraits signifying late-colonial subjectivity.
The denizens of the public house accentuate the sense of the colonial
apparatus by discussing the nearby law-courts, the hanging of crimi-
nals, the government of Ireland, and British empire politics; these discussions elaborate upon the ways in which the population is interpellated
by the colonial power. Lastly, there is the location of Barney Kiernan's
public house: although the most westerly point of Dublin in which any
episode of *Ulysses* is set (and therefore furthest from the center of Empire), it stands in Little Britain Street. In the episode's final phrase,
Bloom is, appropriately, ascending from Little Britain "like a shot off a
shovel."

   This ascension — beyond Little Britain — offers a version of an apotheosis of Bloom: it transforms his representation as a subject. To understand it in its comic resonance is to come to grips with the subject-
categories extrapolated here. Bloom's apotheosis is possible because the
text, flaunting the divided subject(s) of the colonial gaze by exhibiting
the elements of such a subject side by side, frees itself from the embarrassment that resulted when such a split was elided in more covert representations. The episode is liberated to play with these stereotypes to

the full measure of the pleasure of the text. Re-presentation means that identities can be subversively exchanged, roles questioned, and avowed destinies annulled in advance.

The representation of Irish subjects in British discourses — Coleridge on the "Irish problem,"[45] Trollope's Irish novels,[46] references to Irishness in the press — exacerbated even as they seemed to elide the savage/civilian split: Matthew Arnold's mid-nineteenth-century praise for the Celt as a creature full of "ardour, rebellion . . . hauntings, . . . passion for revolt" is exemplary here. Irish writers, even those of the Celtic revival, embarrassed by this but at work within the same terms, had two options: either to agree with the stereotypes, paint the natives as childish and possibly savage — as the popular late-nineteenth-century lyricist Percy French did in his music-hall songs[47] — or oppose them with a heroicized ideal — as in the agrarian novels by the blind Fenian, Charles Kickham.[48] Neither mode escapes a shrillness: their political consciousness, racked by their frustration, is palpable. When "Cyclops" manages, perhaps for the first time in Irish literature, simply to accept the existence of both discourses at once, and to present them side by side, the text achieves a comic liberation of the kind Roland Barthes celebrates as a sort of textual exhibitionism,[49] a blissful transgression of embarrassed representation.

Into this carnivalesque space are led both the British and Irish forces, which would seem at odds if the only level of politics were the nationalist slogans tossed about by the drinkers in Barney Kiernan's pub, or by the critics of "Cyclops" who speak only of Joyce's attack on chauvinist nationalism. Rather, collusion is suggested: the nameless narrator freely admits, in his first words in the novel, that he was "passing the time of day with old Troy of the D. M. P" (U 240); later the Citizen, partisan nationalist, is happy to talk to the clerks from Dublin Castle, headquarters of the British rule he professes to hate. Further, such comic unionism is not confined to overcoming national divisions; it is the license for breaching the expectations of the realist narrative at every level. Consider such wonders as the pound note that Joe produces ("Decent fellow Joe when he has it but sure like that he never has it . . . the sight near left my eyes when I saw the quid" (U 241, 244), the incredible hangmens' letters of application produced by Alf (U 246), and Alf's report of his too recent sighting of "poor little Paddy" Dignam, who had been buried that morning (U 247). Wonders of text, of knowledge, and of authorship abound: the postcard riddle ("Up:up," it read), the fact that the Citizen knows "Tacitus and Ptolemy" (*U* 268), and, most startling, that Bloom "gave the ideas for Sinn Fein to Griffith" (*U* 275)—in effect, that Bloom suggested the very blueprint for achieving Irish independence, a set of proposals being put into practice by the journalist and politician Arthur Griffith and others in Dublin when "Cyclops" was being written.

Extensive magic of this sort enlivens the realism of the Nameless One's narrative; it slides into hilarity in the interpolations. An executioner "step(s) onto the scaffold in faultless morning dress and wearing his favorite flower, the *Gladiolus Cruentis*" (*U* 253). Soon the dog Garryowen is speaking Irish "in a tone suggestive of suppressed rancour" (*U* 256). (By now ressentiment can be laughed at in the text; this may well be the writing degree zero of ressentiment in twentieth-century fiction.) Queen Victoria is remembered "blind drunk ... old Vic, with her jorum of mountain dew and her coachman carting her up body and bones to roll into bed and she ... singing ... come where the boose is cheaper" (*U* 271), and the ranger of the Irish National Foresters is wedding Miss Fir Conifer of Pine Valley.

Rabelaisian carnival, however, is merely the condition of the episode's political effectiveness. Subversions of every hackneyed character of both the empire and its Irish nationalist enemies upturn the text's stereotypes as they are created,[50] but such subversion is never unlimited, never merely subversive for its own sake. (Even Garryowen's howling semiotic is translated back into English.) Rather, the ideological task of the episode is to locate, through patterns in the subversions it displays, novel representational strategies through which subjectivity may be constituted anew. Much of the carnival in fact verges on the viciousness of "displaced abjection"[51]—scapegoating by the oppressed (here, the colonized Irish) of a group among them who have even less access to power (here, Ireland's Jews). Carnival as subversion of colonial authority (say, the bawdy stories about "Old Vic") and carnival as displaced abjection (jokes about the Jewish Dubliner Moses Herzog) are played off each other; the effect is to show how grotesque are the oppositions generated by the initial splitting of colonial "identity," and the bitter irony of the natives learning all too well the use of stereotypes developed to oppress themselves. Further, the episode's initial opposition of the Citizen and Bloom is delineated with increasing urgency even in the midst of carnivalesque disintegrations of lesser characters. This central showdown of subjects is orchestrated by modulating the sympathy of the episode's styles for both the realist and fabulous characters they display.

The two directly opposing styles—the realist narrative of the Nameless One and the heteroglossic hyperbole of the interpolations—seem to correspond to the conflict between Bloom and the Citizen that is mostly described in the realist *récit*. Here too, however, once the division between the styles has been asserted, the episode becomes a divided ground whose borders beg to be transgressed. Trespass is signaled by the profusion of languages seeping into both stylistic arenas: the Citizen contributes Irish ("To hell with the bloody brutal Sassenachs and their *patois*" is his opinion [*U* 266]), Bloom is bid farewell in Hebrew—"Visszonlátásra!" (*U* 281)—while the dead Dignam, appearing in a seance (*U* 284), natters on in a language that looks like Sanskrit but slips off the tongue as Americanese: "alavatar, hatakalda, wataklasat ..." The styles distinguishing the interpolations turn out not to be their province alone: for example, the Nameless One's narrative is replete with documents that also read as set-pieces, like the hangman's letter of application, or the *Irish Independent* obituaries at which the Citizen jeers.[52] (Hunched over the newspaper, the Citizen mimes Joyce himself, who read newspapers of June 16, 1904, with particular care to write this episode.) This interpenetration destabilizes the comparative authority of each discourse: the two styles become mirrors reflecting each other with a surreal distortion. Because this stylistic bravura cannot be matched to the trite dualism of conventional realist subjectivity represented by the savage Citizen and the civilian Bloom, a space is opened in which to envision a reorganization of that subjectivity in Joyce's modernist text.

This mismatch is signaled by a dissonant jerkiness: the text jumps from realist spoken narrative to hyperbolic scripted interpolation without warning, like jump cuts in edited film. (We will later have occasion to note the filmic qualities of the "Circe" episode also.) Even in the *récit* itself, conversation works by interruptions, mostly from looking to commenting, from the specular to the prosaic: The drinkers first see a passerby through the public house window, then discuss him. This stress on the eye peppers the text with analogies to the story of the Cyclops in the *Odyssey*. There, the Cyclops' eye signifies the repressive power of surveillance: when Odysseus puts out that eye, he becomes free.

When the specular is countered with the prosaic here, the ensuing discussion undermines the formation of subjectivity predicated on the eye of surveillance. The jump-cut interruptions interfere not only with the discussion of a character; they open spaces in which characterization as a narrative strategy is undermined.

"Cyclops": Reading for Hegemony and Counterhegemony

Sudden turns, multiplied, leave fault lines in the text that become the starred spaces in which hegemony[53]—the force by which a people is convinced of the naturalness of its situation—is questioned, and the possibility for counterhegemonic agency on the part of late-colonial subjects is discussed. These border zones occur between the installments of the *récit* and the interpolations. They are occupied either by texts embedded in the interpolations that might easily have been part of the Nameless One's tale (the account of the boxing match [U 261] is an example), or by those parts of his tale (for instance, the skit on the African chief's visit to England [U 274]) that might easily have been interpolated texts. The gossipy narrative of the Nameless One—he is the sole first-person retrospective narrator in the whole of Joyce's fiction—supplies a form adroit in delineating character through splitting. The interpolations, by turns outdoing the nameless narrator in hyperbole, formality, and satire, toy with archaic or manifestly more exaggerated modes. The borders between the two literary strands are tense areas of the text, because the heteroglossic, highly permeable stylistic montages do not directly match the stark dualism of the characterizations of Bloom and the Citizen, both subject-constructions erected with the assured "common sense" of realism. In the space between them, most of the accounts of the court cases, court proceedings, and fights are given, culminating, of course, in Bloom's fight with the Citizen. Here too, the subject of British colonial politics is explicitly discussed and the role played by authorship in describing or critiquing this political relation is considered.

When discussions of British-empire politics take place in these border zones between the two styles, they are always allied with the issue of the authorial "I," of the author and his power over the texts within the text. The comic report from a newspaper on a Zulu chief's visit to England read by the Citizen is a skit on colonial relations, the late queen, Manchester businessmen, and the Bible, which the chief celebrates as "the word of God and the secret of England's greatness." Its satire is undercut, however, by the mystery of its authorship:

> —Is that by Griffith? says John Wyse.
> —No, says the Citizen. It's not signed Shanganagh. It's only initialled: P.
> —And a very good initial too, says Joe.
> (*U* 274)

Joe's lost phrase alerts us: the "P" suggests, to him at least, Charles Stewart Parnell, the fallen Irish political leader whose personality haunts the work of Yeats and Joyce. Parnell had died in 1891, but a rumor still circulated (mentioned in the "Hades" episode to Joe Hynes himself [*U* 92–93]) that Parnell was still alive. This living/dead author, this shadowy initial to which a hero of an earlier period of political hope is reduced, signifies at once the ephemeral quality of heroism both in politics and in the authorship of political texts. The text that is next discussed reinforces this theme: the Congo Report written by Sir Roger Casement. This too is a critique of colonialism, but the talkers know almost nothing about the author, except that "He's an Irishman" (*U* 247).

Finally, there is the discussion of Bloom not as author, but rather as the source who "gave the ideas for Sinn Fein to Griffith to put in his paper" (*U* 275). The reference is to Arthur Griffith's *The Resurrection of Hungary;*[54] a set of articles published in 1904 urging that Ireland follow the example of Hungary, which had seceded from direct Austrian rule to become an autonomous part of the Austro-Hungarian Dual Monarchy. These highly important articles were pivotal in the development of radical Irish political consciousness in the years prior to 1922. Griffith suggested that Irish M.P.s refuse to sit in the British parliament, a policy followed in 1919, only months before Joyce began writing this episode. Authorship here, however, is divorced from writing altogether: it is "giving the ideas for," a displaced, doubled affair, in which the dual monarchy, itself a second-order idea borrowed from the Hungarian experience, is the result of two authors. As such, agency-through-authorship is revealed to be barely tenable. The author turns out to be as radically split as any other subject interpellated by the colonial regime. In each of these examples, the concept of authorship as it exists in the first, imperial world, with the author's name emblazoned beneath the title as the guarantee of a work's authentic value, is discounted. Yet, however tentatively, the question of agency, of the possibility of active resistance, is raised. The enabling subject is still, however, relegated to rumor (always the counterdiscourse of the subaltern) and to conjecture. The conjectured author is examined here once again through the discussion of another forum in which the status of the subject is deliberated by the state — the legal system of court cases and trials.

When the courts crop up in "Cyclops," it is in conjunction either with naming (citing known litigants, and offering the full paraphernalia of character-making) or with the defeat of characters' reputations through libel. The culture of the courthouse pervades the episode. Barney Kiernan's, itself known as "The Court of Appeal," stands near Green Street Courthouse, where numerous rebels had been tried and found guilty. Little Britain Street stands in the quarter of Dublin north of the Liffey that boasts the Four Courts and King's Inns, the centers of judicial power in Ireland. Colonial surveillance — a policeman at each corner backed by G-division detectives in the barracks — is suggested, we recall, by a plethora of references to the police. References to the courts occupy whole interpolations and swathes of realist narration. The court hearing in the case *Halliday v. Livingstone* is rendered in biblical terms (*U* 265); we hear talk of the "Canada swindle case" and, afterwards, of the judge's sympathy for Gumley, sued by Reuben J. Dodd. This goes beyond the suggestion of panoptic control to examine, as we will see, the specific means by which the Irish subject is interpellated as an effect of a specific colonial apparatus by the British court system in Ireland.

The legal notion of libel — the act of injuring a person's reputation by something printed or written, or by a visible representation — is used to initiate the discussion in the regime's own terms. Denis Breen is convinced that someone has libeled him with the nonsense-postcard; the discussion of this among the denizens of the public house shows how libel — assailing another's character — makes for revisions of the characters of everyone present. Breen may sue:

> —Ten thousand pounds, says Alf, laughing. God, I'd give anything to
> hear him before a judge and jury.
> —Was it you did it, Alf? says Joe. The truth, the whole truth, and
> nothing but the truth, so help you Jimmy Johnson.
> —Me? says Alf. Don't cast your nasturtiums on my character.
> —Yes says J.J., but the truth of a libel is no defence to an indictment for
> publishing it in the eyes of the law. (*U* 263)

Here, note that the basis for a libel is publication in a text, and the very discussion of Breen's hoped-for mode of redress — the courts and his chances there — lead to insinuations and libelous statements that impugn the characters of a host of others. Accusation pervades the realist strand of the narrative, from the opening sentence, when the Nameless One accuses a chimney sweep of nearly driving out his eye. It undermines any common denominator of "character" (based on a common currency of reputation) from the beginning; as textual strategy, it mimics the prosecution of a legal trial for destabilizing ends.

The courts, when explicitly discussed, are seen as state mediations between accusations and varieties of deception that forestall such attacks. The courts are presented as the arena in which to resolve conflicts between "Irish" and "Jewish" Dubliners, and the nuances of the judgments are considered, in the cases of *Geharty v. Herzog, Gumley v. Reuben J. Dodd, Breen v. his unknown libeler, James Wought alias Shapiro ... v. Zaretsky*. The judge, the wits in the public house would have it, is in turn deceived regarding the characters of the litigants: "Poor old sir Frederick, says Alf, you can cod him up to the two eyes" (U 264). Sir Frederick decides, however, in favor of the Irish: he connives in scapegoating the Jewish minority. For everyone, from Sir Frederick Falconer, one of the chief representatives of British law in its Irish colony, to the denizens of the public house, deception — hiding beneath appearances or documents — completes the cycle of a discursivity based on accusation. Reported deceptions proliferate: the Citizen is in fact a land-grabber (i.e., a farmer who takes the land of an evicted tenant) in Shanagolden (U 269); Bloom's errand of mercy involves deceiving an insurance company, the Scottish Widows, about the widow Dignam's claim (U 257); Blazes Boylan's father "sold the same horses twice over to the government to fight the Boers" (U 262). The feeling is that this duplicity is known ("We know that in the Castle," says Castle clerk Martin Cunningham [U 276] of Bloom's work with the Sinn Feiner Griffith) and practiced both by the forces of surveillance and by those watched. Accusation and deception exist in a misalliance that fosters the milieu of secrecy in which the colonial power operates.

The texts of this border zone, between the doubled presentation of the colonial subject and the heterogeneity of the discourses that underpin it, uncover issues of the subject's interpellation by forces of hegemony. By referring to texts that explicitly critique colonial political regimes, such as those by "P," by Casement, and by Griffith, and by displaying the tenuous nature of their authorship, Joyce asserts the difficulty of effective individual agency, what Gramsci referred to as "war of position" or what is sometimes called "standpoint epistemology."[55]

At the same time, the talk of the courts and of legal trials posits the cynical view of state interpellation as all-pervasive, a regime of accusation and deception that interpellates every colonial subject and text.

The "Cyclops" episode, then, is a realistic rather than realist text: it purveys a hardheaded politics. It uncovers the hegemonic strategies exerted by the empire through its state apparatus of police, courts, and informers upon its Irish subjects, even if some of them professed to disavow that power. Hence the politics of this episode is not a matter of an inevitable confrontation between vicious chauvinist nationalism and rationalist liberalism, as has been claimed by critics who take ideology to be a matter of explicit avowal by authors and characters rather than a matter of implicit forms that interpellate those figures. The episode's uncovering of accusation/deception and the use of it as a narrative mode warn us that the explicit is not to be taken for granted in averring the political. Rather, what emerges as the crux of political agency is the extraordinary difficulty of overcoming—on the part of an individual author embroiled in the ethos of individual subjectivity and his authorial role—the vision of colonial subjectivity preimposed by the colonial regime. The final staged fight between Bloom and the Citizen becomes the text's desperate effort to pitch the two versions of the colonial stereotype against each other in order to envision some form of postcolonial subjectivity to come.

Informing on the Fight Between the Citizen and Bloom

This fight is the episode's culminating conflict: here, the Citizen's accusations are not countered by deception on the part of Bloom. This is the moment when the limits of the objectivity pursued by the text are *shown*—the implication being that they cannot be said, as the saying has become too enmeshed in the round of accusation and deception to be trustworthy. In having the Citizen and Bloom fight, however, *Ulysses* may seem to subscribe to the most vicious form of colonial stereotyping: the image of the colonial natives as a quarrelsome, troublemaking breed, terrorists "by nature." Whether Indians, SWAPO guerrillas, or "fighting Irish," this is the colonial stereotype fundamental to all the others. This fight is one of the two instances of violence between persons in a strikingly peaceful book (the other, when Stephen in "Circe" is knocked unconscious by a British soldier [*U* 490] will be discussed in the next chapter). Does the novel merely mimic or caricature colonial stereotypes here? It is not enough simply to blame the Citizen, for Bloom (quite justifiably) has grown agitated discussing persecution, at first apart from his adversary: "Bloom was talking and talking with John Wyse and he quite excited ... — Persecution, says he ..." (U 271). Critics have noted that this is the episode in which he too grows aggressive.[56] Countless hints in the Nameless One's narrative lead up to this fight, and commentators have replicated that narrative in their criticism by making the fight their focus too.

Remember that this fracas is highlighted by the Nameless One, and as he is the prime mover of the regimen of accusation, he is the least trustworthy narrator of what occurred. Instead, he is an excellent example of the completely interpellated consciousness: the rhetoric of accusation and deception, beholden to the regime of surveillance, is his highly polished patois. He knows everyone's dirtier secrets, admits to a network of informants, and has an insatiable appetite for gossip. He is, in fact, a type of the most notorious accuser in any late-colonial police society, the informer; he would have relished the paraphernalia of informing epitomized by the British poster calling for spies that we looked at in the first chapter. We realize in "Wandering Rocks" that Corny Kelleher, the undertaker (U 185), is a police tout; we may suspect the same of our Nameless One. Thus his is the most duplicitous role in this split episode. He sides with the British colonial regime: indeed never admits to any other allegiance, and grows angry when he contemplates Bloom's/Griffith's plans for Irish self-government (U 275). In the first place, therefore, we should expect him to be eager for such a row: it confirms his prejudices about his countrymen. Second, the round of accusation and deception propeling his talk works by generating fear (of libel, of exposure, of shame); his terrorizing talk grants an inevitability to the outbreak of terror here. On the other hand, we associated the vulgar noise of the Nameless One with the presentation of the Citizen's "savage" Irishness: it would seem, therefore, that the Citizen is more fully interpellated by the rhetoric of surveillance of the ruling power than his nationalist jingoism suggests. His nationalism — the version that became commonplace in late-nineteenth-century Ireland — mimics the homage to race of the colonial master. (Joyce's own aversion to such chauvinism has often been noted.)[57] Finally, if the Nameless One is a police spy, the reader — his listener — is placed in a quandary regarding allegiance. The implied reader here is occasionally addressed by the unnamed narrator: one critic places them in another public house at about nine o'clock that same night.[58] As readers, we are forced to take the part of this listener: that of the G-man police detective listening to the informer's tale. The informer's task is to report trouble, to reinforce the impression of acrimonious natives, and he does so here with the fullest repertoire of story-embellishing skills that he can muster. To avoid taking the G-man detective's point of view, we must stake out a role at a distance from this untrustworthy narrator. The other point of reference for us, clearly, is in the interpolations, which also elaborate upon the event.

These other texts, their authorship ambivalent, hardly seem to offer critiques of the colonial regime or even of the discourse of accusation-deception that represents it. Toward the end of the episode, however, the interpolations and the realist text slip apart, opening a space for the fight between Bloom and the Citizen to be shown in the text. The later interpolations become spread out in geographical territory and historical time: in fact they cover the whole of Ireland (from Kinsale to the Giant's Causeway, County Antrim, in the second-to-last interpolation [U 282]), and the whole of Irish history, from the early Christian period of Saint Columcille to the present of Barney Kiernan's public house (U 287). In this spatial and temporal reterritorialization they remind us of the time and scope, as well as the political stakes, of the episode. Throughout, the interpolations have reminded us of the heroicizing discourses of Irish historiography, even as they mocked them: they served, covertly, to historicize the setting. Now, late in the episode, reminders begin to crop up of the period in which the episode was written (1918) as opposed to that in which it was set (1904). "Cyclops," it is always said, is the violent episode of *Ulysses*. The striking violent event that had occurred in Dublin in the period between when the novel is set and when each episode of the text after "Scylla and Charybdis" was written had been the rebellion of Easter 1916. Hence, the description of the earthquake that accompanies the throwing of the biscuit-tin (U 281–82) strongly suggests the vision of Dublin captured in photographs immediately after the Rising (Figure 4):[59]

> All the lordly edifices in the vicinity of the palace of justice were
> demolished, and that noble edifice itself, ... is literally a mass of ruins,
> beneath which it is to be feared all the occupants have been buried alive.

The course followed by the procession of saints in the fifth-to-last interpolation is precisely that from the center of the rebellion, the General

Fig. 4. O'Connell Bridge, Dublin, looking north to O'Connell Street in the aftermath of the 1916 Rising.

Post Office on O'Connell Street, to Barney Kiernan's, through some of the streets that were worst hit by British shelling in 1916: "by Nelson's Pillar, Henry Street, Mary Street, Capel Street, Little Britain Street ..." (*U* 287). (It is one of the ironies of the Rising itself that Pearse, the rebel leader, surrendered in Britain Street.) The bonfires lit on the hills and coast (or so the third-to-last interpolation would have it) as a farewell to Bloom are also typical of the iconography of Irish rebellion: lit along the coast, they suggest alternatives to the Martello towers of the garrison that also ring the country, one of which had served as the setting for the opening episode of this book. Even the biscuit tin used as a missile, from Messrs. Jacob and Jacob, is a clue: for Jacob's biscuit factory, where the tin originated, was one of the strongholds occupied by the rebels during the 1916 Rising.

For the English audience who read this episode when it was published in the *Little Review* in November 1919,[60] at the moment when the guerrilla war of Irish independence, which followed three years after the fighting in Dublin, was at its height, we can say that not only would they have been treated to what might have been the gratifying spectacle of two Irishmen fighting, but also troubled by what seemed like veiled references, first to the destruction of the city in 1916, and second to Sinn Fein, which by then — for Bloom's/Griffith's Hungarian system had been put into practice — was a name synonymous with guerrilla insurgence and the violent struggle for national independence in Ireland. For us as readers today, the suggestion of the devastating violence in Dublin in 1916, when five hundred people were killed and over two thousand wounded, which occurred two years before the episode was written, casts the throwing of a biscuit-tin in anger in a much more fully comic light. The "Cyclops" violence is revealed as a triviality, as a comic interlude in the face of three hundred civilians dead and the nearby streets destroyed two years before "Cyclops" was written.[61]

For a deeper meditation on the phenomenon of violence among colonized peoples themselves we might turn (as is so often the case in considering the violent interpellative structures of colonialism) to Frantz Fanon. In "Colonial War and Mental Disorders,"[62] he lists the traits that French psychiatry had described as typical of the Algerian psyche, all typical too of the British colonial stereotype of the Irish:

> Complete or almost complete lack of emotivity
> Credulous or susceptible to the extreme
> And earlier:
> The Algerian frequently kills other men.
> The North African likes extremes, so we can never trust him. Today
> he is the best of friends, tomorrow the worst of enemies.

Fanon shows how it serves the purposes of the imperial rulers to display the natives as fighting among themselves: they can thereby justify their continued presence as the forces of law and order. Reading "Cyclops" as a document of its political moment, we might imagine that it colludes with this stereotype. Joyce, however, in his work "to keep the professors busy for a hundred years," also points the way to reread the pseudo-epic battle. First, he teaches us to beware of the Nameless One's narrative, to read with alert suspicion regarding his point of view. Réné Girard in *Deceit, Desire and the Novel*[63] posits a theory of desire predicated on the look of a third party. Consider an analogous theory of repulsion: where enmity is not simply a result of two individuals subjects clashing over liberal principles, but rather a sense that results precisely *because* this gaze, this machinery of surveillance, is in place. Sartre also theorized the dynamics of group formation as communal solidarity in the face of the "look" of a third party. He suggested that after the revolutionary moment[64] a group maintains their tripartite dynamic by integrating a third within itself in a system of "revolving thirds."[65] This theory may be turned inside out to imagine a model for the working of repressive power. In this model, the Nameless One, appropriately anonymous, would be the third figure.

As Fanon points out, the moment of revolution is that which "brings to the fore the true protagonists." This moment is merely hinted at in "Cyclops." It was written just before the Irish War of Independence of 1919–21; Stephen has yet to be knocked down, not by another Irishman, but by a British soldier, as occurs in "Circe." Yet in this episode the beginnings of the new postcolonial subject are visible. First, the interpolations contradict the conclusions of the gaze of the Nameless One. In them, paradoxically, we find the realistic—as opposed to the mimetic—element: the suggestion of the revolution occurring in Ireland while the text was being written. The interpolations have a *counter-interpellative* role: they break the power of the gaze of the third. Smashing the narrative of the Nameless One, they prevent the repulsion between the Citizen and Bloom from seeming more than a spectacle, a spectacle illustrating the stereotypes fostered by the accusations of the colonial regime itself.

The impetus of "Cyclops" is to prize the realist narrative and the interpolations apart: hence a utopian version of postcolonial subjectivity is not to be gleaned in the comic union of two styles (biblical and colloquial) in the very final sentence of the episode. The colloquial style appended at the end has been too deeply interpellated by the colonial regime, the Bible mocked as "the volume of the word of God and the secret of England's greatness" (*U* 274). British master discourses of whatever stamp, this last-minute unionism implies, are still in control of describing Irish realities. Closure here avows itself an ideological act: it is achieved by a last gruff interruption of the Nameless One, the narrator as informer to the colonial regime. Rather, such a postcolonial subject may be discovered in Bloom's avowal of his own different kind of doubled, as opposed to split, subjectivity: his Jewishness and his Irishness. (These "racial" differences, we remember, were the origins of the two styles in the episode, in the speech patterns of Geharty and Herzog.) Bloom's avowal of his own doubled identity is the moment he comes to consciousness, his "conscientization," in Paulo Freire's sense.[66] Bloom declares:

> —Ireland, says Bloom. I was born here. Ireland.

Then:

> —And I belong to a race too, says Bloom, that is hated and persecuted. Also now. This very moment. This very instant. (*U* 272, 73)

The final phrase "This very instant" again alerts us to the double timing of the episode: set in 1904, written in 1918. For once again, historical reality had caught up with the sentiments in the intervening years. In 1904, the Zionist movement was still in its infancy.[67] By 1918 Britain had, in the Balfour Declaration, guaranteed the Jewish people a homeland in Palestine. The intervening years saw a resurgence of anti-Semitism both in Britain and (as *Ulysses* makes plain) in Ireland.[68]

By talking of the Jews as well as the Irish, Bloom moves from the issue of bigotry to, as he himself puts it, that of injustice. He also displaces the discussion of colonial oppression onto the question of the relationship of political power to the discourse of race. He parallels the Irish and Jewish questions as two instances of politically motivated racial injustice. He thereby broadens the question of Irish independence, looking to the moment when it might make common cause with movements of national liberation everywhere. In 1904 both the "New Jerusalem" and the "New Ireland" were still moot. By 1918, however, the British, colonists in both territories, had agreed to the wisdom of a Jewish homeland, but were still recalcitrant on the need for an Irish one. One of the arguments advanced against a British withdrawal at that time was a use of the stereotype that this episode explores—it was suggested that if the peace-keeping and law-enforcing colonists left, the Irish would fight among themselves and there would be a "bloodbath."

It is fascinating to realize that versions of this argument are still being advanced in relation not only to today's Irish "question," but to the question of Israel as well. Today, the Irish Catholics and Protestants and the Israelis and Palestinians are divided into opposite groups that are continually labeled with precisely the barbarian/civilian stereotype that is at least as old as colonialism itself: the old division between law-abider and terrorist. In both Ireland and Israel territorial divisions and the apparatus of patrolled borders split both areas in two, in the way suggested (and perhaps foretold) by Joyce's partitioned text. Even to imagine how these partitions and the need for them may be overcome proves profoundly difficult. To reformulate the split version of the colonial subject that has helped to give rise to them must be a start. It is this revision that we are invited to imagine in reading "Cyclops."

When the "fighting Irish" stereotype leads to no more than the throwing of a biscuit tin, the notion that the role of a colonial administration is to protect the natives from their own proclivity to violence is effectively ridiculed. Nevertheless, there is a sense in which "Cyclops" looks toward the civil war that broke out in Ireland months after the treaty guaranteeing the independence of the Irish Free State was signed. This was a war between the "Die-hards" who felt that the treaty splitting the island of Ireland into two parts was a betrayal, and the moderates, who were willing to accept this condition and get on with the task of setting up a new administration in the southern part of the island. Thus the hardheaded politics of "Cyclops" let its Irish readers (of 1919, of 1921, or since) know that the new community will never be homogeneous, and that new subjects who might hope to escape interpellation by the colonist regime will have been constructed by that regime in the first place. This turns out to be an especially poignant lesson when one remembers that the rationale for the treaty's territorial splitting was another split, between the mostly British-identified Protestants of the northern part of Ireland and the mostly nationalist Catholics of the south. Joyce's partitioned episode ultimately works, for its Irish readers, as a premonition of this split at the center of the Irish postcolonial experience; one may note that it has been key to the post-colonial history of many other of Britain's ex-colonies also. The perspective offered by the "Cyclops" episode, in advance, would appear to be that in the nation that emerges out of the colony, the need is to understand and cope with a collective dynamic, integrating differences and identities long fostered by the ruling power for their own ends, rather than imagining some illusionary collective cohesion premised on the necessary conformity of like-minded postcolonial subjects, a conformity supposedly generated as if by magic in the glorious moment of independence.

Envoi

Roger Casement was a controversial late-colonial subject whose dramatic and various representations in the archive of British colonialism,

Irish anticolonial insurgency, the popular press of the period, and even high modernist poetry, could not in the end manage to paint him as a subject outside the barbarian or civilian stereotypes enforced by the colonist regime. Perhaps only when his quicklime-covered remains were drawn through Dublin in 1966 for his reburial in the postcolonial capital on the fiftieth anniversary of his execution was he in any sense a postcolonial subject, and even then he was still imagined within the heroicizing frame of Celtic revival nationalist hagiography, which, as we have seen, was much beholden to the colonist version of the civil native. The same, however, I submit, cannot be said of Bloom in "Cyclops." In earlier episodes, especially "Wandering Rocks" and "Sirens," we have seen that his relentless and characteristic *flânerie* was a mechanism by which he managed to escape from many of the effects of the pervasive surveillance and interpellation that the successful colonist regime uses to keep the native population in its grip. This regime continues to be displayed in all its ferocious powers of surveillance in "Cyclops," as it will be in each of the succeeding episodes, particularly in the night city of "Eumaeus." Attempting to escape interpellation, literally, by passing it by, Bloon is trapped in the pub in "Cyclops," at the center of such interpellative forces as the watchful eyes and ears of the possible informer, the appropriately named (by the critics) Nameless One, and the not-so-manifestly interpellated figures like the chauvinist Citizen, whose vicious nationalism turns out to be only a more thorough mirroring of the ideology of the ruling power. Trapped, Bloom is forced toward a moment of coming to consciousness, a glorious moment in which his own field of vision of the reality of his situation is brought home to him. As such, "Cyclops" stages Bloom's own potentially revolutionary moment, represented in such a way as to also open the reader's eyes.

4

"The Whores Will Be Busy": Terrorism, Prostitution, and the Abject Woman in "Circe"

First, two scenes from the violence that has occurred since 1969 in Northern Ireland. One is of a young woman, shaven-headed, tarred and feathered, tied to the railings of a church; the other, of a young (male) poet who contemplates her. The tarred and feathered woman, punished for keeping company with a British soldier, stands as one of the most terrifying images of the victim in the Northern Irish fighting. The tar splashed on her skin makes a public spectacle of the moment violence touches the human body. That she is a woman, in an economy of guerrilla violence which, despite its random quality, insists that almost all its perpetrators and victims be male, accentuates the horror of this sullied body-as-spectacle. Yet she has not been assaulted by an alien power or by the "other side" because of her difference; rather, she is a scapegoat displayed by some in her own community. As spectacle of assaulted woman scapegoated by her own people for (as they see it) having "strayed," she stands at that border where their assertion of subaltern identity transforms itself into a rationale for political violence. At this border (which is also that of writing, of communication) her body signifies the urgent necessity, in the time of insurgent violence, for subaltern identity to be more profoundly understood.

Thus we turn to the second image, that of the young male poet, from the same community, who contemplates her. The poet in question is Seamus Heaney, who in his lyric "Punishment" (1975)[1] considers, albeit with subaltern circumspection, how he might react to the tar-splashed woman's body. He mulls two alternatives: "civilized outrage" versus "understanding ... the intimate revenge." These may, however, be excuses, for after opening with a love poem spoken into the past to a young woman who has been buried in a bog in Germany for almost two thousand years, he admits, when he turns to the tarred and feathered woman in the present, that he would be silent:

> I almost loved you
> but would have cast, I know
> the stones of silence ...
>
> I who have stood dumb
> when your betraying sisters,
> cauled in tar,
> Wept by the railings,
>
> Who would connive
> in civilized outrage
> yet understand the exact
> and tribal, intimate revenge.

Listening, we may ask, first, what exactly makes the poet "dumb," and, second, should we accept his silence? Heaney's admitting a wordless complicity is courageous, but his avowal of it—his declaration that he understands but would not speak this community's complicity in this spectacle of violence against one of themselves—is shocking, and must be repudiated. Speaking of the "stones of silence," he calls upon *us* to speak, after we have contemplated further the figure of the assaulted woman and her significance in the economy of violence and insurgency. To begin, we may unpack the suppositions and implications of those discursive options that this male writer gives himself, coming to terms with terrorist violence through an allegory of the assaulted woman: "civilized outrage" on the one hand, "intimate revenge" on the other. Here is another redeployment and reconfiguration of the barbarian/collaborator stereotype discussed in the previous chapter. For a start, note how the poet implicitly disposes these categories through his perception of subaltern practice versus the procedures of those in power: "civilized outrage" is associated with the verbal, the public, and, potentially, the poet, while "intimate revenge" is tied to the figural, the private, and, through the figure of woman, the feminine.

How does a subaltern people, in its texts, represent and understand the terrorist violence of the revolution that leads to independence? I suggest that in subaltern representations of terrorism, the figure of woman is at first willfully erased while realist "outraged" images of the terror dominate, to be deployed later, hysterically, as ambivalent, "intimate" image of collaborator and victim, to explore how violence may be represented and understood. My example of a text written in time of revolution in which this move occurs is the "Circe" episode of James Joyce's *Ulysses*. It is important to remember, I suggest, that "Circe," embodying the most nightmarish moments of *Ulysses,* was written — and rewritten a total of nine times — when the guerrilla War of Independence was at its height in Ireland, and further, that it takes as its material at such a time a fervid hallucinatory account of prostitutes, brothels, and their customers. "Circe," like Heaney's "Punishment," juxtaposes and then merges spectacles of violence and portraits of women at their most exploited; but while the women in "Punishment" are victims of actual terrorist violence, "Circes"'s prostitutes, in their representation, are allegorical of the predicament of the subaltern subject in the terrorist milieu. At issue for any subaltern text written out of the violence of revolution is this: How can the project of liberation, which aims to enable the construction of new subjectivities, exist in the same breath as terrorist violence that is willing to wreck any subjectivity in its path? In the space of this contradiction, masculinist discourses often place the figure of woman.

This substitution occurs in "Circe" as follows. First, written against the background of urban terrorist violence in Dublin, the episode presents us with a series of "terrorist" incidents. (An example is Stephen's fight with the two British soldiers [U 491].) These descriptions are couched in the accents of what Seamus Heaney termed "civilized outrage." The incidents are realistically portrayed (although an element of farce is present); they form part of the realist-romance strand of the episode, and they show only men. (Their subjects are male heroes.) As the realist strand fades into the phantasmagoria of Bloom as flaneur wandering in Nighttown, however, the figure of woman becomes visible, not as heroic individual but rather as the commodity-body of the prostitute, and soon, when the commodities around her come to life against a background of minor incidents of violence, as monster. This is the surreal (i.e., modernist) strand of the episode; it is, I suggest, its discourse on terrorism as (in Heaney's phrase) "intimate revenge"; and it focuses primarily on the figure of woman. Finally, the clash of these realist and modernist modes implicitly challenges the reader to find a level of significance in the text that, as "outrage," homologizes the particular strategies and effects of terrorist violence and, as "revenge" suggests some means by which the commodified feminine, after its erasure under realism and its disfigurement under modernist reification, can assert a potential subjectivity. Three modes of representing terrorism are discernable in "Circe," then, which one might label, in the broadest terms, realist, modernist, and postmodern; the first erases the woman as character, the second uses the figure of woman as ambivalent image, and the third, I suggest, provides a space in which a potential subject-after-subalternity can be imagined as woman. This essay details how each of the three modes achieves its effects.

"Circe" is the novel's most blatantly surreal episode. It highlights the limitations and the possibilities of a modernist text that is transgressive not merely in the service of some impulse to "make it new." Rather, transgressiveness here homologizes the political struggle; this subaltern text was composed during the very months in which the first nation to win independence from the British empire in this century was fighting intensely and with much bloodshed for its political independence. Here is the modernist core of *Ulysses*. Reading it, keep in mind, more than anywhere else in the novel, Adorno's dictum that modernist art is the most transparent of all, but that the truth it represents so plainly is painful for us, so that we repress what is evident.[2] Following Adorno's logic, it may be said that "Circe" is perceived as the most "difficult"[3] and incomprehensible episode in the text precisely because it generates and blatantly flaunts contradictions, forcing them further into the reader's field of perception. The key contradiction epitomized by "Circe" is that between its representation of actual violence on the one hand and potential postcolonial subjecthood on the other. Acknowledging destructive violence and articulating a potentially optimistic vision was fully a problem for Joyce, and has confronted every postcolonial writer working at the moment of independence since.[3]

By focusing on violence, I might seem to be reinforcing the First-World stereotype that often appears to count terrorism as the raison-d'être of postcolonial political life.[4] Yet the subaltern writer has never been unwilling to face up to terrorism, and as critics we must consider how any given text works through it so that it may be understood and overcome. Such working through takes place in "Circe" and in numerous later postcolonial texts by a measured display of the doubly determined subalternity of the figure of woman; this means that the understanding of woman's figural role in the representations of both male and female subaltern writers is crucial if one is to evaluate their potential for the creation of postcolonial subjectivity in general. By considering

"Circe" in the first instance as a text that "reflects-refracts" (Bloom's terms) violence, we pay homage to the historically specific moment of its writing, apparently at the expense of attention to its materials — prostitution in Dublin at the turn of the century. The text's refusal of mimeticism and its assertion of its own excessive possibilities is exactly what must be explored if its versions of violence and subject-making are to be understood.

To see how these representations are configured in the text of "Circe," we first need to consider how the three modes of exploring terrorist violence came to enter the field of vision of this particular subaltern text. By reviewing turn-of-the-century representations of terrorism — itself an invention of the Enlightenment and hence an eminently modernist form of warfare — in high naturalist and modernist texts, I will show that "Circe" occupies a pivotal moment in the history of modernist prose, at which the new narrative forms made possible specifically subaltern representations of the colonial native's most common form of violent insurrection. Then, by considering briefly a contemporary novel — J. M. Coetzee's *Waiting for the Barbarians* — that uncannily repeats the scene of Heaney's poem "Punishment," I will show how the subaltern text specifically (as opposed to the narrative, however benign it may be, of the colonizer) bears the brunt of an awareness of terrorism's effects. Coetzee's images lead to the focus of this chapter: Why and how the figure of woman comes to be deployed as signifier of terrorism from the viewpoint of the colonized.

Terrorism and the Scapegoating of Women

The tripartite discourse of terrorist violence in *Ulysses* is a function of its particular situation in the history of high naturalist and modernist representations of terrorism, stretching from Joseph Conrad's *The Secret Agent*[5] to T. E. Lawrence's various memoirs to Joyce, and on to Max Beckmann's painting *Die Nacht* (1918)[6] and Picasso's *Guernica*. While the origins of terrorism can be traced to the *petite guerre* of postrevolutionary France, it became widespread throughout Europe with the anarchist "propaganda of the deed" in the last quarter of the nineteenth century.[7] At this time, it was a subject for revolutionary manifestos such as Bakunin's *Principles of Revolution* (1869), for police files, and for the new yellow journalism of the gutter press. The London *Daily Mail*, for example, doubled its sales during the Boer War, which witnessed what was perhaps the first full-scale guerrilla campaign.[8] By the turn of the century terror had become the material of high literature, in works such as Joseph Conrad's *The Secret Agent,* Henry James's *The Princess Casamassima,*[9] and Emile Zola's *Paris* (1898).[10] (Later came "insider tales" such as the Irish author Liam O'Flaherty's *The Informer*[11] and J. P. Sartre's *Les Mains Sales.*)[12] The high point of naturalist representations of terrorism came in a work published four years after *Ulysses:* T. E. Lawrence's *Seven Pillars of Wisdom*[13] (first issued privately in 1926). A high naturalist author like Conrad was hampered in showing what he saw as the "otherness" of terrorism because naturalism demanded that there be a hero and that the account be written from within; T. E. Lawrence overcame this by dressing as an Arab and posing as leader of the Arab guerrilla armies. It is impossible now to read Lawrence's cross-dressing into nativism without irony. Yet his unlikely glorification of the Arab guerrillas, particularly estranging to Westerners today in the context of the western media's treatment of Middle Eastern conflicts, pinpoints, at the key moment in the development of this subgenre, how this kind of warfare will always be read according to allegiance; it will be read as "terrorism" by those who fear it, or as a "guerrilla campaign" by those who support it. While the relation between modernism's "revolution of the word" and the terrorist "propaganda of the deed" deserves to be more fully studied, one might note at once that the varieties of perspective offered by estranging representation mean that it was perhaps only in such texts (as in Joyce and Picasso) that the subaltern viewpoint was possible.

Terrorism as amateur, incidental, and unofficial warfare has from its origins been the tactic of the subaltern, the peasant, and the "other." From the viewpoint of those threatened, terrorism is brutal, unplanned, and its acts "disasters." Such disasters, as Maurice Blanchot stated in his *The Writing of the Disaster,*[14] will always be "remembered forgetfully" because they "escape the possibility of experience ... at the very limit of writing." The discourse of terrorism is part of the history of the fear of otherness: its primary rhetorical mode is outrage. Considered from the viewpoint of the subaltern whom the terrorist would represent, on the other hand, the violent act becomes a moment (however much the writer may heroicize or repudiate it) in the history of resistance and in the insurgency that exemplifies that resistance. Consider the opening chapter of Frantz Fanon's *The Wretched of the Earth,* "Concerning Violence,"[15] to which I referred earlier: it simultaneously calls for anticolonial rebellion and struggles to defuse and deny the actuality of the violence it calls up. Its wrenching ambivalence richly exemplifies the mechanics of what Seamus Heaney termed "intimate revenge"—even when the revenge is to be directed (as in Fanon's case) against the colonizing power. T. E. Lawrence cross-dresses himself as the outsider in order to write from within. Seamus Heaney, as an insider, cross-discourses in order to write from without. From their opposing viewpoints, each illustrates how the official discourse of being frightened and the subaltern discourse of resistance need not necessarily be separate: both impulses can invade any given text.

It is the subaltern text that bears the brunt of facing up to this double discourse, however. To show why this is so, I will trace the uncanny reappearance of the scene of Heaney's poem in another recent meditation on how to react to terrorism, J. M. Coetzee's novel *Waiting For the Barbarians*.[16] Coetzee's hero, like Heaney's lover-voyeur, renders his "intimate" voyeurism of the assaulted body of a woman as allegorical of reactions to terrorism. But while we, in turn, look on when he, the magistrate of a colonial town, unties the dirty bandages on the unnamed tribal woman's broken feet, we are aware that, first, this woman has been terrorized by the "official forces" in a rampage of state terrorism, and, second, that the narrator is himself a member of that official state bureaucracy (although a dissident, so that his text becomes liberal remonstrance, with certain of the accents of Conrad). He is relentlessly "civilized"; as a member of the established government, he can dispose of the problem that the woman represents by returning her (at the end of a long pilgrimage of expiation) to her tribe. Heaney, on the other hand, avows his subalternity: this is his courage. He is, in a sense, the representative of the tribe who, in Coetzee's novel, received the lamed woman back from the ruling regime—the tribe who would punish her again, we might imagine, for having strayed. Yet Heaney also avows his civility. The observed body, from the subaltern viewpoint, must, in this sense, always have been received back from the oppressor: in other words, what is seen is always now seen partly through the oppressor's voice and that vision is spoken always, partly, in the oppressor's language and forms. For the subaltern constituency for whom the disaster cannot, in Blanchot's elegant phrase, merely be "remembered forgetfully," some kind of complicity will always cohabit with a version of civilized outrage. Subaltern texts veer between the two modes; only by finding other levels of significance in the disfigured body of the woman can the reader go beyond the contradiction itself.

Why is it specifically upon the spectacle of the victimized body of a woman that this doubleness continues to be rehearsed? The deployment of the figure of woman turns an ethical dilemma into a matter of figuration. It displaces a public problem onto what the writer considers an issue of the space of the private, or, in the term Heaney uses in "Punishment," the "intimate." These, on the one hand, are the kinds of displacements Jameson enumerates as characteristic of Third World novelistic practice;[17] on the other, they are strategies of modernist representation, in which, as the critic Buci-Glucksman puts it, the male-female relation was thoroughly reconsidered, and the space of the feminine became allegorical of modernism's "other."[18] This new othering of woman as figure in both modernism generally and subaltern representations in particular is part of the astounding fear of woman that permeates so many high modernist texts. Specifically, women came to be associated with the most pressing political crises of the early twentieth century—of which the primary symptom was the Great War. The deployment of woman as allegory (in the sense in which Walter Benjamin defines that term) of terrorist violence in a modernist text must be read as part of the dramatic changes in representing women in relation to war generally that occurred in the first decades of this century.

When women in the twentieth century became victims and protagonists of war, the genres that supposedly had shown war in general but which inevitably focused on male subjects were now used to depict women also. In the west, the theater of war has been a male preening place. The woman as spoils and as victim had been a persistent stereotype, notably in neoclassical art; woman as warrior was a rarer subject. Throughout the Victorian era, the Taylorization of the "science of warfare" through military organization further zoned the sexes. Numerous conventions—The Hague (1875, 1899, 1907), Geneva, and so on—invariably passed resolutions aimed at distancing the army from the civilian population, and, ostensibly, at limiting the destruction of war as much as possible to the armed forces. In the First World War the dead were almost all soldiers, and virtually all male.[19] Given the division of risk on the basis of gender in time of war, women's roles were relegated to the conventional female ones of caring (as epitomized by Florence Nightingale, the Lady of the Lamp in the Crimean War), camp-following (consider the 1860–88 legislative experiments[20] to monitor the health of all prostitutes in British and Irish garrison towns), and entertainers (the female stars who sang to the troops in World War II).

Second, with the activity of war a male preserve, woman was bequeathed a symbolic function: she stood for the motherland. Under the aegis of a nationalist "chivalry" purveyed increasingly through the new popular media with full kitsch trappings as the nineteenth century progressed, the woman was made to represent what the men in national armies were fighting for: Britannia for the British, Marianne for the French. With the fall of the first buzz-bombs upon England at the end of World War I, however, the image of woman as individual victim had to compete with the overdetermined icon that showed the unblemished woman as personification of the state. The women who took on "men's work" behind the lines were now part of the war effort.

Next, with the formation of women's corps in the various Fascist citizen's militias that proliferated between the wars, on the one hand, and the acceptance of women as members of guerrilla armies and resistance groups[21] on the other, women had to be represented at last as warriors and as soldiers. At the same time, the increased stasis (as in the trenches of World War I) and increased technologization (as with the tank) of war generally resulted in the end of the conventional battlefield. This meant that war now worked to forestall representation of its aggression as spectacle. (For example, World War I photographs of the front[22] almost invariably show either soldiers waiting in the trenches, or panoramas of a desolate no-man's-land: scenes from before or after the combat.) As only the victims or the actors in the behind-the-lines war effort could be represented in action, images of war increasingly came to show women. With her new roles in warfare, the woman as soldier came to be shown within the stereotypes of representation of the male, while the male war victim might be shown in poses previously used to portray women. Finally, in guerrilla warfare, the terrorist is by definition absent, so that the victim, primarily as abject woman, is central.

The figure of woman as cipher of war's horror, then, became key in metropolitan modernist representations. In subaltern discourses, however, the native writer's more profound ambivalence over whether to express civilized outrage or maintain complicit silence in the face of the terrorist horror turns out to be enacted upon the image of the woman, who comes to be seen at once as both victim and active agent. For the colonized at the moment of anticolonial warfare, the question of allegiance is an intensely urgent one. It is in these contexts that the representation of woman as at once victim and protagonist in "Circe"—a text written against the background of the first full-scale terrorist war in Ireland—may be understood. Written about Dublin in the very years in which that city became the first in this century to experience a protracted period of urban terrorist warfare, "Circe" portrays its violence as a matter which intrudes suddenly and unpredictably upon an apparently peaceful scene, a scene—mostly of victims— populated by women. Although portrayed mainly as victims, these women, who in "Circe" are the prostitutes of Nighttown, turn out to be the site upon which the opposing impulses of the subaltern modernist confronting terrorist warfare vie for predominance. These women are made to represent both the subaltern's fear of colonial power as the imposition of consumer culture, a culture where women's bodies are commodities, and at the same time the site of utter abjection, where oppression seems to legitimize kinds of resistance suggestive of terrorist actions. These two impulses, confronted in the test of "Circe," make way for a third, which as we shall see may allow the women it represents the opportunity to seize a more independent version of themselves as subjects.

The Three Representations of Terrorism in "Circe"

This scene of women, both as epitomizations of the lures of empire and as its most evident victims, needed the defamiliarizing machineries of modernist representation if its subaltern significance was to emerge into the clarity of allegory. In the more resolutely metropolitan empire-centered texts and fragments of modernity that confront terrorism through the figure of exotic and abject woman—from the native woman dancing on the shore of the Congo River in *Heart of Darkness*[23] to the images of young French collaborators, shaven-headed, being hounded through the Paris suburbs at the end of World War II—the supposed mimeticism of the representations, their realism, underpin scenes so shocking that the possibilities for modernist allegory are only intimated, never in fact brought into the field of vision. *Ulysses,* on the contrary, is constructed as a text that opens in realism—the possibilities for allegory of all its representations fully intimated by the symbolist gloss that the reader has come to expect from *Portrait of the Artist*—

and, upon this template, turns to the estranging modes of modernism, in which, in Adorno's terms, the allegory is not implied but all too evident. As such, we can now at last stop wondering (with Pound, among others, who, in a letter to Joyce, criticizes the novelty of the "Sirens" episode)[24] why this realist text-machine needed to disintegrate into the heteroglossia of modernism; rather, we ask why such a modernist text needed as its opening gambit such slices of realism. The answer, clearly, is that the text stages the contradiction between the representational possibilities of the two modes, challenging its readers to envision a space in which one can read the two kinds of configuration at once. The division allowed Joyce to pare down the realism to its most shabby — until it mimicked not some imagined real but rather the most conventional and shop-soiled vagaries of the established realisms, stripping it of the intimations of the symbolic that so encumber a writer like Conrad. Instead, he was free to make explicit in his modernist moments what otherwise he would have needed to intimate.

"Circe" is the fragment of the text in which modernism finally drowns out the realist element; significantly, this occurs in the episode that confronts terrorism. "Circe" first shows the inadequacy of realist representations of this kind of violence. Second, in its modernist representation of the feminine as doubled image of both imperialist oppressor and as colonist native abject, it shows the pervasive effect of terrorism in the subaltern culture. Ultimately, "Circe" calls on us to discover in its radical form a narrative that homologizes a subaltern's response to terrorism as an issue of abjection; to do so, it overcomes the limits of terrorism's representation in both realist and modernist modes. It achieves this by juxtaposing the residue of realism and the trajectory of modernist textuality in the book. To suggest how these levels were realigned, and to show how these juxtapositions were resolutely *ideological,* before turning to "Circe" itself, consider first how to read a short ballad written in 1903 by Oliver St. John Gogarty.

Gogarty was a prominent Dublin doctor, friend and later "betrayer" of the young James Joyce. Gogarty's ballad[25] was not about a terrorist incident: rather, it concerned the return of the troops from the first terrorist warfare of the new century, the Boer War. To celebrate the arrival of a regiment of the British army to Dublin in 1903, Gogarty penned a ballad of welcome that was published, on the day the regiment arrived, in a local newspaper. The poem extravagantly praised the men of the regiment and took pride in their arrival in the city. However, it was soon noted by the keener readers (and not much later, by all of them) that if one took the first letter of each line and read downwards, there immediately became visible a vulgar countermessage: "The whores will be busy." This caused such outrage that the paper was shut down.

Clearly, this ballad was read in three different ways, and each was directly the result of the reader's ideological position. First, there is the loyal British subject, who read the poem literally, as an expression of loyalty to the army. Then there is the Irish nationalist, who read the poem subversively, as a clever text in which the real subtext—the vertical line—is embedded. Finally, it will be read now, by readers who are aware of *both* the overt message and the embedded line. What effect can this text have on such readers, who must read both public and subversive lines at once?

What is striking is that, by being ideological, these are readings that take the ballad to be respectively a realist, modernist, and (latterly one might claim), a postmodernist text. The staunch Britisher, unsuspecting, reads Gogarty's poem as an exercise in realism, mimetic description that recounts an event. The Irish native reader, like Gogarty himself, reads the text as a modernist piece, as a wittily dialogic work in Bakhtin's terms, where the overt discourse is merely a vehicle for another, the more subversive subtext. Finally, contemporary readers have a clever postmodern text, as they read the contradictory and opposing messages, one embedded neatly in the other, at once, and assert that they are at peace with both.

We have three ideological viewpoints, therefore, to which I have mapped three periodizing readings. Such a mapping of ideology to genre to historical moment is no doubt all too ordered; it elides the vivid excessiveness of the sphere of cultural production, in which the role of high culture in historical development might precisely be discovered. Nevertheless, to complete this strategic mapping, if only to outline the base-superstructure model that a text as disorderly as *Ulysses* might exceed, I want to add to the equation the three stages of modern political development to which the ideologies and literary periods I have already enumerated might belong. Fredric Jameson makes such connections when he describes how there is "a first moment of national or local capitalism, to which realism roughly belongs," followed by "a break or restructuration of the monopoly period (or 'stage of imperialism') which seems to have generated the various modernisms." He then characterizes our own period as "the multinational era, whose historical

originality can alone account for the peculiarities of what has now become known as *post-modernism*."[26] To suggest that "Circe" incorporates
the first two of these modes as (roughly) realist and modernist literary
strategies implies that subaltern discourse, far from renouncing the
master-discourses, is condemned to reenunciate them; this is an issue
that preoccupies the opening of the novel. Further, in staging a confrontation of roughly realist and modernist modes that demands what
may be called a postmodern reading, "Circe" may be said to stand at a
key moment of historical change, an epistemic break (that is not necessarily a simple rupture in linearized history) that marks a nexus of the
three historical forces from which the genres of narration, in Jameson's
framework, are generated: those of nation and capital, of empire and
colonialism, and of postcolonialism. This may well be the case: "Circe's"
realist scenarios do inscribe here the great—and final—glory days of
both British and (its inverse image) Irish nationalism; the episode's modernist theatrics celebrate the age of empire while marking its downfall
in the first colony of the modern period to gain independence from
Britain; and the discourse that emerges when these two collide marks
the postcolonial era, implying a time when terrorism will be over and
the "Free State" will come into being. Hence the question of the symbolic status of the feminine under each of the three modes is not only
the issue of woman as erased, as disfigured, or as potential subject and
allegory of terrorism in male representations, but rather the question of
how to represent any "other" group in the successive modes of state
governance that have underpinned stages of high capitalism.

     With this in mind, we will now look closely at "Circe" itself.

"Circe" I: Realist Terrorism

"Circe" was written between June and December of 1920, the most
decisive months of the Irish War of Independence. In this period some
of the worst terrorist and counterterrorist acts of the campaign took
place in Dublin, which had become a city under siege in the same way
as did Belfast in the early 1970s. Since February 1920 Dublin had
been subject to a curfew.[27] Organizations like Sinn Fein, to which
Bloom, as the "Cyclops" informant tells us, contributed key ideas, and
the Gaelic League, about which the Englishman Haines had been en-
thusiastic, had by now been banned in much of the country; by 1920
"Sinn Feiners" largely meant nationalist guerrillas. On October 25,

Terence MacSwiney, Lord Mayor of Cork, died in Brixton Prison after a 74-day hunger strike that caused international outrage; Ellmann tells us how Joyce had followed MacSwiney's fate in the newspapers, and how he would later, in a piece of doggerel verse, cite it as proof of British turpitude. On November 21, 1920, "Bloody Sunday," twenty British secret-intelligence agents were shot at dawn in their beds in lodgings throughout Dublin; that afternoon, in retaliation, civilians were gunned down when the British army fired on spectators at a foot-ball match in Croke Park (a sports field mentioned in "Cyclops" as "Clonturk Park" [U 254]). On December 11, about a week before Joyce wrote in a letter that "Circe [was] finished this morning at last," the Black and Tans, a British Army brigade recruited to fight the IRA, burned down the center of Cork city.[28]

Against this conflagration, Joyce inserted three key scenes of realisti-cally portrayed violence into "Circe," images that break the book's ret-rospection to show what life was like on Dublin's streets when the book was written, rather than when it was set. These show incidents in a ter-rorist war much as they have been shown in countless newspaper pho-tographs, reports, and histories.[29] They constitute, I will suggest, a re-lentlessly masculinist discourse, describing only a world of heroic males; they exploit the salient categories of realist discourse to cover terrorism; and they are deconstructed almost as soon as they arise by the surreal supratext's attention to a pillar of realist representation — the issue of identity.

The first, inserted at the height of the preliminary "trial" Bloom un-dergoes in "Circe," comically portrays the kind of incident common-place today in Northern Ireland or on the West Bank, or at any guer-rilla flashpoint. It is almost midnight on a dark street; two policemen confront Leopold Bloom:

SECOND WATCH
(*points to the corner*) The bomb is here.

FIRST WATCH
Infernal machine with a time fuse.

BLOOM
No, no. Pig's feet. I was at a funeral.

FIRST WATCH
(*draws his truncheon*) Liar!

(U 385)

Here is the "man in the street," going about his business, interrupted by police questioning: the subject of numerous photographs from Dublin during the Irish War of Independence, and a staple image from every guerrilla war zone since. The police suspect that the parcel, which Bloom has thrown to a dog, is a bomb: he matches their fin-de-siècle stereotype of a "dynamitard," a furtive male figure dressed in black.

The second realist scene comes with the raising of a cry: "Dublin's burning, Dublin's burning, on fire, on fire." The "stage direction" reads *"Brimstone fires spring up. Dense clouds roll past. Heavy Gatling guns boom. Pandemonium. Troops deploy ..."* (*U* 488). This is the Dublin of Easter Week, 1916, during the Rising that sparked the insurgency of the next half-decade, and whose outlandish gesture is celebrated in Yeats's famous poem. Central Dublin did burn on the nights of that week: rebel strongholds throughout the city were shelled from a boat on the Liffey. The fires burned most of the buildings along Dublin's most imposing thoroughfare, O'Connell Street, where the General Post Office, which served as the headquarters of the rebellion, stands; this street marked the limit of the zone in which the prostitutes of Nighttown solicited.[30]

The third (and key) realist scene showing the violence of 1920 follows almost immediately; in it, Stephen is knocked almost unconscious by a British soldier. Here is the final blow of the drawn-out struggle:

(*He rushes toward Stephen, fist outstretched, and strikes him in the face. Stephen totters, collapses, falls, stunned. He lies prone, his face to the sky, his hat rolling to the wall. Bloom follows and picks it up.*) (*U* 491)

Private Carr punches Stephen because the young schoolteacher has drunkenly asserted that "I have no king myself at the moment" — that he does not consider himself a British subject; Carr wants to "make a bleeding butcher's shop of the bugger" (*U* 487) because he believes that Stephen is insulting "My fucking king." This is the mawkish realism that renders transparent all too readily its symbolic intent: this version of "one small blow" in the "nationalist struggle" might be Joyce's version of a scene from a novel by the mid-nineteenth-century Fenian writer Charles Kickham, or his dramatization of one of the numberless popular rebel songs of that period in Ireland. Such a scene would have seemed maudlin in some minor nationalist play of these years. Although it is presented here as farce, and is ridiculed by the surreal scene changes surrounding it, it *is* presented in the realist mode at the height of the most surreal episode of *Ulysses*. We are forced to consider its significance over against the surreal phantasmagoria that surrounds it.

How does this moment, along with the other realist scenes, represent the actuality of political violence in Dublin in 1920? They represent it, I suggest, as travesties of such commonplace realist representations of terrorism as newspaper reports. Joyce's scenes resemble newspaper coverage in that they show the terrorist war as a succession of incidents, invariably involving individuals rather than groups: the honest citizen who encounters the police, the young drunk who confronts the soldiers. They correspond to familiar newspaper photos: the civilian being searched, the building in flames. In a terrorist war, an attack can almost never (unless by chance) be photographed or reported while it is in progress. Thus either the attack will be reported afterwards, with images of mourning, which, if possible, show women, or the repeated incidents of the state of siege that citizens endure in a time of terror are taken to represent the suffering as a whole. These latter are what are served us in the realist scenes in "Circe." Yet harassment of a citizen by a vigilant or even brutal policeman, whether in the Gaza strip or in this episode, is only the shadow of the horror of a terrorist or counterterrorist burst of gunfire or bomb explosion. Because of this difference between what gets represented and what is actually experienced, a distance is opened, a space of assuagement that is also the space of ideological interpellation, between the shame of daily harassment that is shown and the horror of a terrorist outbreak that is experienced. In "Circe" this space provides the opening for the subversive heteroglossia undermining the realism, but it also allows a more predictable version of "civilized" ideology to be inscribed upon the realist mode: the images are rendered with a nationalist gloss.

Because nationalism flowered in the mid-nineteenth century under the same cultural and social forces that created the glass armor of the familiar that is realist narrative, narrative realism and nationalist ideology share assumptions about the proprieties of representation: both believe in the inevitability of heroism and agree on the ratio of public and private in creating heroic subjects. (Such proprieties, in turn, are exactly those exploited by terrorism as a mode of warfare.) Hence realistic reportage tends to focus not on the relation between perpetrator and victim, but on that between ordinary citizen and police; it searches for the heroic, finding it in the victim or possibly even in the terrorist; and it plays on the split between public and private lives. Thus reports, whether in newspapers or in "Circe"—Bloom versus the interrogating police, Stephen versus the soldiers, or a child playing on the street near a soldier in a photograph from Northern Ireland—work to symbolically substantiate that high nationalist version of history (advocated by the terrorists) that portrays the guerrilla war as an uncomplicated nationalist struggle between the local population and a brutal occupying military force. In the tableau the "man in the street" will invariably stand for the native subject being harassed by the enemy forces. This means that in "Circe" Joyce's mimeticism could not, ultimately, be achieved without the suggestion of a high nationalist interpretation of the events portrayed, even though we knew that Joyce feared terrorism (as in his fear over Nora's visit to Galway in 1922)[31] and ridiculed rabid Irish nationalism, even in A Portrait of the Artist.[32]

Next, as the representative incident comes heavily freighted with the nationalist symbolism of the victim, this victim will inevitably be constituted as the hero (or antihero) that realism demands. The realist text, demanding the heroic, is functionally assimilative, ill-suited to portraying the radical otherness that its discourse wishes to impute to the terrorist. Thus "Circe" shows the public lives of the male characters (Stephen, Bloom) in confrontation with public forces (the police, the army). Staging this confrontation, "Circe" operates in the ambivalent space where preserving public spheres and preserving private ones are exposed as incompatible projects. What is made clear here is the very end of the viability of the realist romance plot in Ulysses: by pushing the heroes of the realist romance of fathers and sons into the publicity of the terrorized street, "Circe" denies realism's radical separation of public and private lives. This ambivalence over the respective spaces of the public and the private intersects with stereotypes regarding the relation of gender to these spheres. The realist novel from Richardson to James was a key discursive arena in which women came to be constructed (often in masculinist narratives) as bourgeois subjects; this genre's focus of fulfillment was the domestic, the home, posited as the arena of private and interior life. Joyce, on the contrary, following a parallel tradition extending from a text about which he wrote—Robinson Crusoe—to Conrad's Lord Jim (the tradition of colonist literature) abducts the novel as a genre populated almost wholly by men, whose locus is the thoroughfare, whether it be sea lane, mountain pass, or street. In "Circe," however, the street is the place of the dangers of terrorism, so that when Bloom is questioned by the police we watch him frantically attempt to reground the basis of his realist bourgeois subjecthood, his "identity," first in *British* colonial stereotypes, and next, in the domestic space that, for the male realist, is the space of women.

The concreteness of these scenes is set against the realist baggage of "Circe" that Joycean critics have rendered familiar, especially the story of the relation between Bloom as father and Stephen as son. The interest in this relation exists in the text as the insistent trace of an archaism, a vestigial formation left over from a previous era's configuration of significance. This level of the text has held the deepest attraction for virtually all the critics of the episode (predictably enough, given the interest in post-Freudian "anxiety of influence of key" postformalist criticism). Its apparently hallucinatory mode has rendered it particularly susceptible to psychoanalytic readings.[33] In readings of the episode as a meditation of the growth of a father-son relationship, where "Circe" is considered a sort of vaudeville reversal of Edmund Gosse's bitter novel *Father and Son* that celebrates male fellow-feeling across the generations, the confrontations with the forces of the law are considered important only as accessory plot mechanisms. By bringing the *Bildungsroman* hero and the paternal antihero together, these incidents are seen to contribute obligingly to the males-only family romance. Yet in snatching the heroes of this domestic (yet male) Utopia out of their private trances to reconstitute them, for a moment, as heroes of public and political tableaus, "Circe" stages a contradiction in realist representation, in which what Jameson calls "the radical split between the private and the public, the poetic and the political, between what we have come to think of as the domain of sexuality and the unconscious and that of the public world ... of political power" must be maintained at all costs.[34] Mimetic representations of terrorism, both in "Circe" and in the press, show private lives in confrontation with public forces. Terrorism itself insures its impact by breaking the division between the private and public lives of its victims: it violates the private space of a random few to force change in the public sphere. In a sense, this is what Joyce does here to the realist tale: when he shows the two heroes confronting the police and army, he splinters that realist strand of the tale with an all-too-realistic violence that the tropes of realism cannot recontain. Hence we watch the first realist scene splinter into surrealism as the text explores the primary pillar of the realist mode—the one that bridges the gap in realism between the public heroic and the private significant—the issue of identity.

Questioning identity renders blatant the contradiction between the use of mimeticism as a vehicle for the family romance plot on the one hand and the depiction of public political troubles on the other. Stephen fights privates Carr and Compton as an Irishman against two Englishmen: the division of identities is clear. As he lies unconscious in the street, however, when the two policemen who have arrived try to discover his name, Bloom attempts to divert them (*U* 493). The situation is saved (as a realist narrative would put it) by Corny Kelleher, the undertaker, who (we are aware from a scene in "Wandering Rocks") is a tout in the pay of the police. This should alert us to the importance of covert information and its relation to naming in any society subject to terrorism. Covert information is the basis of terrorist surprise, and at the heart of the surveillance that elicits this information is the name. Remember that, earlier, when the police asked Bloom for his name, he lied:

FIRST WATCH
Come, name and address.

BLOOM
I have forgotten for the moment. Ah yes! (*He takes off his high grade hat, saluting*) Dr. Bloom, Leopold, dental surgeon. You have heard of Von Blum Pasha. Umpteen millions. . . . Cousin.

FIRST WATCH
Proof.

(*U* 371)

Bloom, terrified, goes through a series of poses in quick succession: a colonial officer, a mason, even a "respectable married man" (*U* 373). He knows he has to prove himself to be a loyal British subject. And in the end he comes out with it: "I'm as staunch a Britisher as you are, sir" (*U* 373). He then tries to prove this by acting the part of a series of stereotyped heroes of the latter-day empire. No one is deceived, but he offers us, incidentally, a reprise of the subgenres into which English naturalism splintered at the end of the nineteenth century: he would be the hero of a Conradian sea-yarn ("Its a way we gallants have in the navy" he cries [*U* 372]), of a Conan Doyle mystery ("Mistaken identity: . . . . We medical men. By striking him dead with a hatchet" [*U* 372]), of a Kiplingesque colonial tale ("The royal Dublins, boys, the salt of the earth. . . . I did all a white man could" [*U* 373]). This occurs in a lengthy trial— "Bloom versus the King" — in which Bloom's mimicry of every

colonist stereotype is interspersed with his promises to live the life of a
hero of domestic fiction. At this, he is accused by one Philip Beaufoy,
appropriately in a pronounced British accent, of being a plagiarist, of
"the Beaufoy books of love and great possessions ... a household word
throughout the kingdom" (U 374)—love, great possessions, and the
household, the reader may take it, being the cardinal points of desire in
any realist narrative. It is as if the text acknowledges that in this kind of
realism even the family romance, let alone the violence of a war, can
only be played out in resolutely British accents. Bloom, meanwhile,
tries to salvage his status as realist subject by reinvoking domestic longings: "*he had seen ... glimpses,*" he states "*through the windows of
loveful households in Dublin city and urban district ... scenes truly
rural of happiness ..., innocent Britishborn bairns lisping prayers....*"
(U 377). Even in the gendered terms of the trajectory of realism in
Ulysses, the space of the feminine (which is, in realism's terms, the
space of the home, the domicile) has been opened up.

"Circe" II: Surreal Terror

The masculinist realist narrative that predominates in the opening stages
of "Circe" is thoroughly undermined. The way in which the violence of
the street is represented exposes its hero-making as vulgar stereotyping,
its subjectivity as mere farcical mimicry of the models provided by the
colonial masters, and its romance plot of father and son as a Utopia for
males only. Yet it still manages to reconcile itself with the sphere of the
domestic on its own terms. This is epitomized, above all, by the brothel
itself, which is both home and men's club, with its parlor, its pianola,
and its women. The brothel is a public space for men that pretends to
be home. The brothel in "Circe" is not a place in which any of the male
characters is eager for sex: indeed, any heterosexual sex here would interfere with the wholly male camaraderie in which the realist trajectory
is interested. While even the nationalist rendering of woman as symbol
of the motherland is satirized here as "Old Gummy Grammy Ireland"
(U 485)—a (per)version of the mother as "mother country"—the
women as prostitutes are doubly abject figures in the male carnival. As
prostitutes, in the fake home of the brothel, they are portrayed as victims.
As consumers, and as commodities themselves (the body of the prostitute as commodity), they are seen as collaborators in that they stand for
the reification that the modernist strand of "Circe" inaugurates as its

analysis of the social condition of the subaltern group. As signs of the reification of social life are juxtaposed with minor acts of violence, the episode actively demonstrates how the violence of a guerrilla campaign percolates into multiple aspects of the people's lives. In the peculiar reconfiguration of reification and incidental violence by which the body of the prostitute becomes the site on which reification is made visible, "Circe" takes the feminine, to this point marginalized in *Ulysses*, to be the cipher of the forces that have made revolutionary violence inevitably a part of people's lives.

Commodities proliferate in the modernist strand of the episode. They first appear as markers of male identity within a pastiche of realist expectation regarding caste, nation, and name, but then come to be more and more associated with women, women first as consumers and then as bodies—as commodities themselves. Take, for example, the comic preoccupation with hats in the episode. Bloom, when questioned by the police, reappears as Von Blum Pasha in a fez; later Richie Goulding is discovered with "three ladies' hats pinned to his head." Soon, we have Bloom's mother in "pantomime dame's stringed mobcap," followed by Molly in a "turreting turban." Earlier, Bloom had reminded Mrs. Breen of an outing:

> "And you had on that new hat of white velours with a surround of molefur that Mrs. Hayes advised you to buy because it was marked down to nineteen and eleven, a bit of wire and an old rag of velveteen." (*U* 366)

The hat is first of all a marker of caste and identity; furthermore, it is a commodity, something on sale, to be bought. This is true also of the extensive clothing and costume described throughout the episode, and even more strikingly true of the jewellery. When Bloom tells Mary Driscoll (a maid whom he had harassed in Eccles Street) "I gave you mementos, smart emerald garters," (*U* 376) it is only the beginning. When Molly appears as oriental houri, for example,

> (... *A coin gleams on her forehead. On her feet are jewelled toerings. Her ankles are linked by a slender fetterchain.... her goldcurb wristbangles angriling....* (*U* 359)

Mrs. Yelverton Barry steps forward

> (*in a lowcorsaged opal balldress and elbowlength ivory gloves, wearing a sabletrimmed brickquilted dolman, a comb of brilliants and panache of osprey in her hair*).... (*U* 379)

The most heavily decorated woman stalking the episode must be Bella Cohen:

> (*... Bella Cohen ... massive whoremistress, enters. She is dressed in a three-quarter length ivory gown, fringed around the hem with tasselled selvedge, and cools herself flirting a black horn fan like Minnie Hauck in Carmen. On her left hand are wedding and keeper rings. Her eyes are deeply carboned.... She has large pendant beryl eardrops.*) (U 429)

These descriptions project female figures that are denied any subjectivity by being submerged in overdecoration; an analogy in visual art might be the fantastically draped women in some of the vast canvases of Gustave Moreau.

Soon we are given intimations of how the commodity can mediate in relations between men and women, when Bloom's fetish potato, "a relic of poor mamma," is taken from him by the prostitute Zoe when she propositions him. The scene in which Bloom "gently" (as the text puts it) asks for it back may indeed be one of the most intimate moments in the episode, even in the whole book (*U* 453). But the kind of relation that commodities mediate is more often overtly oppressive; for example, that between Bloom and Bella/Bello is mediated by Bella's fan. Bello tortures Bloom, yet it is not (s)he but her fan which speaks. (The fan tells Bloom: "We have met. You are mine. It is fate." [*U* 450]) The most notorious example of the commodity coming to life, however, came earlier, when "*A cake of new clean lemon soap arises, diffusing light and perfume.*" The soap sings:

> We're a capital couple are Bloom and I.
> He brightens the earth. I polish the sky. (*U* 360).

This is a turn-of-the-century flash advertisement, and it fully epitomizes the modernity of the episode. It is what the materialist critic Franco Moretti[35] considers "the unsurpassed literary celebration of commodity fetishism" in "Circe."

Commodity fetishism is the outcome of the process of reification in the material bases of society, the process by which the value of the relation between human beings becomes invested, instead, in commodities. Briefly, it comes about (as Marx explains it in the first chapter of *Capital*)[36] because the commodity, a product of human labor, manages no longer to bear the stamp of that labor. A social relation between people comes to assume, in their eyes, as Marx puts it, "the fantastic form of a relation between things." In terms of Weber's concept of rationaliza-

tion, "the older, inherited ways of doing things are broken into their
component parts according to the instrumental dialectic of means and
ends, a process which amounts to a virtual bracketing or suspension of
the ends themselves."[37] Moretti, writing on *Ulysses,* accounts for this
happening at the turn of this century, and for its becoming perceptible
to the point where it might enter the field of vision of the literature of
the period, by noting that at this historical moment occurred "the interruption of the process of the circulation of commodities ... the crisis of
overproduction: that is, the seemingly paradoxical condition of the co-
existence, on the one hand of unsold goods, and on the other, of unsat-
isfied needs."[38] This crisis of overproduction in early twentieth-century
Europe is what gave rise to modern mass advertising, as advertisers
sought novel ways to persuade customers to purchase unsold merchan-
dise. Moretti borrows Dangerfield's slogan — "the strange death of liberal England"[39] — as he explains how the British economy at the turn of
the century continued to hold to the free market modes that had served
it brilliantly in the first industrial revolution, and thus fell behind in the
efforts at systematic economic concentration — the formation of syndi-
cates and monopolies — that fueled the boom in Germany and the United
States in these years. He reads the Circean carnival of commodities,
then, as a vision of a dead-end British economy turned inward, reveling
simply in consumption — implying a critique quite similar to that offered by Lenin, in his tract *Imperialism,*[40] when he blasted the British
for so conspicuously taking their leisure.

Moretti's examination of the functioning of this carnival of commodities within the political unconscious of "Circe" is incomplete, however,
because he does not take account of the specifically late-colonial situation of Dublin as capital of Ireland that Joyce describes. "Circe" is not,
after all, set in London; rather, it casts its eye over the first city of the
imperial periphery. Moretti's invocation of the Leninist critique is in
this sense appropriate, in that Lenin's analysis of imperialism is more
interested in the effect of imperial expansion upon the metropolitan
centers than in the overall effect of such expansion on global conditions
and the lives of people in the peripheries. If we shift the focus from
metropole center to peripheral outpost, while still recognizing that
commodity fetishism, focused on the figure of woman, is the dominant
trope of "Circe," how do we account for its exposition in the episode —
and for the violence that stands as its mirror-image in the text? This
violence is the element Moretti ignores; he is content to see the text's

heterogeneous dissociations as an appropriate homology of the failure of early twentieth-century British society to arrange its system of economic relations in a stable system of function and meaning. *Ulysses* no doubt does reflect this, but it does so, I hope to show, by representing an alternative reality, the other "disorder" of the colonial hinterland.

The issue of how commodity fetishism, advertising, and *flânerie* coexist in the colony has already been discussed in chapter 2. The question for a subaltern reading of "Circe" as a text of commodity fetishism is this: How does the commodity itself operate in the imperial periphery? In the colony, the product, in the first place, is likely to have been imported from the imperial center. This is evidently the case with the commodities of "Circe": the soap reminds us inevitably of Pears soap, one of the first British consumer products to be mass-advertised: the raw material for its manufacture, cocoa oil, came from the African colonies, but it was made in Leverhulme, near Liverpool.[41] When Bloom, in his first trial, describes his utopian longings for an ideal suburban home, his description of a melodeon trails off into an advertisement for the instrument: "with four matching stops and twelvefold bellows, a sacrifice, greatest bargain ever ..." (*U* 377). He has just remembered that it is "Britanniametalbound." The association of desired commodities and advertising underlines the sense that these products are part of the excess goods of the crisis of overproduction. This is a crisis of the home country, the imperial center. If we move from Leninist analyses of imperialism, and those of the classical theorists of the Great War period that followed his "export-of-capital" line of analysis, however, and concentrate instead on less totalizing theories of imperialism such as that of Rosa Luxemburg, which turn out to be interested in specific economic conditions in the peripheries rather than merely in the symptoms of economic decay in the core, then we can understand how the commodity, as the dumped surplus of the metropolitan crisis of production, acts as an utterly alienating and disrupting force in the fragile system of relations that constitutes the colonial reality.

Luxemburg's key theorizing of imperialism, *The Accumulation of Capital*,[42] was published in 1913. In it, taking as her starting point what she considered an error in Marx's analysis, she explains the need of capitalism to *realize* its surplus. Marx describes surplus value as being realized when the products at the end of a period of production are sold and the profits returned to expand production. In a context of overproduction, however, she concluded that the only way for the excess to be realized was by finding consumers outside the established capitalist relations of production. The remorseless drive toward expansion by capitalism is not, she insists, a search primarily for raw materials or labor but rather for customers. She saw the colonies as necessary to the capitalist centers primarily as markets, as pools of potential consumers. Most striking, however, and pertinent to the purposes of this reading, she sees the penetration of the "natural" economy of the peripheral territory as a dynamic and brutally violent struggle. The commodity economy must destroy the preexisting "natural" economy of the colony not only to gain possession of its resources and to "liberate" its labor power and coerce it into service, but, ultimately, to introduce a commodity economy. The violent form this introduction has often taken is suggested by the historical example she chooses to illustrate her point: Britain forcing China to open its borders to the trade in opium in the nineteenth century in the Opium Wars.

This analysis seems to me particularly applicable to Ireland at the turn of the twentieth century. Luxemburg sees gaining possession of the colonies' resources and the "liberation" of labor power as the first steps in the imperial penetration of a colony: these are the mechanisms represented, for example, in Conrad's *Nostromo* or *Heart of Darkness,* where silver and ivory are the raw materials being removed and the native population is being coerced into performing this work. These steps, however, had been put into effect in Ireland two centuries earlier; given the particular history of "uneven development" in the Irish colony, it was only by the turn of the twentieth century that the country finally appeared ready for an economy centered on commodities. The 1890s, for example, had finally witnessed, with the successive Land Acts culminating in the Wyndham Land Act of 1903 (which marked the end of the landlord system) the creation of a new petit-bourgeois class of small landowners.[43] A new small-merchant class, a "shopocracy," had come into being. This was the class which was the target of Yeats's scathing attack in his poem "September 1913":

> What need you, being come to sense,
> But fumble in a greasy till
> And add the halfpence to the pence ...? (CP 106)

These are of course the merchants whose names ring through *Ulysses* and particularly in "Circe": we hear of "*Dockrell's wallpaper at one and ninepence a dozen*" (*U* 377), "Derwan the builder," "bottles of Jayes Fluid" (*U* 396), and "expensive Henry Clay cigars." Joyce in later life would ask visitors from Dublin if they could, as he was able to do, name from memory all the shops up one side and down the other of the well-known shopping streets. Between the time in which *Ulysses* was set (June 16, 1904) and the time in which it was written (1914–21), the structures were set in place so that Ireland would become what, in Luxemburg's view, the colonies were expected, ultimately, to become: a culture and economy of consumers. It was perhaps the first modern colony in which the local culture could be successfully penetrated in precisely this manner. As in the metropolitan centers of empire, these consumers were from the first taken to be women.

Why does "Circe" place over against a striking carnival of these commodities only recently made available to the Irish natives a plethora of scenes of violence? We have seen how reification and subsequently the fetishization of commodities in First-World economies resulted when the relation between the producer's labor and the end product (the commodity) is no longer evident, so that, for the producers, "the sum total of their own labor is presented to them as a social relation existing not between themselves, but between the products of their labor" (Marx). In the Irish situation of 1904–21, the question of labor or production does not even arise, as many of the products were produced elsewhere—generally in Britain. Hence the actual alienation existing between the consumer and the product (whatever the superficial desire) was necessarily intense, in that the sum total of the labor represented by the product, if it is visible at all, is simply labor produced by the imperial peoples upon the backs of those in the colonial periphery. Thus the relationship that the fetishized commodity comes to mediate, in the last instance, is that between the native consumer and the alien producer. What occurs in "Circe" is that the fetishized product, once it is allowed (literally) a life of its own, inevitably takes on the life and traits of the imperial producer, and proceeds to bully, in various ways, the native would-be consumer. He or she must be violently coerced into being a consumer. The native, then, may respond in anger; in either instance there results what the media calls "an unacceptable level of violence."

It is in this light that we may read what is generally regarded as the most vicious confrontation and bizarre reversal in the episode, the sadomasochistic domination of Bloom by Bella Cohen. In such a quasi-allegorical reading, Bella Cohen is exposed as a monstrous late-capitalist Britannia. Predictably, although she herself arrives as a heavily bejewelled presence at the beginning of the set-piece, she does not herself address Bloom: rather, it is her fan, and then her "hoof," that hector the submissive Bloom. It is Bloom himself, as the native consumer, who cries "Enormously I desire your domination," while the fan—image, in a more coquettish fiction, of shyness and evasion—assumes here, with its tapping, its full role as repressive commodity. Bloom wishes that "I had not parted with my talisman"—the shriveled black potato, emblem and relic of that natural economy which, with the Irish potato famine in Ireland in 1845–47, had been laid open for dismantling with one excruciating jolt. He gives a rich demonstration of the extent to which the Edwardian Irish citizen of empire had been interpellated at multiple levels of public and private experience by a consumer fetishism based on the desire to be cosmopolitan and upper-class, as he kneels to tie Bella's boot:

> To be a shoefitter in Manfield's was my love's young dream, the darling joys of sweet buttonhooking, to lace up crisscrossed to kneelength the dressy kid footwear satinlined, so incredibly impossibly small, of Clyde Road ladies. Even their wax model Raymonde I visited daily to admire her cobweb hose and stick of rhubarb toe, as worn in Paris (U 432).

Above this native-as-consumer, Bella becomes Bello, a male dominator and torturer, and as such dominates Bloom, now female. The images and words of Bello might easily have come, in fact, from early twentieth-century cartoons of the exploiting capitalist by artists such as Georg Grosz:

> (*squats with a grunt on Bloom's upturned face, puffing cigarsmoke, nursing a fat leg*) I see Keating Clay is elected vicechairman of the Richmond asylum and by the by Guinness's preference shares are at sixteen three quarters. Curse me for a fool that didn't buy that lot Craig and Gardner told me about. Just my infernal luck, curse it. And that Goddamned outsider *Throwaway* at twenty to one. (*he quenches his cigar angrily on Bloom's ear*) Where's the Goddamned cursed ashtray? (U 435)

In British entrepreneurial accent he refers to cigars, preference shares in the most thriving Irish company, chairmanships and racing bets, while Bloom, the colonial abject par excellence, constitutes his discourse as a matter of the sensitive body ("Every nerve in my body aches like mad!" [U 435]), personal guilt ("a small prank …" [U 437]), and callow mimicry of the colonist's imagined virtues ("It was the purest thrift" [U 437]).

Here, the spectacle of commodity fetishism is not undermined by violence: on the contrary. The violence too is generated as spectacle, as advertisement: this is narrative exposition with the communicative status of advertisement. For a First-World audience, it first advertises the acts committed and the causes they advertise. Second, as this audience is usually proffered its spectacle of otherness as one of violence, where the fetishized commodity and the reification of human relations at home is made more palatable by the coexisting spectacle of violent otherness elsewhere, it advertises the instability of worlds elsewhere in order to accentuate the feeling of security and superiority in the utopia of commodities at home.

Yet when this violence, as in the Bella/o series of scenes, becomes transmuted primarily into spectacle, and a "society of the spectacle" (to use Guy Debord's famous formulation),[44] whether it be of commodities or of violence elsewhere, is created, the text has, as it were, again surrendered to the cultural logic of the imperial homeland. This would be entirely appropriate if the novel were about the imperial home country, the ruling center (as Moretti would wish it to be), but I suggest that instead the narrative turn in the text shows that it is aligned, rather, with the concerns of the colony. What occurs in "Circe" is that the commodity spectacle (and the whole episode, itself a kind of screenplay, seems to yearn toward the condition of spectacle) is derealized and fades, while a series of set-pieces showing violence in every mode — the pelting of Bloom out of the brothel, the execution of the Croppy Boy, the sighted burning of the city, Stephen's smashing of the lampshade in the brothel parlor — takes its place.

Before exploring the effect of this proliferation of acts of violence as the final mode of portraying a state of terrorism, we need to understand the use to which the figure of woman as prostitute has been put in the modernist mode of portraying violence here. When the woman is rendered as body-as-commodity, what we witness is a shocking representational crossover from a scattered focus on the decorated, bejeweled body as a locus of highly reified (male) desire to a vision of a reified female body (that of Bella) as terrifying monster/master. This body as monster is here an *embodiment* of the most pervasive form of inherently violent imperial power: the imposition of a full commodity culture. What the modernist text gives us, then, is an astute analysis of the violent interpellation by the imperial center of the peripheral colony, which in turn implies the validity of the violence of the insurgency as reactive strategy.

This subaltern analysis, however, is constructed at the expense of the active degradation of the signifier(s) of the feminine. If the reign of terror of the Irish War of Independence is translated, perhaps wistfully, at one level here, into a Bakhtinian carnival of commodities, then the women in the episode become targets of what Peter Stallybrass has termed "displaced abjection," the phenomenon by which an oppressed group uses carnival to invert its own low position with respect to another even weaker group in "a ritual or game of nasty victimization."[45] The fact that the women who populate "Circe" are prostitutes is highly useful to the text's allegorical project: the prostitute represents the body that proffers itself (or so it seems to the male "artful voyeur") as commodity.[46] "Circe"'s modernist mode allows us to see not only the doubly abjected woman of Heaney's poem "Punishment," but rather that woman as the awful threat that she is really taken to be by the "artful voyeur." This is a multiple threat: that the pervasive violence of the imperial power (which in the text's symbolic schema the women have come to epitomize) will defeat or contaminate the subaltern insurgent, and that the violence of this insurgent will turn upon itself and be self-defeating. Ultimately it is the threat that, as one violence fades into another, the more abject the subaltern the more likely she is to represent nothing more than a (per)version of the imperial power. If you are an extremely forgiving critic you may want to see Bella Cohen as the tarred-and-feathered young woman's revenge. More likely, however, you will be inclined to see the Bella-Bloom imbroglio as another male modernist version of the scene of erotic cruelty that transfixes again and again all of male modernism's "great transgressors";[47] Baudelaire, Lautreamont, Artaud, Bataille, and latterly Burroughs and Pynchon.

"Circe" III: Simulation and Speaking Subalterns

Just as Joyce refuses to realize the heroicization of the male subject in his realistic portrayals of violence, however, so too, in his modernist mode, he draws back from a full realization of the figure of woman as the horror of either imperial or insurgent violence. The moment at which the modernist tableau of Bella/Bloom becomes spectacle matches that at which, in the realist scenes, the police demand Bloom's name: both bring modes of representation to points that a subaltern discourse cannot abide. What remains beyond these points is what Derrida, speaking on *Finnegans Wake*,[48] has called "the (asymptotic) totality of the equivocal," at which, he says, Joyce "tries to make outcrop, with the greatest possible synchrony, at great speed, the greatest power of meanings buried in each syllabic fragment, subjecting each atom of writing to fission in order to overload the unconscious."

Such fission, clearly, would be "Circe"'s postmodern moment; it occurs, I suggest, along the lines of the original division of potential reactions described by Heaney in his poem "Punishment" as "civilized" and "tribal" respectively. On the one hand the "civilized" "Circe" works to dematerialize the visions of the subaltern subject that both realist and modernist modes of representation in the episode have striven to reconstruct: it does so by constructing a more thorough homology — perhaps a Baudrillardian simulation — of terrorist outrage out of the architectonics of *space* in the episode. Here the image of the prostitute is forgotten; rather, it is the red-light district itself as signifier of "other" territory that is key. On the other hand, the "tribal," subaltern "Circe" works to posit, however timorously, some notion of agency from the doubly abjected and scapegoated figure of the woman as prostitute, to begin to present the woman as active individual speaking *agent* who can take her place in the postcolonial free state.

A homology of terrorism in the postmodern level of the episode is made possible in the first instance through a radical estrangement of the spatial certainties of the episode's setting, a denial of the familiar or the expected in the perspective of the very scene itself. This begins with a disruption of the division between indoors and outdoors in the opening of "Circe." The scene where Bella harasses Bloom is set indoors, in the parlor of the brothel; the fight between Stephen and the soldiers takes place in the street. But on other occasions — when Bloom, for example, is crowned king of the "Nova Hibernia of the Future" — the setting is left unnamed, unframed. The outdoors-indoors distinction is everywhere underlined, so that the *threshold* becomes a privileged place: where the prostitutes stand to advertise for business, where the nervous customer scuttles out. Bloom has to be coaxed into the brothel by Zoe, and is chased out the same door later. (Notice, in the very presentation in print of the episode, how common is the parenthesis — marker of the threshold in syntax.) Soon our conventional expectations of inside and outside are undermined: while the pianola is played indoors, as we

might expect, a gramophone drones in the fog without. Such contradictions contribute to our uncertainty about the setting of the episode as a
whole. Nighttown is the *other* space of *Ulysses*. The novel as a whole is
a text obsessed with an exact realism in delineating its setting, but
Nighttown is cut off from that realist city; appropriately, it is today the
part of central Dublin that, gutted and rebuilt as worker's housing since
World War II, least resembles the city Joyce describes. "Circe" sep-
arates this zone from the rest of the urban fabric by speaking of the
"... entrance to Nighttown ... before which stretches uncobbled tram-
siding set with skeleton tracks, red and green will o' the wisps and danger signals. Rare lamps, with faint rainbow fans ..." It is a strange
night-space, peopled with a troop of grotesques worthy of an Ensor
etching. It is an example of what Foucault termed a heterotopia,[49] an
"other" space against which the society defines its familiar scenes and
the values they represent. Foucault spoke specifically of both the red-
light district and the colony as two of the most suggestive heterotopias
in western culture; he also compares them, and such an analogy is, I
suggest, the implicit analogy in "Circe" also. Once the status of the setting of the episode comes into question, however, we have reached the
end of spectacle (for the setting itself is the primary scene of this spec-
tacular episode) and reached the moment when a postmodern representation of violence in the *form* of the episode is possible.

Once we stop taking the spectacle of banal violence and that of commodity fetishism for granted, once they lose their superficial wonder,
we are left with the mechanics of the episode's form. This mechanics
acts to fabricate a simulacrum[50] of terrorism itself. The *modernist* portrayal of terrorism in "Circe" is comparable to the interest in violence
shown by movements such as Marinetti's Futurism; think of Sorel's
treatise, *On Violence* (Mussolini's favorite reading), Celine's controversial fascism, or Breton,[51] who once said that the ultimate artistic act
was to run downstairs and fire into the crowd. In *postmodern* form,
however, the text stages an apocalypse of the age of mechanical reproduction: not of explosions, or spectacle, but rather of movement-as-dis-
appearance: the truly tragic minimalism of the moment in the December
1988 Pan Am "explosion in the sky" when the radar blip fragmented
and disappeared from the screen.[52] In "Circe," scene after scene literally
disappears, as a realist scene replaces a surreal stage-set and in turn is
replaced by a snatch of realism without notice. Characters arrive and
disappear without warning, and nobody ever exits, ever crosses the

kind of threshold that might allow us, who read our realism and our modernist surrealism at once, to make a choice. It is a seriality of unconnected disappearances, and it is very much a machinery of fear—it induces in the reader the fear of "remembering forgetfully" the terrorism that is hardly representable in writing, and on the verge of occurring. "Circe" is very much the first talking film, in which we can experience the fear of the audience at the first talkie, who had become used to the exaggerated spectacle of silent gesture. Unlike a film, however, "Circe" perversely refuses to be realized as image, so that it is always continually adverting to its own disappearance, even as it is produced. And unlike a "talking picture," its voices also (because they are merely written) continually disappear into their own silence. There is no terrorist violence here: rather, what is allowed is the calmness of absence, which is the very condition needed by terrorism if its surprise is to be sprung. Terrorism operates its regime of power by inducing fear of secretly planned accidents, and that is also exactly how the narrative logic of "Circe" operates, in a series of accidental arrivals and disappearances that have the arbitrary quality of modern serial interaction in the crowd.

This rarefied atmosphere of simulated terrorism is very much part of the rhetoric of fear in the face of outrage, a rhetoric I earlier described (in terms of Heaney's division) as characteristic of "civilized" discourse. In "Circe"'s anonymous cityscape of appearing and disappearing figures, those that stand apart are the lonely figures of the prostitutes. It is they alone who will articulate a version of their own subjecthood here. The modernist discourse of terrorism and its perpetrators and victims comes to an end in the episode when, underlining the feminization and then extinction of the male as heroic subject here, Bloom as orientalized widow is sacrificed on a "suttee pyre" (*U* 444). At this point "The Nymph"—in fact the figure "clad lightly in teabrown colors" (*U* 444), in a print that hangs over Molly's and Poldy's bed in Eccles Street—taken from the magazine *Tidbits,* appears in discourse with Bloom. She is, at last, the image of woman wholly reduced to advertisement, and she complains of the company she was forced to keep in the magazine: "proprietary articles and why wear a truss with testimonial from ruptured gentleman.... Rubber goods. Neverrip brand as supplied to the aristocracy.... Unsolicited testimonials for Professor Waldmann's chest exuber. My bust developed 4 inches in 3 weeks, reports Mrs Gus Rublin with photo" (*U* 445). Bloom, as she tells him, "with

loving pencil ... shaded my eyes, my bosom, and my shame" but it is
she who reverses the "artful voyeurism" of the male discourse that has
produced her and the whole critique of commodity as woman's body
here: she turns to gaze upon him:

THE NYMPH

(covers her face with her hands) What have I not seen in that chamber?
What must my eyes look down on?

(*U* 446)

At this turning point, the figure of the feminine strikes back: though
wholly commodified, she takes her reification to the point where she
asserts her subjecthood yet retains her femininity (Bella had only done
so by becoming Bello, horrendously male). Although Bloom hysterically fights back against this threat by imputing to his nymph-ideal of
femininity a rabid sexual appetite (*U* 541–42), the prostitutes Zoe and
Bella come forward now to reclaim their own version of reality: they
demand money, they speak of work, and the issue of a specific national-
ity — Irishness — surfaces in the episode.

Irishness arose inconspicuously as an issue with the mention, while
Bloom was being humiliated by Bello, of "Mrs. Keogh, the brothel
cook" (*U* 435). Here is the Irish working-class woman, the Irish maid
of the Dublin, British, or North American bourgeois household, her
position much the same as that of Nora Barnacle before she went off
with James Joyce to Trieste, Zurich, Paris. Her name reminds the
reader of the mean-spirited Shawneen Keogh of J. M. Synge's *The Play-
boy of the Western World*. Although it has been asserted of *Ulysses* that
there is not a single worker in the book, Mrs. Keogh appears here
*"wrinkled, greybearded, in a greasy bib, men's grey and green socks
and brogues, floursmeared, a rollingpin stuck with raw pastry in her
bare red arm and hand ..."* (*U* 435). She is a grim socialist-realist incar-
nation of the near-sentimental Gaelic revival milkwoman of the "Telemachus" episode.

Although "Irishness" is soon abducted as a question of nationalism
here by the latter-day version of male heroics resurfacing at the end of
the episode (Stephen's tussle with the British soldiery and the horren-
dous pseudo-apocalyptic black mass conducted by the men upon the
body of a pregnant woman), this happens only after the question of na-
tionality has been connected, through Mrs. Keogh, to that of the worker.
The question of ethnicity is shown to be a red herring as Stephen, with

his display of "parley-vous," implies that advertising peep-shows is a French occupation, and Zoe points out again that she is an English-woman (the pianola plays "My Girl's a Yorkshire Girl" [*U* 469]). As soon as ethnicity has been proven nebulous, Bella asks "Whos paying here?" and Stephen hastens (despite his disdain for payments) to fumble for his money. Bloom intervenes in his cautious way: "(*quietly lays a half-sovereign on the table between Bella and Florry*) So. Allow me.... We're square" (*U* 455). The woman as prostitute is no longer simply commodity, she is a paid worker as well. Once this is clear, the doubly abject prostitute does now speak:

ZOE

(*lifting up her pettigown and folding a half-sovereign into the top of her stocking*) Hard earned on the flat of my back. (*U* 454)

The episode rolls on, toward violence in the brothel, the male carnival of nationalism that is the fight, and the closing tableau, a *pieta* with men, with father Bloom, the fallen son Stephen, and Rudy, the lost son, nonprodigal, as mechanical doll. Yet the speaking women are the text's gift to the subaltern reader from Nighttown. I have tried to show here how the figure that the male writer introduces to signify violence may turn into a subject almost against the grain of the text. This is the moment at which the episode imagines some kind of agency: it is the moment at which Heaney's tarred and feathered woman *speaks back*. To close, I will quote a recent account of a Northern Irish woman describing how the occasion on which she was silenced turned into the moment when she became politically aware:[53]

One night in November, about tea time, I'd done the dishes and thought I'd go out and get the paper and some sweets for the kids. There was a river and a little bridge, and ... two or three long-haired lads came along in the dark saying "Hiya Hester." ... In the minute or two that I'd said "Hello"—or seconds—they'd grabbed me and said "We know you've been helping them, now c'mon" and pushing and shoving. I was frightened as Hell's gates, I tried to shout but it wasn't a scream that was coming out, it was "Mammy" and it sort of came out like a croak. I got pushed right underneath this bloody bridge. As a foot-patrol was coming up—must have been high on the bridge and we were underneath, you see—they threw me hard, I sort of hit a rock, and they ran across the river.... I don't know how long I lay there before I came out. I knew I was wet and sore and I tried to walk.... I knocked at the first house. The woman screamed when she saw me. I think she thought I'd been tarred and feathered.

After this, Hester became the organizer of a Protestant political group. The women scream at the sight of a woman tarred and feathered; the men (even the poets) are silent, avowedly complicit. But it is possible (even for a male writer) despite Gayatri Spivak's insistence, and perhaps despite the representational ethos of Joyce's "Circe," to imagine that the abject woman as subaltern can speak.

5

Molly Alone: Questioning Community and Closure in the "Nostos"

Both Marxism and psychoanalysis, in their concepts of labor and of individuation and gender formation, depend on the plot of original unity out of which difference must be produced and enlisted in a drama of escalating domination of woman/nature.

Donna Haraway ("A Manifesto for Cyborgs,"
in *Simians, Cyborgs and Women*)

And I asked him with my eyes to ask again ...

Molly Bloom ("Penelope" [*U* 644])

"Members of Cumann na mBan, Irishwomen's Council, waving encouragement to Mountjoy prisoners over top of prison wall": this, one of the most singular photographs[1] from the archive of the revolutionary years in Dublin, was taken in 1921, when Joyce was working on the closing episodes of *Ulysses,* including "Penelope," in Paris (Figure 5). The incident shown occurred outside Mountjoy prison, only a short distance north of Eccles Street, and not far from the house in Phisborough where James Joyce's mother died in 1903. The photograph epitomizes the ambivalence of the roles played by women both in the revolution itself and in the economy of images deployed to represent it. On the one hand, the figure of a lone woman had again and again been enlisted as allegory of the Ireland for which (male) rebels had died. As either old woman (Yeats's Countess Cathleen) or young girl (the figure of Ireland represented on numerous monuments erected in the first quarter of the twentieth century to fallen heroes in Irish towns and villages) this solitary figure was less a representation of the community out of which the rebels came than a personification of the abstract

Fig. 5. "Members of the Cumann na mBan, Irishwomen's Council, waving encouragement to Mountjoy prisoners over top of prison wall," from de Valera et al., Fig. 6, *The
Irish Uprising, 1916–22* (New York: C.B.S., distributed by Macmillan, 1966).

nation for which they had died. On the other hand, the Troubles of
1916–21 saw the participation of many women, who acted mainly as
soldiers, transporters of arms, keepers of "safe houses" for guerrillas on
the run, or as nurses. To an extent the urgency of revolution swept gender distinctions away; one of the 1916 commandants and leaders of the
Easter Rising was the Countess Markiewicz, who in 1918 became the
first woman to be elected to the British parliament, and who became
minister of labor in the first Dail, the Irish parliament, in the same year.
Still, the fact that her sentence of death as an insurgent had been com-
muted[2] "solely on the basis of her sex" while all but one of the other
leaders of the rebellion were summarily executed should alert us to the

limitations and possibilities that accompanied women's participation in a revolution by a patriarchal subaltern culture against an even more thoroughly masculinist colonial regime. The women in this photo, then, have their backs toward us, their foothold on the roof of the carriage is precarious, and their gesture — waving a cloth tied to a stick before the massive-walled apparatus of the prison system — seems futile and ineffectual. The Irish anticolonial revolution leaves us with two images of women: lone women as allegories of an abstract nation, and small groups of women who seem united, but not in the resolute groupings that would suggest the kind of communities that might epitomize the new state. Women were deployed as key signifiers of the nation itself in the representational economy of the revolution, yet paradoxically it was only as lone figures that (in masculinist narratives) they were allowed to suggest the new nation. And this was the representational principle followed in the creation of the most brilliant and notorious image of a woman in Irish literature in 1921: Molly Bloom herself.

In looking at this photograph as readers of Joyce's work, we see the postman walking toward us, staring into the camera, as a man who might be carrying the sorts of letters that Bloom wrote to Martha Clifford, Boylan to Molly, the hangman of "Cyclops" to the Mountjoy prison authorities — or the letter from the informer to the British authorities, to be sent to "some well-disposed friend in England," which we encountered in the notice in chapter 1. He is, indeed, Sean the Post, Joyce's own figure of an author who wanders through *Finnegans Wake*. If *Ulysses* is an anticolonial novel, however, the author's gaze at the close of the narrative had to turn (unlike that of the postman here) toward an image at once of resistance and of a potential new community. The text denies us a community of women; instead, as in the memorials in Irish villages, it chose the image of a lone woman. Molly, like the women in this photograph, waves back at the panoptic might that bears down on much of the masculinist culture represented in the novel. Armed with the subversive bravado also practiced by these women, she effects a particular communication between divergent elements of the culture, marking the sign of a potential solidarity — and equality — in the community and the text.

This chapter considers the closure of *Ulysses*. In postcolonial writing that operates as homology of the forces in conflict during the revolution, the struggle is represented as a new beginning. The past is, relatively, disregarded: in *Ulysses*, especially in the first two opening episodes of the text, the accepted version of nationalist history is ridiculed as a pastiche of a series of mythologies, most of them mere faked copies of imperial originals that had been developed in the first place to subjugate the peripheral peoples. Rather it is the future, and the possibility of imagining a newly independent national community that will take shape in that future, which preoccupies the work. For the postcolonial author working up the first tentative texts in the new voices of a national culture, it might appear that the beginning of a narrative would have been most difficult. In practice, however, the writer sustained the act of beginning as a concerted effort to displace those hackneyed discourses of "history" that had already been set in place to narrate the potential new nation. Instead, it is the conclusion of the text, as the test case in the narrative for the successful imagining of a new community, that is difficult.

Closure in any text that is preoccupied with marking a new beginning will not be easy; in one with the skeptical political sensibilities marking *Ulysses,* it was almost impossible. Both Joyce and Yeats in their later work (*Finnegans Wake* and *A Vision*) would circumvent this demand for closure by invoking respectively notions of Viconian cycles and occult "gyres"; in *Ulysses* the author is, as it were, caught unawares without such a commodious philosophy of history, and the issue of how the future might be envisaged must be dealt with in the face of the closure of the text. Hence the usefulness of the ploy of documenting only a single day: besides effectively devaluing the perspective of history or the past in the work, it meant that the book was forced to end, literally, once night fell. Still, the importance of closure in *Ulysses* for its author may be gleaned in the fact that, to effect it, he invoked a principle of radical difference. He turns around what he had up to now composed as a masculinist narrative, to close with a monologue by a woman. Joyce himself termed the "Penelope" episode the "indispensable countersign" to *Ulysses;*[3] when Molly Bloom, at the last moment, presents an other viewpoint in the text, she questions much more thoroughly than before the possibility of envisioning a national community, beyond masculinist fellowship or the lack of it in this novel.

Closure marks the success or otherwise of imagining a new national community; the text's utopian project is at stake. I suggest that *Ulysses,* given its author's distance (as modernist "exile") from the events it encodes, rather than fretting over the imagining of such a community, instead poses the more radical question of whether in fact, at the moment of revolution, such an entity can be imagined at all. Consider the impulses toward an imaginary community in this novel; the full comic impetus in *Ulysses* to bring subjects together as empathetic groups. In the male-centered narrative occupying the greater part of the text, this is focused on the tentative relationship, developed through a series of coincidences, between Stephen and Bloom. Even if what we are given at this level is a figural, rather than an actual, father and son, and if their paths cross only by chance, by webs of coincidence rather than by a symbolic filiation in the way that Bloom himself would like to imagine (see "Eumaeus"), here is still the pattern, however distant and faded by replication, of a key thematic of nineteenth-century realism. Because it is a very late copy, with much of its supporting sensation-text stripped away, we are allowed continually to see the underlying panoptic regime of surveillance. I have shown how this regime is exposed to us in the "Cyclops," "Sirens," and "Circe" episodes of *Ulysses*. Because the panoptic regime is rendered visible, this form of late realism is highly effective as a late-colonial text: it uncovers again and again the brutally tight control exerted by the colonial government over the native subjects under its rule. The colonial police state mediates the intersubjective relations not only between colonist and native, but also among the natives themselves. If we take the "Nostos," the final three episodes of *Ulysses,* as the strategic closure of the novel, then "Eumaeus" clearly brings to a crisis both the father-son relationship and the regime of colonial surveillance portrayed in this aspect of the narrative. On the one hand, Bloom and Stephen at last sit opposite each other and talk; on the other, this takes place in an atmosphere of suspicion, rumor, and even pseudo-political intrigue that marks the apogee of the panopticist motif in the text.

Underlying this fundamentally male-centered, realist narrative, which is at its strongest in the opening episode of *Ulysses* but survives, despite a panoply of defamiliarizing onslaughts in episode after episode, at least until the very end of "Eumaeus" in the novel, there is threaded through the text the second narrative impulse, modernist in form, which identifies more thoroughly with the subaltern predicament and which, significantly, is centered on a series of images of women. If the male-centered realist-inspired narratives work (in the novel written at the moment of decolonization) as critiques of colonialism's exercise of power and management of knowledge of the social sphere, then this second strand of the novel (that for which it is considered "difficult" and for which it is truly notorious) works to give voice to versions of subaltern difference that tentatively but uncompromisingly enter the novel's field of vision.

From the moment the old milkwoman—less a pathetic and ignorant victim than a canny manipulator of clichéd realist expectations about what she represents—steps into the Martello tower in the opening "Telemachus" episode, it is around images of women that the innovative modernist trajectories of the text adhere. "Aeolus," the first episode in which the smooth face of the narrative is shattered (here by the jocoserious headlines), culminates in "The Parable of the Plums," a murkily allegorical tale about two midwives who toss plumstones from atop the column commemorating Nelson, British seaman and "onehandled adulterer" (U 121), in O'Connell Street. "Sirens," the first significantly obscure episode (as Ezra Pound noted) centers on the two barmaid-sirens, Miss Douce and Miss Kennedy. Note that all of these women in the first half of the novel are workers, in fact very clearly members of the working class. Most of the male characters who figure in the first half of the novel are either bohemians or petty bourgeois. Thus a gendered division of labor in the colony is implicitly posited early in the novel. "Nausicaa," its style contorted into a pastiche of Victorian kitsch romance, eulogizes Gerty MacDowell, while "Oxen of the Sun," the novel's modernist tour-de-force exposition of successive literary styles, is meant to tell of Mrs. Mina Purefoy giving birth. These women are not paid workers as are, for example, the barmaids; rather, they are shown as the bearers and minders of children. Seeing this portrayal against that of the earlier women, however, these bourgeois women who are wives and consumers seem all the more abject.[4]

Every one of these women are abjects, more thoroughly interpellated by the various hegemonic forces controlling the culture than are any of the men here: as such, the scenes of the women are the scenes of the most thoroughly delineated subalternity in *Ulysses*. And the text, facing this subalternity in all its vividness—from that of the milkwoman, whose own viewpoint we are barely allowed to glimpse, to that of Molly, whose viewpoint is directly her own—has invariably to cast about to find new and more appropriate ways to narrate this abjection.

I have worked to demonstrate how, in both realist and more markedly modernist episodes of the novel, the critique of oppression on the one hand (in, for example, the split subjectivity displayed in "Cyclops") and the delineation of subalternity on the other (as in the regimes of surveillance shown in "Circe") are both transformed through the novel's comic impetus by flashes of a vision of postcolonial subjectivity. As regards the utopian potential of the text to imagine many such subjectivities into a new community, the reader can hardly hope that the male-centered realist narrative, copied from models that celebrated an imperialist nationalist world, will prove an appropriate vehicle. Once "Eumaeus," where that realist narrative reaches its climax, is over, it is dispersed; hence Stephen blithely walks away from Bloom in the stylistically uncompromising "Ithaca" episode. The question that then remains about the women-centered moments of the text is this: to what extent do these representations of abject women go beyond delineating the grimness of abjection to foster notions of a novel community of those once downtrodden? *Ulysses* in its latter moments presents us with a portrait of a lone woman, Molly, rather than of a group of women together, and it never allows the abject women it represents (with the exception of the Nighttown prostitutes of "Circe," discussed in chapter 4) to come together in the work. This is indicative, I suggest, of a text that does not ultimately present us with a readymade new community but rather poses the more difficult question of what such a community might imply.

The reader must seek the roots of the novel's reticence on this score in both the general difficulty (especially in leftist critiques) of ever imagining the Utopia that should follow a revolution, and, more specifically, in a strain of pessimism infusing any colonial subaltern political sensibility. This sensibility, although made famous by Joyce as his vaunted rejection of Ireland's political and cultural narrowness, was by no means specific to him alone. The issue of a utopian component in materialist thought has always been contentious; Marx's own writing is vague about what the world under the rule of the proletariat might resemble. Leftist critics have always looked with a certain envy upon the utopian appeal of such secular religions and galvanizing forces as nineteenth-century nationalism. The argument about whether an avowal of utopian longings as a component of a materialist critique does not represent a shameful sliding into a discredited idealist liberalism has gained new urgency with the birth of the various structuralist and poststructuralist versions of Marxism, particularly in France and Britain, during the last two decades. Critics such as Fredric Jameson have argued cogently for a utopian dimension as a fitting acknowledgment of the component of desire in western materialist thought,[5] if only in the sense that any ideological trajectory must awaken utopian desires in order to critique them. (Stuart Hall, in similar vein, following Gramsci, has controversially urged that British leftists might learn from the appeals to popular longings manipulated by resurgent British conservatism.)[6] At the same time, an infusion of the radical philosophic spirit of what Gayatri Spivak characterizes as Derrida's geo-deconstruction[7] into the newer leftist critiques has made many of these latter-day appeals for leftist utopianisms seem like last-ditch retrenchments; the new work has begun to question the grounds of any materialist assumption of a utopian future time. Thus the feminist historian of science Donna Haraway,[8] for example, attacks both Marxism and Freudianism, the nineteenth-century theories of the social and psychic body, as themselves thoroughgoing realisms that emphatically replicate the mirage of original unity of every imperial cultural formation, so that a hypothetical ultimately unified community must be suspected as merely a projection of what should have been abandoned. This is the point at which I wish to situate my own reading of the plot of closure in *Ulysses*. Against a nostalgia for such an original unity, as expressed in the realist tale of Bloom the would-be father encountering Stephen the figural son, *Ulysses* is well equipped to show the difference between this desire and the regime in which it exists, but, I suggest, it balks at the prospect of allowing its most obvious subaltern subjects, the women it portrays, any potential unity beyond colonial interpellation. As such it merely proposes to the reader the more stark and profound question of whether such a unity can be imagined in any real sense at the moment of anticolonial revolution.

In the second place we must consider the text's refusal to end by imagining a novel community as proof once again of the difficulty of overcoming the pessimism of subaltern politics in the late-colonial period. The perspective I have in mind is less the youthful Dedalus's "*Non serviam*," which personalizes and psychologizes one response to the national political dilemma, than the pervasive skepticism regarding anticolonial revolution suggested, for example, in such texts as the following epigram by Yeats, published in his *Last Poems* of 1939:

Parnell
Parnell came down the road, he said to a cheering man:
"Ireland shall get her freedom and you still break stone."
(CP 309)

Joyce's youthful political pessimism, as the careful researches of Dominic Manganiello have shown,[9] was first evidenced in his interest in the socialist doctrine of his day; when he later discovered himself as an artist—if we are to take *A Portrait* as biographical manifesto—this pessimism reformulated itself as a late example of the alienation of the romantic artist. Both manifestations are similar even if, in conventional political terms, one seems the avowal of political involvement and the other its repudiation, in that they both represent a young colonial subject's pessimism in the face of rule, as Stephen himself puts it, by "the imperial British state" (*U* 17). As such they foreshadow the disillusion that Joyce as well as Yeats, whose politics noticeably evolved over the decades, came to feel for the "New" (i.e., independent) Ireland. (Yeats's cheering man is the poet's counterpart to Molly Bloom, because here too, close to the end of his poetic-political testament, he focuses his gaze upon a lone and abject figure rather than the cheering crowd or community one expects to find standing before the pontificating politician. Molly, however, might well have sneered where Yeats's old man cheered.) As such also we might infer that Joyce's refusal at the end of *Ulysses* to postulate a new community in solidarity was prescient about the actual conditions of the independent postcolonial state that was founded after the treaty of 1921. Neither Saorstát Eireann, the new Irish Free State, nor Northern Ireland—the two political entities into which the island of Ireland was split by the treaty—lived up to the utopian ideals of the revolutionaries. The Free State itself was immediately torn in a civil war over whether the territorial split agreed on in the treaty was acceptable; this was the first legacy of the treaty that was negotiated in London while Joyce was finishing his novel across the Channel.

Still, it would require an undue pessimism on our own part to read Joyce's refusal to imagine a real community outside abjection as a failure of the novel's political project; rather, it aptly represents the mixed idealism and limitations of the new Irish Free State itself. In this sense Molly Bloom as representative Irish subject acts to taunt—as *Ulysses* has taunted from its first moments—nationalist stereotypes of Irish identity, while still retaining, as did the new state, a consciousness of her continuing subalternity. With the novel ending, however, just as the new state was about to come into being, the text effectively replaces the issue of difference based on colonial power versus native abjection, which the novel, like the treaty itself, has resolved in favor of a limited new national subjecthood for most of the inhabitants of the island, with the issue of difference among the native subjects themselves, which it epitomizes through difference based on gender. In this sense, if *Ulysses* is read as "national allegory,"[10] then Molly, in the "Nostos" of *Ulysses*, is a mirror image, in the text's depiction of home, of Deasy, the schoolmaster of the opening "Telemachiad." For Deasy is the Protestant and Orangeman in the largely Catholic Dublin of *Ulysses*, and it was unresolvable differences between the mostly Protestant unionists who wished to remain with Britain and Catholic nationalists who wished for an independent Ireland that led to the civil war between different nationalist factions in 1922, as it has led to much strife between nationalists and unionists in Northern Ireland since. Molly's insistence on her difference based on gender may be paralleled with Deasy's avowal of his difference based on politics and creed. What we are presented with at the end of the novel is its focus on the continuing oppression of the figures of the most abject subalternity here, and the fact that this abjection is based on difference in gender is accentuated. With Molly as the "indispensable countersign," "Penelope" is the most challenging, the most radically interrogative, moment of the text. With this in mind, let us now turn to a more particular reading of the "Nostos" episodes.

Suspicion and Difference

At the outset I stressed the radical interrogativity of *Ulysses* as a whole: its determination to question every implication of representation. This turns the text in the first instance toward a paranoid mimeticism, an eagerness to be correct with every timetable and house number on the one hand, and a desire to undermine every protocol of realist narrative on the other. Interrogativity, relentless questioning, takes over as the very engine of the text in the final three episodes comprising the "Nostos"; it is most evident in the central set-piece, "Ithaca," where stark question-and-answer is posited explicitly as the episode's form, but it is none the less pervasive in "Eumaeus" and "Penelope." In "Eumaeus," set in the murky cabman's shelter on the Dublin quays between 12:40 and 1:00 A.M., this questioning takes the form of suspicion regarding identity. It is also the questioning through which Bloom and Stephen come to know each other (to the extent that they do). Theirs is a vestigial community of two, the only community engineered by the realist strand of the novel, which is inaugurated against a fitting background of an intense police and judicial presence reflecting the pervasiveness of colonial state power. What "Eumaeus" proves is that their gesture of coming to know one another is acted out against a background of politically charged suspicion which is in turn depicted as a microcosm of the pervasive suspicion of the colonial regime.

The cabman's shelter is a new kind of setting in the successive urban locales of *Ulysses,* and one that effects an important strategic compromise between what was alien and familiar in a turn-of-the-century city like the Dublin Joyce describes. Up to now the novel in this regard has had it both ways: appearing to be a modernist metro-text that describes life in the increasingly crowded city, we might have expected it to show a world of strangers and alienated inhabitants. On the contrary, *Ulysses* has delineated a milieu in which almost every major character turns out to be familiar with the others, either through acquaintance or family relationship—the kind of world we expect to encounter in a nineteenth-century realist novel. Bloom, for example, is troubled, as we discover in "Ithaca," by one question: "Who was McIntosh?" (*U* 600), the only person whom he did not know at the funeral of Paddy Dignam; Richie Goulding, with whom Bloom ate dinner earlier in the Ormond Hotel, is, we realize in the same episode, the husband of Stephen's Aunt Sara (*U* 547).

The cabman's shelter as setting, however, effects a compromise between the alienated urban scene and the typical realist locale of familiar characters, for it is a small room in which strangers are expected to be familiar with each other. The shelter is late-colonial Dublin's grim version of cafe culture, the setting for encounters between strangers appropriate to the great imperial metropolises. (In such late nineteenth-century metropolitan realist fictions as the detective story, settings such as "the club" and the railway carriage were likewise used as locales that sustained strands of a parlor familiarity and a street anonymity at once.) Thus Tonnies's *Gemeinschaft/Gesellschaft* division is broken down here, as a group of strangers are brought together to speak to one another, but the kind of forced community thus created is a highly uneasy one, charged with the kind of suspicion often bred of a fear of violence.

This suspicion is generated against a background sense, strongly suggested especially in the opening pages of "Eumaeus," of a heavy police presence. Approaching the shelter, Stephen and Bloom wander through "Store St., famous for its C division police station" and moments later

Bloom is "recalling a case or two in the A division in Clanbrassil St." where a policeman "admittedly unscrupulous in the service of the crown ... [was] prepared to swear a hole through a ten gallon pot" (*U* 502). Not only do these passages give a strong sense of the police network in the city, but, as in the above lines, they associate this official surveillance with untrustworthy tellings and false knowledge. Further suspicion and efforts to guard against it are suggested by the presence of the corporation watchman under the dark Loop Line Bridge, who turns out to be "the eldest son of inspector Corley of the G division" (*U* 504)—the G division was the police undercover detective agency. By now the episode has mentioned each of the best-known police divisions in central Dublin. The police presence, heavy throughout *Ulysses*—in "Lestrygonians" Bloom had watched a phalanx of Dublin Metropolitan policemen march out of College Street police station (*U* 133)—is accentuated here, as it was in "Cyclops." This underlines the real stakes, for the society, of the suspicion soon to be generated among the characters in the shelter.

What these stakes might be is suggested by the discourse of conventional politics infiltrating this episode. The way in which strangers are forced to be familiars in the cabman's shelter acts as a license for political figures to be discussed as familiars also. Hence Charles Stewart Parnell is the subject of more explicit extended discussion here than in virtually any other episode.[11] Also, the immediacy of insurgent political action is brought home to us here through Bloom's suspicion that the keeper of the shelter is none other than "Skin-the-Goat," once a member of a secret terrorist group of the 1880s, the Invincibles. "Skin-the-Goat" was said to have driven the horse and car of the assassins who killed Lord Cavendish and T. H. Burke, the chief secretary for Ireland and his undersecretary, in the infamous "Phoenix Park Murders" of May 6, 1882.[12] (Remember that this episode was being written at a time when the guerrilla War of Independence in Ireland had grown so intense that the British army and authorities were forced to sue for a cease-fire, at a time when assassinations and attempted shootings in Dublin were daily occurrences.) When the supposed ex-Invincible, who still harbors patriotic views, and the drunken sailor D. B. Murphy, who has just been discharged from the British merchant marine and who speaks of "our empire" (*U* 524), begin to argue, the level of political discourse that is given an airing is merely the stereotyped sloganeering which we have already heard from the Citizen in "Cyclops" or at moments in Joyce's *Dubliners* story "Ivy Day in the Committee Room"; it is quickly dismissed by Bloom's private thoughts in the narrative. Rather, the flashpoint occurs when the ordinary suspicions harbored by the various strangers in the shelter regarding one another unwittingly touch upon the notoriety of Skin-the-Goat's terrorist past. This, as we will see, also turns out to be the first empathetic moment between Stephen and Bloom.

The sailor is telling of a murder he witnessed; this leads to a discussion about knives. Someone notes that "that was why they thought the park murders of the invincibles was done by foreigners on account of them using knives" (U 514). Up to now, Bloom has encouraged Stephen to speak, but the younger man has responded without spirit. At this point, however, the text draws back to record one of their first mutually empathetic moments:

> At this remark passed obviously in the spirit of *where ignorance is bliss* Mr B. and Stephen, each in his own particular way, both instinctively exchanged meaning glances, in a religious silence of the strictly *entre nous* variety however, towards ... Skin-the-Goat (U 514)

Here is the first and indeed one of the very few points at which Bloom and Stephen appear to agree; less forceful than the tableau of father and fallen son at the end of "Circe," it is nevertheless perhaps the most touching moment in the strand of the narrative that celebrates the meeting of these two. What is striking about this throwaway mutual glance, however, is that it shows the two agreeing only on an issue drawn from the conventional discourse of Irish political and insurgent affairs.

This is appropriate, since the realism that has fostered Bloom and Stephen as characters is also most at home with the hackneyed versions of Irish political discourse. This nevertheless marked a failure of the realist masculinist plot to bring the two together on (in its own terms) a more "meaningful" level; their only opening to empathy takes place at the most conventional plane of Irish politics, and furthermore, one that has been denigrated by the realist strand of the novel itself from its opening pages. This is borne out in "Ithaca," where the most profound material the two find to discuss as they drink Epps cocoa in the kitchen of 7 Eccles Street is the characteristics of the race to which each professes to belong: the discourse of racial character, as "Cyclops" has proven, being closely related to that of jingoist nationalist politics. It is fitting therefore that Stephen does not spend the night under Bloom's roof, and that the spell of the realist pseudo-family romance is finally broken. Bloom succumbs to a yearning to simulate the fundamentally *Gemeinschaft* world of the realist novel within this text, but Stephen is too ferociously modern to accept this. He pushes nastily at the borders of tolerance while Bloom and he, seated in Eccles Street, discuss their respective races: he sings a song about a Jewish girl who kills a neighboring boy (*U* 566), and plays the Jew's harp, apparently as a kind of taunt when, having left Bloom, he walks away down the dark alley (*U* 578). Stephen's departure and implicit disavowal of the possibility of any real connection with Bloom clearly came none too soon; the implication of the postcolonial text is that no new national community will be envisioned within the terms of the realist narrative of relationships invented and perfected by the imperial culture.

Apart from documenting Bloom's and Stephen's failure to empathize, moreover, the text of "Eumaeus" had been preparing us for this split by thematizing the doubtfulness of the identity of virtually everyone mentioned in the episode. Old versions of identity, devastated as early in the novel as "Cyclops," are now in full rout in the masculinist strand of the text. Already in "Cyclops," identity based on nation per se is reviled; here in "Eumaeus," the garrulous narrative becomes entangled in continuously repeating its doubts about the identity of all the strangers who are brought together in the dank shelter and asked to be familiar with each other. Often this makes for comedy: the drunken sailor, for example, tells Stephen that he knows Simon Dedalus, but his Simon turns out to have "toured the wide world with Hengler's Royal Circus," (*U* 510) and was seen by the sailor in Stockholm. Later, when Bloom notices that the postcard the sailor displays was addressed to one "*A Boudin*" (*U* 512), he begins to doubt that the drunkard's name is Murphy, although the latter has just shown off his discharge papers to prove it. Bloom himself is referred to as "L. Boom" (*U* 529) in the *Evening Telegraph* report on Dignam's funeral, while "Skin-the-Goat" is seldom mentioned here without the addition of the phrase "assuming he was he" (*U* 523). All in all, every male identity is undermined, especially in this self-conscious narrative, so that by the end we can easily agree with Bloom's proposition that "when all is said and done the lies a fellow told about himself couldn't probably hold a proverbial candle to he wholesale whoppers other fellows coined about him" (*U* 520). When we remember that a stable sense of identity (i.e., an identity based on norms that a particular community implicitly agrees to accept) whether personal, national, or "racial," is integral to sustained realist narration, we can appreciate how the suspicions generated by the conflation of a *gemeinschaftlich* easy familiarity and the *gesellschaftlich* alienation of a modernist metro-text here effectively forestall the attainment of a sense of community acceptable within the realist tradition.

It is appropriate, given the nostalgia in "Eumaeus" for a community recognizable within realist expectations, that most of the questions asked in the episode should be part of an effort to get to know the strangers present; even more appropriately, given the fact that such a community does not materialize, most of these questions are either sidestepped or ignored. Characteristic is Stephen's laconic reply to the sailor on being asked if he knows Simon Dedalus: "I've heard of him," Stephen says (*U* 509). Later the sailor refuses to answer Bloom's re-peated inquiries about whether he has seen the Rock of Gibraltar. Con-versely, given the episode's impulse to document an alienated world of passing strangers, it fits that most of the thoroughgoing discussions re-garding identity concern not any of the individuals present but rather celebrity court cases, of which those in the shelter might have read in a newspaper. We hear of the "Cornwall case" (*U* 528) and the "Tich-borne case" (*U* 531) — the second of which involved the issue of a claimant's real identity — and above all of the divorce case of Kitty O'Shea, Parnell's lover.

Parnell here is the heroic identity whose fall might be said to have presaged the fragility of all the identities on display in nighttime Dublin. To preserve his reputation, he had, we are told, started "to go under several aliases, such as Fox and Stewart" (*U* 530). What is done systematically to the memory of his reputation here is that it is removed from the public, political sphere and, processed in Bloom's mind, is transformed into a clichéd love story from the genre of realist romance: the kind of tale that Gerty McDowell might have enjoyed reading. When Bloom extracts from Parnell's fall the moral that here was "The eternal question of the life connubial.... Can real love, supposing there happens to be another chap in the case, exist between married folk?" (*U* 532) he has posed the last question in "Eumaeus" from the realist plot that seeks closure in a conforming marital relationship. The effect is extraordinarily comic not merely because the question is hackneyed in the extreme, but because it confronts us in a text that also portrays a twentieth-century alienated world. Conversely, the last memorable question in "Eumaeus" comes out of that urban milieu of alienated *flânerie:* Stephen's query as to "Why they put tables upside down at night, I mean chairs upside down, on the tables in cafés?" (*U* 539). This is mordantly comic here (it might have rung somewhat differently, for example, in a French existentialist novel of thirty years later) simply because it is a flaneur's question in what still appears a family-romance text, the sort of novel in which the work of the servants (sweeping the floors in the morning) is taken for granted. The fact that the furniture is upside-down, however, and the fact that it is not disposed in a drawing-room but in the new urban world of the streets, is an apt image of the confusion of realist narrative regarding its function at this stage in the novel.

It is in this context that we can begin to understand why the novel undertook the "Ithaca" episode in the form of a stark series of questions and answers. The function of "Ithaca" may be grasped as an effort to bridge the different literary trajectories of "Eumaeus" and the closing episode "Penelope," which are, respectively, the male- and female-centered worlds of the "Nostos." In the masculinist "Eumaeus," as we have seen, the realist world of a web of relations based on familiarity is not, despite a stitching of questions, reconciled with the modernist metro-text that documents the alienating city. The realist narrative, telling centrally the story of Bloom as father and Stephen as son, proves incapable of creating a satisfying community of father and son in this context; the modernist city-text that defeats it, on the other hand, is more appropriate for describing a grand European capital than a backward late-colonial metropolis. In "Penelope," as I will show, there is staged on the contrary an altogether more novel strategy, which poses the possibility of community as an issue rather than hankering after it nostalgically as a utopian possibility. "Penelope" too might seem a realist parlor-romance, set in the boudoir and bedroom of its seductress, but Bloom discovers that the furniture of that boudoir has been moved about by Molly, and, comfortable in the dark with his old expectations, he bangs his head in finding this out (U 579). The bridge episode of "Ithaca" is devoted primarily to making a last-ditch effort to complete the novel's realist project, and latterly, to setting the conditions for the unique narrative of "Penelope." In pursuing these objectives, "Ithaca" exposes the regimes of surveillance that are the political unconscious of the realist tale of "Eumaeus" and, in uncovering the materials of this realism in its final phase, it shows off the material bases on which Molly's monologue is built. In a sense "Eumaeus" poses the question of the possibility of community under the old realist rubric, to which "Ithaca" responds with a negative answer; it implies that for the subaltern, strict realism (here pared down to the question-and-answer of the police interrogator and suspect) will never escape the panoptic intent of those in power who invented it. "Penelope" then reformulates the question and the terms under which the utopian project of subsequent postcolonial narratives should operate.

The marshaled questions of "Ithaca" let us know that Stephen and Bloom found little to discuss beyond the defunct prestige of racial characteristics. They allow us to contemplate Stephen's refusal of Bloom's hospitality without having to dwell on the rejection of a comfortable realist close that this gesture represents. More importantly, they allow us to glimpse in its thoroughness the collection of information on which realist narrative is built. "Ithaca" is generally termed a catechism, and is taken to mimic both collections of Catholic doctrine (the Maynooth Catechism, for example) and nineteenth-century popular compendiums of scientific information. But the first half of "Ithaca," while it appears to be presenting lists, dicta, and accounts of sins or experiments (as in the church and scientific catechisms), instead described what two men, both clad in black, were doing on the streets of Dublin and in an Eccles Street basement between one and two o'clock in the morning. As such, it is more accurately the account of a police investigation with model answers — the transcript of an inquiry that might have taken place, let us imagine, in the interrogation room of Store Street divisional police station, which Bloom and Stephen passed on their way to the cabman's shelter.

The questions about how Bloom entered his own home (he climbed over the railings, let himself fall into the area, and entered through the area door), for example, have all the eagerness of a police detective investigation of suspicious movements: "Bloom's decision?" "Did he fall?" "Did he rise uninjured by concussion?" "Did the man reappear elsewhere?" (*U* 546–47). Hence it is in "Ithaca" that the massive regime of surveillance of the colonial state is made explicit in the form; we are confronted with a series of questions and answers that is at once a catechism (implying a compendium of the important knowledge of the culture) and a police interrogation (implying the grip of the panoptic regime upon the dispersal and even the very existence of the culture's pool of knowledge). As is fitting in this *envoi* to the novel's realist narrative, the apparently "obscure" (modernist) text has seldom, throughout the whole book, been so literally transparent. A keyword in "Eumaeus" had been "Sherlockholmesing" (*U* 519); this is made the operative principle of "Ithaca" itself. Note too that this police-interrogation continually suggests a threat of violence that contrasts painfully with the coziness of the cocoa-drinking scene being described.

It is in the second part of "Ithaca" that we realize what its role as *envoi* of realism in the novel entails. When we are shown Bloom alone here, we are forcefully reminded of the utterly interpellated subjectivities to which the regime of surveillance encoding the whole episode gives rise. We are given a list of Bloom's books (*U* 582), his budget for the day with debits and credits noted in the best accounting order (*U* 584), and his ambition — to own a suburban villa ("Bloom Cottage. St. Leopold's. Flowerville" [*U* 587]) complete with water closet, tennis court, shrubbery, and facilities for "snapshot photography" and the "comparative study of religions" (*U* 587): the chosen field of many an enlightened retired colonial official. The wedding presents, pieces of furniture, papers, and *bibelots* of the Bloom household are all catalogued. What the novel returns to at this finishing-point of realist narration — perhaps a closing point in high literature for the genre itself — is the spirit informing its beginning in Britain almost two hundred years earlier in the early days of Britain's colonial expansion, in the fictions of one of Joyce's favorite authors, Daniel Defoe.

Molly Bloom, cleverly placing herself inside and outside her own text at once, both an admirer and a critic, tells us that she doesn't like "books with a Molly in them" and refers us to Defoe's *Moll Flanders*, whose heroine she remembers "always shoplifting anything she could cloth and stuff and yards of it" (*U* 622). (Molly remembers Moll as a deviant consumer rather than as an aggressive businesswoman — or she may imply a comic conflation of both roles.) She had earlier folded the form of "Ithaca" back upon itself and ensured that it ended as a remarkably self-reflexive text, by posing to Bloom a succession of questions about his day. Molly's inquisitiveness means that the last part of "Ithaca" becomes a series of questions about a series of questions. Its realist relentlessness is enervated by a spiral of conditional tenses supplanting interrogative forms, as in the wistful late question, "If he had smiled why would he have smiled?" (*U* 601). Through flashes of extra-textuality of this sort — at another point, squatting on the chamber pot, Molly calls on "Jamesey" (i.e., Joyce as author, perhaps) to "let me up out of this" (*U* 633)—Molly as subject is granted a mercurial, shifting position both inside and at once outside the text she is destined to carry to its conclusion.

What is striking, however, is the extraordinary particularity of the material base on which such a mercurial subjectivity is constructed. Interpellated by the pleasures of middle-class commodity culture quite as thoroughly as is her husband, Molly too thinks of the furniture (the jingly old bed, for example), bibelots, and advertised clothing, as in "one of those kidfitting corsets Id want advertised cheap in the Gentlewoman with elastic gores on the hips ... what did they say they give a delightful figure line 11/6 obviating that unsightly broad appearance across the lower back ..." (*U* 618). (Like Bloom, she too has an eye for advertisements). Her speech is a palimpsest of middle-class clichés ("sure you cant get on in this world without style" [*U* 618]), so that her voice never sounds less than directly derived from that of others ("of course hed never find another woman like me to put up with him the way I do" [*U* 613]). Molly Bloom is, therefore, both the image of the wholly interpellated subject, a type of the ideal colonial native, and simultaneously a shifting signifier that is at flash-moments deployed at a distance from the text altogether. It is in the space between these two roles that the voice of Molly as interrogator of postcolonial community operates.

Molly Bloom is an ideal colonial subject to such a degree that she may be compared to Kimball O'Hara, the "Kim" of Kipling's novel of the same title.[13] Like Kim, she is the daughter of an Irish colonial soldier in the British army. As offspring of colonial soldiers and, apparently, "native" women (in both cases the identities of their mothers are kept vague), Kim and Molly are curiously both members of the colonist and native cultures at once. This is underlined in both cases by the darkness of their skin: Kim seems to be "a young heathen" to the British officers who offer to educate him, while Leopold Bloom is proud that Molly, from Gibraltar, is "a Spanish type" (*U* 533). Both Kim and Molly represent on the one hand a utopian ideal of assimilation of the colonist masters and native colonial subjects; on the other, they transgress a boundary that, because the rigid division between colonists and natives sustaining the empire had to be kept up, was the greatest taboo of all to cross.

Further, Molly as a native of Gibraltar who now lives in Ireland— that is, a person from one colony or outpost of empire who now lives in another — has also successfully transgressed the unspoken rule that the natives of that colony will keep to their own territory. Benedict Anderson, in *Imagined Communities*,[14] his study of the relation of nationalism and imperialism, points out that a key way in which the imperial power reinforced local chauvinisms, as well as its own tacit belief in the particular inferiority of each colony compared to the center, was to forestall any mixing among the colonial peoples: an Indian functionary, for example, even after a standard "British" education, would never have been encouraged to go to work in Hong Kong. Molly Bloom, however, has evaded this stricture. Thus just as Bloom, in "Cyclops," stands for the principle of oppressed peoples who must, he implies, be in solidarity with each other ("And I belong to a race too ... that is hated and persecuted" [*U* 272]), Molly signifies the principle of native oppression rather than the ideological narrowness of any particular national chauvinism. Unlike Bloom, however, she does not focus on this oppression as the enabling integer of her subjectivity.

Further, with her father as Irish soldier in the British colonial service and her mother possibly a Jewish Spaniard, her family history marks her at once as a figure who will never be allowed, even if she had wished, to represent herself as an "authentic" nationalist. Earlier we saw how Bloom, as a politically conscious Jew ("though in reality I'm not" [*U* 525] he tells Stephen in "Eumaeus") and an Irish person, stands not for a single chauvinist nationalism but, in his interest in the future of a Jewish state as well as an Irish one, rather for the more magnanimous principle of national independence for all oppressed peoples. Now we see that Molly is not a native of one colonial territory, but rather, with her heritage of Ireland and Gibraltar, is a subaltern native of the empire itself: she becomes a signifier of colonial subalternity in general.

Moreover, as a woman in a male-dominated colonial system that almost always assigned women the lowest rung in the hierarchy of power, Molly is the last of a line of women in *Ulysses* who are the text's most abject subaltern subjects. This series began with Stephen's sick mother, whose grim degrading death is reported in the opening pages of the text, and continued with such figures as the poor milkwoman, who is merely interested in being paid; Mrs. Breen, the harried "melancholily" (*U* 129) wife of Denis, the victim of the "U.P.: up" postcard; Gerty McDowell, wistful, limping, poorly educated and dreamy on Sandymount strand in contrast to Stephen's well-read cockiness on the same beach earlier; Mina Purefoy, who is giving birth to her ninth child in Holles Street Hospital; Mrs. Keogh, the brothel cook in "Circe"; and "the partially idiotic female," a prostitute whom Bloom encounters along the quays in "Sirens" and who, "glazed and haggard under a black straw hat, peered askew round the door of the shelter" (*U* 517) in "Eumaeus."

The degree of abjection under which these women suffer at the hands of the patriarchal colonial culture is perhaps most ferociously suggested by the "Oxen of the Sun" episode of *Ulysses*. The important event reported in this stretch of narrative is the birth of a boy to Mina Purefoy after a long labor; the great bulk of the episode, however, is given over to an account of a bawdy group of medical students in the hospital dayroom, whose jokes are related in a compendium of pastiche styles that represent key stylistic turns in the history of the English literary canon. It is as if such styles, the styles of England's literary history, could not be brought to bear on a description of a woman in labor in one of England's colonies, so that they can only refer to the lives of women as fleetingly glimpsed background figures in a world of men.

Molly Bloom, as the first woman in the text to be allowed to think for an extended period in her own voice, is as interpellated by the colonial patriarchal culture as these women, but she exceeds it as well. She too is an abject; in contrast to Poldy, she is limited in her movement to the grim Eccles Street house, so that her night thoughts often turn to escape into the city streets in a *flânerie* similar to that her husband has practiced all day — she thinks of setting out for the market in the morning, for example. She has few friends, and if loneliness is to be considered the pervading sensation of this text, she has surely much more reason to be lonely than Bloom. ("They have friends they can talk to weve none either" [*U* 640]). On the other hand, she has been successfully interpellated as an ideal colonial subject from the colonizer's viewpoint: she is struck, for example, by the pageantry of "the prince of Wales own or the lancers O the lancers theyre grand or the Dublins that won Tugela" — referring to different regiments in the British army (*U* 617) — and, more important, she fulfills the role of the eager native consumer of colonial commodities: she and Boylan ate the jar of Plumtree's Potted Meat together, and she wishes that Bloom would allow her more money for clothes (*U* 618). In other words she may strike us as an extraordinarily acquiescent, even eager, late-colonial native subject.

Further, she is a woman alone, not part of any group that might suggest the solidarity of resistance. She is markedly apolitical in any con-

ventional sense, jeering at Bloom's suggestion that Arthur Griffith, the
Sinn Fein leader, is the coming man ("well he doesnt look it that's all I
can say" [*U* 616]). (Events that occurred before Joyce wrote this episode
proved Bloom right here; Griffith, a marginal figure in Irish politics in
1904, had become a central figure in the founding of the Irish Free
State.) This, taken together with her unrepressed thoughts on sexuality
as well as her unpunctuated flow of language, seems to imply a rejection of the public and the communal in favor of the personal or the
erotic. Yet just as Stephen's corresponding "Proteus" monologue is not
as introverted as it might have seemed, what is striking about Molly's
thoughts is that she reconnoiters her aloneness, her apoliticality, her
sexuality, and even her self-presentation as a matter of information and
its control by those who have power to manipulate it. Against regimes
of information she uses interrogativity as a striking rhetorical feature of
her thought, in order to present us, at the end of the novel, with a fully
subaltern perspective on the opinions, prejudices, and beliefs of the
Dublin of her day. In the first place, she recounts a series of scenarios in
which men are tiresome questioners. She remembers Bloom "drawing
out the thing by the hour question and answer would you do this that
and the other with the coalman yes with a bishop yes" (*U* 610), and on
Breen's mystery postcard she opines "wouldnt a thing like that simply
bore you stiff to extinction" (*U* 613). She knows much about the skill-
ful use of information: she laughs at Josie Powell "because I used to tell
her a good bit of what went on between us but not all just enough to
make her mouth water" (*U* 612–13). At the next level, she remembers
throughout the episode scenes where men holding officially sanctioned
positions questioned her. Molly represents these as occasions on which
she either kept her distaste to herself, or cleverly acted as an innocent to
enjoy a joke of her own at the questioner's expense. Thus she thinks of
the gynecologist on the Pembroke Road (*U* 633–34), and of Catholic
confession:

> when I used to go to father Corrigan he touched me father and what
> harm if he did where and I said on the canal bank like a fool but
> whereabouts on your person my child on the leg behind high up was it
> yes rather high up was it where you sit down yes O Lord couldnt he say
> bottom right out and have done with it (*U* 610)

Lines like this ("and I said on the canal bank") are probably the best
uses of subaltern carnival discourse in either western or postcolonial

modernism. They aptly represent the strategies that the abject colonial native, denied direct access to her own speech and language which is instead mediated to her through the searching interrogations of those in power, brings to bear to subvert the oppressor's words. The comedy of "Penelope" (and it is by far the most humorous episode in this intensely comic work) is again and again derived from the kind of knowing yet apparently innocent subversion of the words and actions of those in power: if Molly could not find an appropriate muttered line at the time to respond to a condescending interrogator, she invents such lines now, describing the solicitor Menton "and his boiled eyes of all the big stupoes I ever met and thats called a solicitor" (*U* 609), and observing of Bloom himself "somebody ought to put him in the budget" (*U* 621). The "Penelope" episode, then, points us to the very principle of difference that will undermine any postcolonial imagined utopian community by granting the last word in what has been a resolutely male-centered text to a woman; further, it shows this woman as a more profoundly interpellated subaltern subject who actively works in her use of language to subvert the tropes that would either create a colonial pseudo-community (the "Commonwealth of Nations" or "Family of Man") or imagine its postcolonial mirror image ("the Irish Free State").

It is with the depth of Molly's abjection as a colonial native woman in mind that we can appreciate the effect of her controversial "Yes," which rings through her narrative and eventually closes her text. Remember the scene this episode depicts: it is of a woman lying in bed, near sleep, between 1:45 and 2:20 A.M. on June 17, 1904. In fact not one word is uttered aloud during this episode. Here is interior monologue brought to its logical conclusion — the utter silence of the thinking subject — and it makes us realize the peculiar appropriateness of this form of narration for colonial subjects — the subaltern whom the colonial master would ideally render silent and of fixed abode. As in the culture of slavery, the only word the native is expected to utter is the token of acquiescence in response to an order — a servile "yes." Molly, at the end of *Ulysses*, renders the very act of accepting Bloom in marriage a part of this colonial question-response when she utters her "yes" in answer to his question. Yet she also toys with the question, tosses it back at him, using the subversive ruse of the subaltern to turn the voicing of that "yes" into an effect suggesting equality. She herself *also* asks — if silently — and they first utter the yes together:

yes he said I was a flower of the mountain yes ... that was one true thing
he said in his life and ... I gave him all the pleasure I could leading him
on till he asked me to say yes and I wouldnt answer first only looked out
over the sea and the sky I was thinking of so many things he didnt know
of ... and I thought well as well him as another and then I asked him
with my eyes to ask again yes and then he asked me would I yes to say
yes ... and his heart was going like mad and yes I said yes I will Yes. (*U*
643–44)

The truth is that we can never know whether the "Yes" that marks the
end of the book is the *last* acquiescence of the most deeply interpellated
colonial abject, marking a new equality that will now mean that the
freed subjects can henceforth pose questions to each other, or whether
it is merely one more acquiescence that marks another turn in the repetitive cycle of oppression. Yet, with the necessity to accept difference
among the native group, through the force of this episode, now thoroughly in place, a community, if it is to be created, will be built on the
acceptance of equality between different but equal groups and subjects
rather than on any ill-defined utopianism that would likely replicate the
fake community of the empire itself. That such a state will come about
is augured by Molly Bloom's spirited deployment of the carnival of subaltern language. Hers is not some lapse into the "flow" of the personal
and the apolitical, but rather the subaltern's deft redistribution of forces
in the language-economy of late-colonial power.

Envoi

Molly Bloom appears to the reader as the most completely interpellated
subaltern in this subaltern text. With her, the novel confronts the most
sacred image of Ireland in the nationalist canon, the image of the nation as "pure" woman, as virgin or mother, and wholly subverts it, re-
placing the servile smile with subversive laughter. Here, *Ulysses* rejects
with a vengeance a key nationalist icon, just as, in the opening episodes
of the novel, it had exposed the whole panoply of Irish nationalist assumptions and mores as an imitation of chauvinist versions of national
community provided by British imperialism. The novel, at its close,
leaves its reader with a realistic image of a fraught but viable subaltern
subjectivity. Molly is a subject deeply interpellated by the colonial power;
she refuses to be interested in politics as such; she is voiceless and
shown as a lone body thinking in the dark. At the same time, she is
thoroughly conscious of her subservience and is willing to experiment

with modes of questioning authority that generate for her a sense of independence and personal dignity. Her thoughts close the book as a strong challenge to recognize that although "national independence" may be won by adhering to an ideology that is derivative, and, in the fullest sense, reactionary, the true independence of each citizen of the postcolonial state is possible only after the accomplishment of the more difficult task of working through all the levels of oppression, in both the public and private spheres, to which the political reality of colonialism gave rise.

Joyce's *Ulysses,* the greatest Irish novel, was written in 1914–21, the years Ireland gained its independence from Britain after the 1916 Rising and the War of Independence of 1919–21. Even if its author had not been as obsessively interested in his homeland and its capital city as he was, this congruence of creativity and political change in itself would be grounds for reading Ireland's emergence into postcolonial statehood as the political unconscious of *Ulysses.* As it turns out, *Ulysses* is notably reticent about the historic changes taking place in Dublin while the book was being written; however, I suggest that this by no means lessens its value as a text that, written against the background of colonial violence in Ireland, meditates upon the forces of colonial rule that must be overcome and the trajectories of independence that must be devised if a postcolonial state acceptable to all of its citizens is to come into being.

Because the novel is set in 1904, it works as a very careful documentation of the forces of policing and surveillance through which the British empire exercised its power in its closest colony. In episodes such as "Lestrygonians" and "Eumaeus," we are made aware of the pervasive police presence in Dublin. In "Sirens" we are shown how the colonizing power would turn its most developed colony into a consumer culture akin to its own, but could not manage to do so while enforcing the poverty of its subjects. "Cyclops" demonstrates how colonist stereotypes of the natives, who are imagined as either dangerous barbarians or collaborating civilians, thoroughly interpellate the local population, so that its members' first impulse is to act out imperial stereotypes of themselves. In the opening episodes of the novel, we are shown convincingly that even the nationalist ideology and iconography developed by the Irish themselves is little more than a reflection of British imperialist nationalism, embodying most of its expectations and chauvinisms. Especially in the characters of the women, from the old milkwoman to the prostitutes of "Circe" to Molly Bloom, and also in the poverty and hopelessness of many of the male characters, the novel amply documents the way in which the colony maintains the native population as an underclass. *Ulysses* works as a thorough indictment of the colonial administration of Britain's oldest colony, pictured at a late moment of that regime.

Yet in keeping with the fact that it was written in the very years when Ireland was achieving postcolonial independence, *Ulysses* also maps strategies through which the subalternity stamped by the colonial regime on the lives of its subjects might be overcome. Merely by presenting—even in such introverted episodes as "Proteus," but most evidently in "Wandering Rocks"—a myriad of individuals going about their own business independently of each other, and imagining them as a single community, the novel works to represent this community in the way in which the new nation will envision it. More fundamentally, *Ulysses* employs a whole series of modernist strategies of defamiliarization to represent aspects of this community in all its diversity. It uses the trope of *flânerie,* embodied in Leopold Bloom, to imagine a new kind of independent subject, one who can walk by the nets of surveillance and persuasion laid down by the colonial regime and those who are interpellated by it. It uses complex narrative strategies to force into conflict some of the discourses invented by the colonists to characterize the natives; in "Cyclops," for example, the barbarian and civilian discourses are brought face to face, and both seem paltry. The hint of violence, in this episode and elsewhere, appears to alert the text to the urgency of its task of inventing narrative forms complex enough to characterize the possibilities of independence for the citizens of the postcolonial state.

Behind each of the text's projects to imagine models of Irish postcolonial subjectivities lie hints of the violence occurring in Ireland at the time that the text was being written. In the face of this violence, the novel's attempts to envision subjects sometimes falter. In "Circe," for example, where *Ulysses* comes close to depicting the violence that was widespread throughout Ireland while that episode was in progress, the prostitutes of Nighttown are scapegoated as participants in Ireland's colonial subservience; there is enacted here a scapegoating of abject women of a kind mostly practiced by the nationalist ideology Joyce condemns as derivative of an imperial original. Nevertheless, in the figures of the abject women throughout the book, *Ulysses* displays not only the fullest horror of the effects of colonial power but also, especially in the thoughts of Molly Bloom, a sense that out of this abjection might come a consciousness that would lead to independent action. This is an antinationalist text in that it is highly suspicious of a bourgeois ideology that it implicitly condemns as a callow copy of empire prejudices — but there are more ways than one to be interested in a nation. *Ulysses* casts a cold eye on the subalternity wrought by the colonial administration, and invents forms to imagine ways in which this subalternity might be overcome.

Notes

Introduction

1. The study that is least faithful to this view is, appropriately, the one that has studied Joyce's own political views most thoroughly, namely, Dominic Manganiello's excellent *Joyce's Politics* (London: Routledge and Kegan Paul, 1980).

2. Excellent studies that trace when each episode of *Ulysses* was written are A. Walton Litz, *The Art of James Joyce: Method and Design in Ulysses and Finnegans Wake* (New York: Oxford University Press, 1961), and Michael Groden, *Ulysses in Progress* (Princeton: Princeton University Press, 1977).

3. For a good account of the human and physical cost of the Easter Rising see Joseph V. O'Brien, *"Dear Dirty Dublin," A City in Distress, 1899–1966* (Berkeley: University of California Press, 1982), pp. 241–74.

4. See, for example, *Nation and Narration*, ed. Homi K. Bhabha (London: Routledge, 1990).

5. See, for example, Fredric Jameson, "Cognitive Mapping," in C. Nelson and L. Grossberg, eds., *Marxism and the Interpretation of Culture* (Urbana: University of Illinois Press, 1988), or his recent book (on film), *The Geopolitical Aesthetic: Cinema and Space in the World System* (Bloomington: Indiana University Press, 1992).

6. Quoted in Fredric Jameson, *The Political Unconscious: Narrative as a Socially Symbolic Act* (Ithaca, N.Y.: Cornell University Press, 1981), p. 294.

7. Ernest Mandel, *Late Capitalism* (London: New Left Books, 1975).

8. For a summary of his argument see Fredric Jameson, "Cognitive Mapping," in Nelson and Grossberg, eds., *Marxism and the Interpretation of Culture*, pp. 347–60.

9. Frantz Fanon, "On Violence," in *The Wretched of the Earth*, trans. Constance Farrington (New York: Grove Press, 1968), pp. 249–310.

10. See Georg Lukács, "Reification and the Consciousness of the Proletariat," in *History and Class Consciousness: Studies in Marxist Dialectics*, trans. R. Livingstone (Cambridge, Mass.: MIT Press, 1985), pp. 83–148.

11. Hugh Kenner, *Ulysses*, rev. ed. (Baltimore: Johns Hopkins University Press, 1987). For example, see p. 102, where he speaks of "a continuous rhetoric of evasion." Kenner shows how "the [later] episodes draw apart from one another not only in character but in narrative time" (p. 101).

12. Colin MacCabe, *James Joyce and the Revolution of the Word* (London: Macmillan Press, 1979), p. 3.

13. See M. M. Bakhtin, *The Dialogic Imagination: Four Essays* ed. Michael Holquist, trans. Caryl Emerson and Michael Holquist (Austin: University of Texas Press, 1981), especially "Discourse and the Novel," pp. 259–422.

14. See Gisèle Freund, *Gisèle Freund, Photographer* (New York: Harry N. Abrams, 1985), pp. 88–93, esp. p. 89

15. This letter by W. B. Yeats, dated August 28, 1915, responded to Edmund Gosse's objection that Joyce had not stated his loyalty to the Allied cause in the First World War. As Gosse had been the author who had been chosen by Yeats to recommend Joyce to the Royal Literary Fund, Yeats is clearly on the defensive here, to ensure that Joyce will be granted an award.

16. See Manganiello, *Joyce's Politics*, p. 162, quoted from *Letters I*, p.118. The original is in French.

17. Herbert Gorman, *James Joyce: A Definitive Biography* (London: John Lane, The Bodley Head, 1939), p. 232.

18. Frank Budgen, *James Joyce and the Making of "Ulysses"* (1934; rpt. Bloomington: Indiana University Press, 1960), p. 152.

19. Ibid., p. 152.

20. Stanislaus Joyce, *My Brother's Keeper: James Joyce's Early Years*, ed. Richard Ellmann (New York: Viking Press, 1958), p. 34.

21. See Litz, *Art of James Joyce*; and Groden, *Ulysses in Progress*. For a comprehensive listing of the important dates in Irish history in the years 1914–22, see *A New History of Ireland*, ed. T. W. Moody and J. F. Beirne, vol. 8 (Oxford: Clarendon Press, 1982), pp. 386–403.

22. See Manganiello, *Joyce's Politics*, pp. 167–69, for an account of and a transcription of part of this speech, which was given in French, and for a translation into English of the quoted extracts.

23. The phrase is from Walter Benjamin, "On Some Motifs in Baudelaire" in *Illuminations* (New York: Schocken Books, 1969).

24. Rosa Luxemburg, *The Accumulation of Capital* (New Haven: Yale University Press, 1981).

25. See Abdul JanMohamed, "The Politics of Manichean Allegory" in *Race, Writing, and Difference,* ed. Henry Louis Gates (Chicago: University of Chicago Press, 1985).

26. See the portrayal of the character Wanja in Ngugi Wa Thiong'o, *Petals of Blood* (New York: Penguin Books, 1991).

1. Mimic Beginnings

1. The text reads as follows:

During the last twelve months innumerable murders and other outrages have been committed by those who call themselves Members of the Irish Republican Army. Only by the help of self-respecting Irishmen can these murders be put a stop to.

It is possible to send letters containing information in such a way as to prevent their being stopped in the post.

If you have information to give and you are willing to help the cause of Law and Order act as follows.

Write your information on ordinary notepaper, being careful to give neither your name nor your address. Remember also to disguise your handwriting, or else to print the words. Put it into an envelope, addressed to:

D. W. ROSS
Poste Restante
G. P. O., LONDON

Enclose this envelope in another. (Take care that your outer envelope is not transparent). Put with it a small slip of paper asking the recipient to forward the D. W. ROSS letter as soon as he receives it. Address the outer envelope to some well disposed friend in England or to any well known business address in England.

You will later be given the opportunity, should you wish to do so, of identifying your letter, and, should the information have proved of value, of claiming a REWARD.

The utmost secrecy will be maintained as to all information received.

2. It is interesting to note that in the very years in which notices in Ireland called upon Irish informers to pass on information by writing to an address in England, Joyce was sending his own information about Ireland — the text of his new novel *Ulysses* — to his readers in England, especially Harriet Weaver and Ezra Pound.

The main sign of the coming political violence in Ireland in the years 1914–15 was the growth of the Irish Volunteers in the Catholic south and the Ulster Volunteers in the mainly Protestant north of the country: two large militia forces, the first group determined to support "Home Rule" for Ireland and the second equally determined to oppose it. Both sides engaged in large-scale illegal gunrunning. A moment representative of the political tenor of these years in Ireland was the huge funeral of the old Fenian Jeremiah O'Donavan Rossa in Dublin on August 1, 1915; at the graveside, Pearse delivered a fiery and passionate oration.

3. For an excellent discussion of the ways in which nationalist discourse, so apparently antagonistic to imperial modes, is doomed to imitate them, see David Lloyd, *Anomalous States: Irish Writing in the Post-Colonial Moment* (Durham, N.C.: Duke University Press, 1993), esp. pp. 42–47.

4. See, for example, Tom Paulin, "The British Presence in *Ulysses*," in *Ireland and the English Crisis* (Newcastle upon Tyne: Bloodaxe Books, 1984), pp. 92–100.

5. Joyce told Budgen in June 1918: "Stephen no longer interests me. He has a shape that can't be changed." Quoted in Richard Ellmann, *James Joyce* (Oxford: Oxford University Press, 1959), p. 473.

6. Hugh Kenner, *Ulysses* (Baltimore: Johns Hopkins University Press, rev. ed., 1987), pp. 34–35.

7. Anthony Trollope, *The Kellys and the O'Kellys* (New York: Garland, 1989) and *The MacDermotts of Ballycloran,* ed. Robert Tracy (Oxford: Oxford University Press, 1989).

8. Quoted in Dominic Manganiello, *Joyce's Politics* (London: Routledge and Kegan Paul, 1980), p. 168.

9. See ibid., pp.161–64, for the most cogent exposition of the politics that Stephen professes in the opening episodes of *Ulysses*.

10. On the successive Celtic revivals, see Seamus Deane, "The Literary Myths of the Revival," in *Celtic Revivals: Essays in Modern Irish Literature, 1880–1980* (London: Faber and Faber, 1985), pp. 28–37.

11. Chidi Amuta, *The Theory of African Literature: Implications for Practical Criticism* (London: Zed Books, 1989), p. 63.

12. Ibid.

13. A typical text of this type would be David Lamb, *The Africans* (New York: Vintage Books, 1987).

14. See, for example, Conor Cruise O'Brien, *States of Ireland* (London: Hutchinson, 1972).

15. Benedict Anderson, *Imagined Communities: Reflections on the Origin and Spread of Nationalism* (London: Verso, 1983).

16. Ibid., p. 145

17. For a summary of the views of both Luxemburg and Lenin on nationalism, see Tom Nairn, *The Break-Up of Britain: Crisis and Neo-Colonialism* (London: New British Library, 1977), p. 83.

18. Anderson, *Imagined Communities*, p. 142.

19. Fredric Jameson, "Third-World Literature in the Era of Multinational Capitalism," *Social Text* 15 (Fall 1986), pp.65–88.

20. Ibid., p. 68

21. Ibid., p. 69.

22. Michael Sprinkler, "Marxism and Nationalism: Ideology and Class Struggle in Premchand's *Godan*," in *Social Text* 23 (Fall/Winter 1989), p. 23.

23. Ibid., p. 60; and Jameson, "Third-World Literature," p. 68.

24. Jameson, "Third-World Literature," p. 65.

25. Sembene Ousmane, *Xala,* trans. Clive Wake (Westport, Conn.: Lawrence Hill, 1976), p. 69, quoted in F. Jameson, ibid., p. 80.

26. Anthony Brewer, *Marxist Theories of Imperialism: A Critical Survey* (London: Routledge and Kegan Paul, 1980), is the best survey of materialist theories of colonialism from Marx to "dependency theory."

27. For studies that compare models of exploitation and oppression as these forces relate to social classes and their formation, see Erik Olin Wright et al., *The Debate on Classes* (London: Verso, 1989).

28. Sembene, *Xala,* p. 80.

29. Aijaz Ahmad, "Jameson's Rhetoric of Otherness and the National Allegory," *Social Text* 17 (Fall 1987), pp. 3–25.

30. Lu Xun, *Selected Short Stories of Lu Hsun,* trans. Gladys Yang and Yang Hsien-yi (Beijing: Foreign Language Press, 1972), p. 5, quoted in F. Jameson, "Third-World Literature," p. 75.

31. F. Jameson, "Third-World Literature," p. 75.

32. This definition comes from F. Jameson, p. 76. See Antonio Gramsci, *Selections from the Prison Notebooks,* trans. Q. Hoare and G. N. Smith (New York: International Publishers, 1971).

33. See Annie E. Coombes, "The Franco-British Exhibition: Packaging Empire in Edwardian England" in *The Edwardian Era,* ed. Jane Beckett and Deborah Cherry (London: Phaidon Press and Barbican Art Gallery, 1987), pp. 152–66. On eugenics, see p. 161.

34. See J. A. Froude, untitled article, in the *London Times* (December 3, 1880), p. 3, and Charles Kingsley, *His Letters and Memories of His Life: Edited by His Wife* (London: H. S. King, 1877), vol. 2, p. 107.

35. See James L. McLoughlin, "The Race Type in Celtic Literature," in *New Ireland Review* 5 (1896), pp. 26–38, 81–94.

36. A. E. Coombes, *Franco-British Exhibition,* p. 164, n. 9.

37. W. B. Yeats, "The Irish Dramatic Movement" in *The Autobiography of William Butler Yeats* (New York: Collier, 1969), p. 378.

38. Roy Foster, "Anglo-Irish Literature, Gaelic Nationalism and Irish Politics in the 1890's," *The Political Culture of Modern Britain: Studies in Memory of Stephen Koss,* ed. J. M. W. Bean (London: Hamish Hamilton, 1987), p. 100.

39. J. A. Hobson, *Imperialism: A Study* (London: G. Allen and Unwin, 1902).

40. Quoted in Penny Summerfield, "Patriotism and Empire: Music Hall Entertainment 1870–1914," in *Imperialism and Popular Culture*, ed. John McKensie (Manchester: Manchester University Press, 1986).

41. See L. H. Platt, "The Buckeen and the Dogsbody: Aspects of History and Culture in 'Telemachus,' " *James Joyce Quarterly* 27, no. 1 (Fall 1989), p. 82.

42. B. Anderson, *Imagined Communities*, p. 139.

43. For a quoted verse of the ballad, see Paulin, "The British Presence in *Ulysses*," p. 92.

44. R. Foster, "Anglo-Irish Literature," p. 99.

45. Ibid.

46. Ibid., p. 98.

47. Quoted in Mark Tierney, *Modern Ireland, 1850–1950* (Dublin: Gill and Macmillan, 1972), p. 108.

48. Platt, "The Buckeen and the Dogsbody," p. 83.

49. For this detail and others, see Mark Bence-Jones, *Twilight of the Ascendancy* (London: Constable, 1987), pp. 109, 137.

50. Douglas Hyde, *Abhrain Grádh Chúige Connacht or Love Songs of Connacht* (London: T. Fisher Unwin, 1895), p. 59.

51. Patrick Pearse, *Poems*.

52. See Bence-Jones, *Twilight of the Ascendancy*, pp. 91–93.

53. Shari Benstock and Bernard Benstock, *Who's He When He's at Home: A James Joyce Directory* (Urbana: University of Illinois Press, 1980), p. 96.

54. Platt, "The Buckeen and the Dogsbody," p. 83.

55. See, for example, Flann O'Brien, *The Poor Mouth* (New York: Viking Press, 1973), pp. 42–43. This is a translation by P. C. Power of *An Béal Bocht*, O'Brien's satirical look at rural Gaelic-speaking Ireland. On pages 42–43 there is a story of how a folklorist mistakes a pig for the most fluent Irish speaker in a crowded and rowdy cottage.

56. See Coombes, "The Franco-British Exhibition," p. 166.

2. Traffic Accidents

1. See Paul Virilio, *Speed and Politics*, trans. Mark Polizzitti (New York: Semiotext[e], Foreign Agents Series, 1986), pp. 4, 153.

2. Walter Benjamin, "On Some Motifs in Baudelaire," pp. 155–200, in *Illuminations*, ed. Hannah Arendt, trans. Harry Zohn (New York: Schocken Books, 1969), especially pp. 166–80.

3. Manfredo Tafuri, "The Dialectic of the Avant-Garde," *Architecture and Utopia, Design and Capitalist Development* (Cambridge, Mass.: MIT Press, 1987), pp. 78–103.

4. Walter Benjamin, "Paris—The Capital of the Nineteenth Century," *Charles Baudelaire: A Lyric Poet in the Era of High Capitalism*, trans. Harry Zohn (London: Verso, 1983), pp. 115–76.

5. For material on the Kildare Street Club, see Mark Bence-Jones, *Twilight of the Ascendancy* (London: Constable, 1987), especially pp. 53–56. On the club during the 1916 Rising, see p. 176. Yeats's jokes about the leaders of the Rising would have been appreciated there at any time: during the rebellion itself, pageboys with bread and tea, Bence-Jones reports, were sent out to British soldiers stationed nearby in the grounds of Trinity College.

6. Marshall Berman, *All That Is Solid Melts into Air: The Experience of Modernity* (New York: Simon and Schuster, 1982).

7. Georg Simmel, "The Metropolis and Mental Life," in *Images of Man: The Classi-*

cal Tradition in Sociological Thinking, ed. C. Wright Mills (New York: George Braziller, 1960).

8. On the political and social uses of these works, see Eric Hobsbawm, "Mass-Producing Traditions: Europe, 1870–1914," *The Invention of Tradition,* ed. E. Hobsbawm and Terence Ranger (Cambridge: Cambridge University Press, 1983), pp. 263–308.

9. See Mark Anderson, "Kafka and New York: Notes on a Travelling Narrative," *Modernity and the Text: Revisions of German Modernism,* ed. Andreas Huyssen and David Bathrick (New York: Columbia University Press, 1989), pp. 142–61.

10. See Hobsbawm and Ranger, *Invention of Tradition.*

11. Walter Benjamin, quoted in Tafuri, "Dialectic of the Avant-Garde," p. 79.

12. Oscar Bie, *Der Gesellchaftliche Verkehr* (Brad Marquardt), p. 3, quoted in Anderson, "Kafka and New York."

13. Rural or peasant life, interestingly, has not been treated in this way. Fin-de-siècle delineations of peasant life, rather, were concerned to show the uniqueness of each peasant community (compare Hardy's peasants to those of Synge, for example) while delineations of urban life, under the rubric of "the universality of modernity," have worked to accentuate what seemed standardized.

14. Virilio, *Speed and Politics,* p. 1.

15. Oscar Bie, quoted in Anderson, "Kafka and New York," p. 144.

16. T. S. Eliot, *The Wasteland,* text of the first edition, in *The Wasteland, A Facsimile and Transcript,* ed. Valerie Eliot (New York: Harcourt Brace Jovanovich, 1971), p. 136.

17. See "The Judgment," in Franz Kafka, *The Complete Stories* (New York: Schocken Books, 1976).

18. Quoted in Anderson, "Kafka and New York," p. 146.

19. In fact, the timeball told Greenwich time for mariners, while the clock-face told Dunsink time for pedestrians. For more of Bloom's meditations on this matter, and the relation of both his thoughts and the clock's actions to the notion of "parallax" that Bloom has been mulling over, see Hugh Kenner, *Ulysses* (Baltimore: Johns Hopkins University Press, 1987), p. 75.

20. A. Conan Doyle, from "A Case of Identity," quoted in Franco Moretti, "Clues," *Signs Taken for Wonders* (London: Verso, rev. ed., 1988), p. 136.

21. The Lawrence Collection is a major collection of photographic plates in the National Library of Ireland, Dublin. Numerous photographs from the collection are reproduced in *Faces of Ireland, 1875–1925 — A Photographic and Literary Picture of the Past,* ed. Brian Walker, Art O'Broin, Sean McMahon (Belfast: Appletree Press, 1984).

22. The fact that Mrs. Dalloway is a woman, however, makes her an atypical figure of western *flânerie.* The *flâneuse* may be read from a feminist perspective as an emancipated subject. Her place, however, is certainly at the geographical center of the British Empire.

23. Tafuri, "Dialectic of the Avant-Garde," p. 89.

24. Guy Debord, *Society of the Spectacle* (Detroit: Red and Black Press, 1983). For interesting comments on the function of the modern and postmodern city, see especially paragraphs 165–79. For a documentation of suggestive work by the Situationists in this area, see "Psychogeographic Maps of Venice," Ralph Rumney, 1957, in *An endless adventure ... an endless passion ... an endless banquet ...: A Situationist Scrapbook,* ed. Iwona Blazwick (London: I.C.A./Verso, 1989), pp. 45–49.

25. Franco Moretti, "The Long Goodbye: *Ulysses* and the End of Liberal Capitalism," in *Signs Taken for Wonders,* pp. 182–208.

26. See Fredric Jameson, *Modernism and Imperialism,* in the series "Nationalism,

Colonialism and Literature," Field Day Pamphlet Number 14 (Derry, Northern Ireland: Field Day, 1988).

27. Frantz Fanon, *The Wretched of the Earth,* trans. Constance Farrington (New York: Grove Press, 1968).

28. This typology of colonial penetration comes from the work of Rosa Luxemburg. For an account of her contributions to materialist theories of imperialism, and the relation of these theories to the conditions in which she herself wrote, see Derek Brewer, *Marxist Theories of Imperialism* (London: Routledge and Kegan Paul, 1980), pp. 61–78. Luxemburg's work on imperialism has been underrated; in some of its aspects it foreshadows the recent work on multinational geocapital by David Harvey and others. I will have occasion to refer to it again in chapter 4 of this study.

29. One might think of the figures in Futurist art and writing as resulting from a modernist movement that, in the wake of Marinetti's famous manifesto, professed to be drunk with movement. Futurism's kinetic figures are speeded-up versions of the flaneur. They may be read as a (desperate) attempt to recapture mobility as a subject's mode of empowerment at the very moment when that mobility was being violently curtailed, as, for example, in factory assembly lines, where the commodity and not the producer moved along, or the mammoth static battles of the First World War, where a machine—the tank—was invented so that the soldiers might move.

30. As a figure in an evolutionary series of representations of the modernist subject foregoing consciousness, the flaneur's most striking feature is mobility in the crowd. The western bourgeois novel has always—from *Don Quixote* to Tobias Smollett's and Henry Fielding's picaresques to R. L. Stevenson's adventure tales to the well-heeled middlebrow tourists invoked by E. M. Forster and Henry James—been committed to the movement of its characters in travel as a prime form of education. (As such Woolf's first novel, *The Voyage Out,* its subject educational travel, opens where Joyce's first novel, *A Portrait,* ends, with its advertisement of the young artist's exile.) The flaneur, locked into a compulsion to move, is a logical culmination of this tradition: in his sole reliance on movement (on foot) as a form of action, however, he also marks its conclusion. The compulsive walking of the lone flaneur marks the end of the effort on the part of the "character" to sustain individuality in the face of the mass of commodities-as-spectacle that, literally, demands that one linger, that one stop (to buy) and enjoy.

31. For Bloom's own budget for June 16, 1904, see *U* 584.

32. Gayatri Chakravorty Spivak, "Subaltern Studies: Deconstructing Historiography," in *In Other Worlds: Essays in Cultural Politics* (New York and London: Methuen, 1987), p. 210.

33. A. Conan Doyle, "The Adventure of the Blue Carbuncle," in *The Sherlock Holmes Omnibus: A Facsimile of the Original "Strand Magazine" Stories, 1891–93* (New York: Bramhall House, 1975), pp. 85–97.

34. Edward W. Soja, *Postmodern Geographies: The Reassertion of Space in Critical Social Theory* (London: Verso, 1989), p. 2.

35. For exact times in which each episode of *Ulysses* is set, see Clive Hart and Leo Knuth, *A Topographical Guide to James Joyce's "Ulysses"* (Colchester: A Wake Newsletter Press, 1975), pp. 23–25.

36. Conan Doyle, "Blue Carbuncle," p. 91.

37. Ibid., pp. 89–90.

38. Moretti, *Signs Taken for Wonders,* p. 151. Moretti's essay "Clues" is invaluable on the politics of the detective story, and on that genre's role as avatar of other popular-culture forms.

As for the conditions of production of the carbuncle in this story, Holmes hints at its inevitable colonial origins when he tells Watson, "It was found in the banks of the Amoy River in southern China ..." (p. 90).

39. *Signs Taken for Wonders,* Moretti, pp. 134–41.

40. Conan Doyle, "Blue Carbuncle," p. 90.

41. Ibid., p. 86.

42. Ibid., p. 85.

43. Ibid., p. 88.

44. Ibid., p. 96.

45. Ibid., p. 86

46. Michel Foucault, "A Preface to Transgression," in *Language, Counter-Memory, Practice: Selected Essays and Interviews,* ed. Donald Bouchard (Ithaca: Cornell University Press, 1977), pp. 29–52.

47. See Jean Baudrillard on the significance of "gadgets" in *For a Critique of the Political Economy of the Sign,* trans. Charles Levin (St. Louis: Telos Press, 1981), p. 32.

48. Marilyn French, *The Book as World: James Joyce's "Ulysses"* (London: Sphere 1982), p. 132.

49. See ibid., p. 127.

50. Jean Baudrillard, *The Ecstasy of Communication* (New York: Semiotext[e], 1988).

51. See Max Horkheimer and Theodor Adorno, "The Culture Industry: Enlightenment as Mass Deception," in *Dialectic of Enlightenment* (New York: Continuum, 1987), p. 148.

52. See Richard Ellmann, *James Joyce* (Oxford: Oxford University Press, 1959), p. 174. The *Freeman's Journal* praised Joyce's singing, and commented that he "gave a pathetic rendering of 'The Croppy Boy.'" Joseph Holloway, however, spoke of the song merely as "the item programmed over the singer's name." It is not clear from his account, quoted by Ellman, that Joyce actually sang the song.

53. See Raymond Mander and Joe Mitchenson, *British Music Hall* (London: Century Books, 1974), p. 107. Here is given the text and cover prints from the music sheets of two "Irish ballads" sung in British music halls in the late nineteenth century: "Only a Few Miles of Water," a sentimental emigrant lament originally sung by Miss Nellie Cannon in 1895, and "What Do You Think of the Irish Now?" a song originally sung by Pat Rafferty in 1900, praising the Dublin Fusiliers for their heroism in South Africa during the Boer War.

54. For the words of the song, and a note on its composition, see Georges-Denis Zimmerman, *Songs of the Irish Rebellion: Political Street Ballads and Rebel Songs 1780–1900* (Hatboro, Pa: Folklore Associates, 1967), pp. 288–89. This song was first published in *The Nation,* the patriotic newspaper of the mid-nineteenth century, on January 4, 1845. For another "Croppy Boy," see pp. 161–65.

55. Ellmann, *James Joyce,* p. 473.

56. Ibid., p. 474. This is a phrase from a letter by Joyce in which he appears to be quoting Harriet Weaver's earlier letter to him.

57. Chakravorty Spivak, "Subaltern Studies," p. 210.

58. See Erik Olin Wright et al., *The Debate on Classes* (London: Verso, 1989).

3. "And I Belong to a Race ..."

1. See Joel Peter Witkin, ed., *Masterpieces of Medical Photography* (Pasadena, Calif: Twelvetrees Press, 1987), 34.

2. See L. P. Curtis, *Apes and Angels* (Washington, D.C.: Smithsonian, 1971).

3. For a reproduction of this photograph, see *The Oxford History of English Literature*, ed. Pat Rogers (Oxford: Oxford University Press, 1977), p. 355.

4. E. O. Somerville and Martin Ross, *Some Experiences of an Irish R.M.* (London: Longman, 1890).

5. For a critical overview of much of this work, see Paul Smith, *Discerning the Subject* (Minneapolis: University of Minnesota Press, 1988).

6. Theodor Adorno, *Negative Dialectics* (New York: Seabury Press, 1973), p. 140.

7. Michael Ryan, *Marxism and Deconstruction* (Baltimore: Johns Hopkins University Press, 1982), p. 76.

8. Adorno, *Negative Dialectics,* p. 140.

9. Fredric. Jameson, "Foreword," to Jean-Francois Lyotard, *The Post-Modern Condition* (Minneapolis: University of Minnesota Press, 1984), p. ix.

10. Adorno, *Negative Dialectics,* p. 140.

11. Peter Stallybrass and Allon White, *The Politics and Poetics of Transgression* (Ithaca: Cornell University Press, 1986).

12. Fredric Jameson, *The Political Unconscious: Narrative as a Socially Symbolic Act* (Ithaca: Cornell University Press, 1981), p. 294.

13. Ibid., p. 95.

14. D. O. Mannoni, *Prospero and Caliban: The Psychology of Colonization,* Pamela Powesland, trans. (London: Methuen, 1956).

15. Seamus Deane, "Civilians and Barbarians," in Seamus Deane, Seamus Heaney, et al., *Ireland's Field Day* (Notre Dame, Ind.: University of Notre Dame Press, 1896), pp. 33–42.

16. Homi K. Bhabha, "Signs Taken For Wonders: Questions of Ambivalence and Authority under a Tree Outside Delhi, May 1817," *Critical Inquiry* 12, no. 1, (1985), pp. 197–221. Also Gayatri Chakravorty Spivak, "Subaltern Studies: Deconstructing Historiography," in *In Other Worlds: Essays in Cultural Politics* (New York and London: Methuen, 1987) pp. 197–221.

17. Seamus Deane, "Civilians and Barbarians," p. 38.

18. M. Arnold, *On the Study of Celtic Literature* (London: Smith, Elder, 1867).

19. Seamus Deane, "Arnold Burke and the Celts," in *Celtic Revivals: Essays in Modern Irish Literature 1880–1980* (London: Faber and Faber, 1985), pp. 17–27.

20. Richard Kearney, "Myth and Motherland," in S. Deane, S. Heaney, et al., pp. 61–80; Beckett is cited in p. 72.

21. Seamus Heaney, "Station Island," in *Station Island* (New York: Farrar, Straus and Giroux, 1985), p. 93.

22. Peter Singleton-Gates and Maurice Girodias, *The Black Diaries: An Account of Roger Casement's Life and Times, with a Collection of His Diaries and Public Writings* (New York: Grove Press, 1959).

23. Quoted in Rene McColl, *Roger Casement: A New Judgment* (London: Hamish Hamilton, 1956), p. 268.

24. B. L. Reid, "Bibliography," in *The Lives of Roger Casement* (New Haven, Conn.: Yale University Press, 1976), pp. 517–20.

25. Georg Lukács, "Reification and the Consciousness of the Proletariat" in *History and Class Consciousness: Studies in Marxist Dialectics,* trans. R. Livingstone (Cambridge, Mass.: MIT Press, 1985), pp. 83–148.

26. W. B. Yeats, "The Ghost of Roger Casement," and "Roger Casement" in *The Collected Poems of W. B. Yeats* (New York: Macmillan Press, 1956).

27. Ruth Dudley Edwards, *Patrick Pearse: The Triumph of Failure* (London: Gollancz, 1977).

28. Jeanne Sheehy, *The Rediscovery of Ireland's Past: The Celtic Revival 1830–1930* (London: Thames and Hudson, 1980).

29. For a reproduction of this painting, see the cover of Heaney, *Station Island*, 1985.

30. Kearney, "Myth and Motherland," p. 71.

31. Hugh Kenner, *A Colder Eye: The Modern Irish Writers* (London: Alan Lane, 1983), p. 175.

32. Walter Laqueur, ed., *The Terrorism Reader: An Historical Anthology* (Philadelphia: Temple University Press, 1978).

33. T. E. Lawrence, "The Science of Guerrilla Warfare," *Encyclopedia Britannica*, 14th ed. (1929).

34. Max Horkheimer and Theodor Adorno, *Dialectics of Enlightenment*, trans. J. Cumming (New York: Continuum, 1987), pp. 15–16.

35. Frank Budgen, *James Joyce and the Making of Ulysses* (Bloomington: Indiana University Press, 1960), p. 146.

36. For example, see David Hayman's essay "Cyclops," in *James Joyce's "Ulysses," Critical Essays*, ed. Clive Hart and David Hayman (Berkeley: University of California Press, 1974), pp. 243–74.

37. Hugh Kenner, *Joyce's Voices* (Berkeley: University of California Press, 1878), p. 78.

38. David Hayman, *Ulysses: The Mechanics of Meaning* (Englewood Cliffs, N.J.: Prentice Hall, 1970), p. 70.

39. Colin MacCabe, *James Joyce and the Revolution of the Word* (London: Macmillan Press, 1979), p. 79.

40. Michael Seidel, *Epic Geography: James Joyce's "Ulysses"* (Princeton: Princeton University Press, 1976), p. 197.

41. Harry Blamaires, *The Bloomsday Book* (London: Methuen, 1966), p. 257.

42. Kenner, *Joyce's Voices*, p. 80, and Hugh Kenner, *Ulysses* (Baltimore: Johns Hopkins University Press, rev. ed., 1987), p. 93. Kenner's similar attitude to Ireland in his work *A Colder Eye* is wittily discussed by Denis Donoghue in *We Irish: Essays on Irish Literature and Society* (Berkeley: University of California Press, 1986), pp. 177–78. Donoghue notes that "Kenner encourages his reader, an American apparently, to believe that Ireland is a crazy country from which, believe it or don't, a number of extraordinary writers have emerged" (p. 177).

43. Franco Moretti, "The Long Goodbye: *Ulysses* and the End of Liberal Capitalism," in *Signs Taken for Wonders*, trans. S. Fischer, D. Forgras, and D. Miller (London: Verso, 1983), pp. 186–208.

44. Kenner, *Joyce's Voices*, pp. 39–63.

45. See Deane, in Deane, Heaney, et al., *Ireland's Field Day*, p. 34.

46. See, for example, Anthony Trollope, *The Kellys and the O'Kellys* (Oxford: Oxford University Press, 1951).

47. Brendan O'Dowda, *The World of Percy French* (Dundonald, Northern Ireland: Blackstaff Press, 1981).

48. Charles J. Kickham, *Knocknagow* (New York: Garland Publishing, 1979).

49. Roland Barthes, *The Pleasure of the Text*, trans. R. Miller (New York: Hill and Wang, 1975).

50. See Patrick McGee, "Introduction" to *Paperspace: Style as Ideology in Joyce's Ulysses* (Lincoln: University of Nebraska Press, 1988), pp. 1–11, for a discussion of the limited political value of deconstructive criticism of Joyce.

51. See Allon White, "Pigs and Pierrots: The Politics of Transgression in Modern Fiction," *Raritan* 2, no. 2 (Fall), pp. 51–70.

52. Marilyn French, *The Book as World: James Joyce's Ulysses* (London: Sphere Books, 1982), p. 148.

53. For one recent discussion of the implications of Gramsci's concept of hegemony, see Ernesto Laclau and Chantal Mouffe, *Hegemony and Socialist Strategy: Towards a Radical Democratic Politics* (London: Verso, 1985), esp. pp. 65–71.

54. Arthur Griffith, *The Resurrection of Hungary,* 3rd ed. (Dublin, 1918).

55. For discussions of the subject as agent in feminist criticism, see Nancy K. Miller, *Subject to Change: Reading Feminist Writing* (New York: Columbia University Press, 1988).

56. Marilyn French, *The Book as World,* p. 156.

57. Dominic Manganiello, *Joyce's Politics* (London: Routledge and Kegan Paul, 1980).

58. For a discussion on this, see Paul Von Caspel, *Bloomers on the Liffey: Exegetical Readings of Joyce's "Ulysses"* (Baltimore: Johns Hopkins University Press, 1986), p. 180.

59. See too Hugh Kenner, *A Colder Eye* (London: Allen Lane, 1983), pp. 175–76: "Joyce records the devastation wrought [in the Rising] by the biscuit-tin the Citizen threw at Bloom."

60. *Little Review* 1–12, 1914–29 (New York: rpt. ed., 1967).

61. See Joseph V. O'Brien, *"Dear, Dirty Dublin": A City in Distress, 1899–1916* (Berkeley: University of California Press, 1982), p. 263, for a detailed account of the numbers of those killed in the Easter rebellion.

62. Frantz Fanon, *The Wretched of the Earth,* trans. Constance Farrington (New York: Grove Press, 1968), pp. 249–310.

63. Réné Girard, *Deceit, Desire and the Novel,* trans. Y. Freccero (Baltimore: Johns Hopkins University Press, 1961).

64. J. P. Sartre, *Critique de la raison dialectique,* Vol. 1 (Paris: Gallimard, 1960).

65. Fredric Jameson, *Marxism and Form* (Princeton: Princeton University Press, 1971), pp. 244–58.

66. Paulo Freire, "Cultural Action and Conscientization" in *The Politics of Education,* trans. D. Macedo (Boston, Mass.: Bergin and Garvey, 1985), pp. 67–98.

67. Conor Cruise O'Brien, *The Siege: The Saga of Israel and Zionism* (New York: Simon and Schuster, 1986).

68. See Colin Holmes, *Anti-Semitism in British Society, 1876–1939* (London: Edward Arnold, 1979). See pp. 97–99 for an account of the Creagh affair, an outbreak of anti-Semitism in Limerick in 1904.

4. *"The Whores Will Be Busy"*

1. Seamus Heaney, "Punishment," in *North* (London: Faber and Faber, 1975).

2. Theodor Adorno, *Aesthetic Theory,* ed. G. Adorno and R. Tiedemann (London: Routledge and Kegan Paul, 1970), p. 262. "Conversely," Adorno comments, "what our manipulated contemporaries dismiss as unintelligible secretly makes very good sense to them indeed." He compares these contemporaries' reaction to art to the feeling Freud described as "the uncanny."

3. See, for example, Philip F. Herring, *Joyce's Notes and Early Drafts for "Ulysses": Selections from the Buffalo Collection* (Charlottesville: University Press of Virginia, 1977), p. 191. Herring describes "Circe" as "the longest and probably the most difficult chapter in a very complex novel."

4. See Edward Said, "Identity, Negation and Violence," *New Left Review* 3 (Sept./ Oct 1988), pp. 46–62. "Terrorism has regularly appeared in contemporary conjunction with stigmatized groups ... The point is that there are ... so few enunciative opportunities to oppose such arguments about terrorism without seeming to be *for it*."

5. Joseph Conrad, *The Secret Agent* (New York: Doubleday, 1953).

6. On the artist Max Beckmann, see Von Benno Reifenberg and Wilheim Hausenstein, *Max Beckmann* (Munich: R. Piper Verlag, 1949). See plate 15, "Das Nacht," and plate 57, "Abfahrt" (1932–35).

7. See Walter Laqueur, *The Age of Terrorism* (Boston: Little, Brown, Rev. ed., 1987), p. 15.

8. Jeremy Tunstall, *The Media Are American: Anglo-American Media in the World* (London: Constable, 1977), n. 10, p. 98.

9. Henry James, *The Princess Casamassima* (New York: Macmillan Press, 1948).

10. Emile Zola, *Paris* (Paris: Bibliotheque Charpentier, 1898).

11. Liam O'Flaherty, *The Informer* (New York: Knopf, 1925).

12. Jean-Paul Sartre, *Les Mains Sales* (Paris: Gallimard, 1948).

13. T. E. Lawrence, *Seven Pillars of Wisdom* (London: Jonathan Cape, 1935).

14. Maurice Blanchot, *The Writing of the Disaster*, trans. Ann Smock (Lincoln: University of Nebraska Press, 1986), p. 48.

15. Frantz Fanon, *The Wretched of the Earth*, trans. Constance Farrington (New York: Grove Press, 1963), pp. 35–106.

16. J. M. Coetzee, *Waiting for the Barbarians* (London: Secker and Warburg, 1980).

17. Fredric Jameson, "Third World Literature in the Era of Multi-National Capitalism," in *Social Text* 15 (Fall 1986), pp. 65–88.

18. Christine Buci-Glucksmann, "Catastrophic Utopia: The Feminine As Allegory of the Modern" in *The Making of the Modern Body*, ed. Catherine Gallagher and Thomas Laqueur (Berkeley: University of California Press, 1987), pp. 220–29.

19. On women's roles in World War I; see *Behind the Lines: Gender in the Two World Wars*, ed. Margaret R. Higonnet, Jane Jenson, Sonya Michel, and M.C. Weitz (New Haven: Yale University Press, 1983).

20. See "Prostitution," *Encyclopedia Britannica*, eleventh ed., vol. 22, pp. 457–64. The Irish garrisons mentioned in the legislation included Cork, Queenstown, and the Curragh.

21. Consider, for example, Countess Markiewicz, one of the leaders of the 1916 Rising in Dublin. See *Cry Blood, Cry Erin* (London: Barrie and Rockcliff, 1966).

22. Examples of these genres of photographs are to be found in Paul Fussell, *The Great War and Modern Memory* (London: Oxford University Press, 1975), pp. 45 and 140, and in Paul Virilio, *Guerre et Cinema I* (Paris: Editions de l'Etoile, 1984), fig. 2. This book has been translated by Patrick Camiller as *War and Cinema* (London: Verso, 1989).

23. Joseph Conrad, *Heart of Darkness* (New York: Norton Critical Editions, 1971).

24. Richard Ellmann, *James Joyce* (London: Oxford University Press, 1959), p. 473. He describes how Pound complained that "a new style per chapter [is] not required."

25. Ibid., p. 378. Ellmann tells this story as proof that the brothels thrived partly because of the British garrison in Dublin. He says that the ballad is generally attributed to Gogarty.

26. Fredric Jameson, "Cognitive Mapping" in *Marxism and the Interpretation of Culture,* ed. Cary Nelson and Lawrence Grossberg (Urbana: University of Illinois Press, 1988), pp. 347–64. See especially pp. 349–350.

27. See pp. 386–403 of *A New History of Ireland*, ed. T. W. Moody, F. X. Martin, and J. F. Byrne, vol. 7 (Oxford: Clarendon Press, 1982), for a synopsis of these events.

28. For a detailed discussion of when "Circe" was written, and a survey of Joyce's reports on his progress in his letters, see Michael Groden, *Ulysses in Progress* (Princeton: Princeton University Press, 1977), pp. 166–78.

29. For such photographs of the Irish War of Independence, see *Cry Blood, Cry Erin*.

30. See Peter Somerville-Large, *Dublin* (London: Hamish Hamilton, 1979), chap. 13, "From Parnell's Death to 1916." He quotes the Reverend J. Gwynne, S.J., writing about Sackville (now O'Connell) Street: "From the Coombe and other parts of the city [come] ... these crowds of young girls who take possession of the city when darkness comes, and whose demeanor by no means suggests the modesty and decorum we are wont to regard as inseparable from the Irish maiden." See also Joseph V. O'Brien, *"Dear, Dirty Dublin": A City in Distress, 1899–1916* (Berkeley: University of California Press, 1982), esp. pp. 189–95.

31. See Ellmann, *Ulysses*, p. 548.

32. See *A Portrait of the Artist as a Young Man* (New York: Viking Critical Editions, 1964), p. 247.

33. For example, see Daniel Ferrer, "Circe, Regret and Regression" in *Post-Structuralist Joyce* (Cambridge: Cambridge University Press, 1984), pp. 127–45.

34. Jameson, "Third World Literature," p. 69.

35. Franco Moretti, "The Long Goodbye: *Ulysses* and the End of Liberal Capitalism," in *Signs Taken for Wonders* (London: Verso, 1983), pp. 182–208. On "Circe," see p. 185.

36. Karl Marx, *Capital*, vol. 1 (New York: Vintage 1977), "Part One: Commodities and Money," pp. 125–78.

37. Quoted from Fredric Jameson, *The Political Unconscious* (Ithaca: Cornell University Press, 1981), p. 220, discussing Max Weber, *The Theory of Social and Economic Organization* (New York: Free Press, 1947).

38. Moretti, "The Long Goodbye," n. 35, p. 184.

39. Roger Dangerfield, *The Strange Death of Liberal England* (New York: Perigee, 1980), first published 1935.

40. V. I. Lenin, *Imperialism, The Highest Stage of Capitalism* (Peking: Foreign Languages Press, 1975).

41. See Valerie Pakenham, *Out in the Noonday Sun: Edwardians in the Tropics* (New York: Random House, 1985), pp. 135–40.

42. Rosa Luxemburg, *The Accumulation of Capital* (New Haven; Conn.: Yale University Press, 1981).

43. See F. S. L. Lyons, *Ireland Since the Famine* (London: Collins, 1973).

44. Guy Debord, *Society of the Spectacle* (Detroit: Black and Red, 1983).

45. Allon White attributes this idea to Peter Stallybrass in "The Politics of Transgression in Modern Fiction," *Raritan* 2, no. 2, p. 67.

46. See Buci-Glucksmann, "Catastrophic Utopia," p. 224.

47. See White, "A Preface to Transgression," n. 47, p. 65.

48. Jacques Derrida, "Two Words for Joyce," in *Post-Structuralist Joyce*.

49. Michel Foucault, "Of Other Spaces," in *Diacritics* 19.

50. See Jean Baudrillard, *Simulations* (New York: Semiotext[e], 1983).

51. White, "A Preface to Transgression," p. 48.

52. See *Newsweek* (Jan. 2, 1989), pp. 14–23, and cover. The *Newsweek* articles contain good examples of most of the "realist" strategies for reporting terrorist attacks that I

have described here in relation to the representation of realist violence in "Circe." Examples are: the portrayal of woman as mourner, the static "aftermath" scene, the focus upon the police questioning of witnesses.

53. This quotation comes from Sally Belfrage, *The Crack: A Belfast Year* (London: Andre Deutsch, 1987), pp. 105–6.

5. Molly Alone

1. The photograph is reprinted in Eamonn de Valera, Thomas P. O'Neill, et al., *The Irish Uprising, 1916–22* (New York: Macmillan Press, 1966), p. 103. This book is a good source for photographic material from the years 1916–21 in Ireland.

2. Mark Tierney, *Modern Ireland* (Dublin: Gill and Macmillan, 1972), p. 117.

3. Quoted in Bonnie Kime Scott, *Joyce and Feminism* (Bloomington: Indiana University Press, 1984), p. 156.

4. On how the culture of consumption interpellates women in *Ulysses*, see Thomas Richards, *The Commodity Culture of Victorian England: Advertising and Spectacle, 1851–1914* (Stanford, Calif.: Stanford University Press, 1990).

5. See especially chapter 6, "Conclusion: The Dialectic of Utopia and Ideology," in Jameson, *The Political Unconscious* (Ithaca: Cornell University Press, 1981), pp. 281–99.

6. Stewart Hall, "The Toad in the Garden: Thatcherism among the Theorists," in *Marxism and the Interpretation of Culture,* ed. Cary Nelson and Lawrence Grossberg (Urbana: University of Illinois Press, 1988), pp. 35–57.

7. Gayatri Chakravorty Spivak, "The Political Economy of Women as Seen by a Literary Critic," in *Coming to Terms: Feminism, Theory, Politics,* ed. Elizabeth Weed (New York: Routledge, 1989), pp. 218–29.

8. Donna Haraway, "A Manifesto for Cyborgs: Science, Technology and Socialist Feminism in the 1980's," in Elizabeth Weed, ed., *Coming to Terms,* pp. 173–204. See p. 175.

9. Dominic Manganiello, *Joyce's Politics* (London: Routledge and Kegan Paul, 1980), pp. 67–114.

10. Fredric Jameson, "Third World Literature in the Era of Multinational Capitalism," *Social Text* 15, (Fall 1986), pp. 65–88.

11. On the significance of the changing attitudes to Parnell represented in *Ulysses,* see my "Parnellism and Rebellion: The Irish War of Independence and Revisions of the Heroic in *Ulysses,*" *James Joyce Quarterly,* 19, no. 3 (Fall 1990).

12. Tierney, *Modern Ireland,* p. 32.

13. Rudyard Kipling, *Kim,* ed. Edward Said (London: Penguin, 1987).

14. Benedict Anderson, *Imagined Communities: Reflections on the Origin and Spread of Nationalism* (London: Verso, 1983), p. 105.

Index

Enda Duffy is an assistant professor of English at the University of California at Santa Barbara. He has written numerous articles on refugee textuality and representations of space in modernist and postcolonial cultures.